Cooter • Flynt • Cooter

# The Flynt/Cooter Comprehensive Reading Inventory-2

## Assessment of K–12 Reading Skills in English and Spanish

**Second Edition**

**Robert B. Cooter, Jr.**
*Bellarmine University*

**E. Sutton Flynt**
*The University of Memphis*

**Kathleen Spencer Cooter**
*Bellarmine University*

**PEARSON**

Boston   Columbus   Indianapolis   New York   San Francisco   Upper Saddle River
Amsterdam   Cape Town   Dubai   London   Madrid   Milan   Munich   Paris   Montréal   Toronto
Delhi   Mexico City   São Paulo   Sydney   Hong Kong   Seoul   Singapore   Taipei   Tokyo

**Vice President, Editor-in-Chief:** Aurora Martínez Ramos
**Associate Sponsoring Editor:** Barbara Strickland
**Editorial Assistant:** Laura Marenghi
**Executive Marketing Manager:** Krista Clark
**Production Editor:** Cynthia DeRocco
**Editorial Production Service:** S4Carlisle Publishing Services
**Manufacturing Buyer:** Linda Sager
**Electronic Composition:** S4Carlisle Publishing Services
**Cover Designer:** Diane Lorenzo

Illustration Credits: pp. 76–81, 83, 84, 86, 88, 90, 92, 94, 96, 148–153, 155, 156, 158, 160, 162, 164, 166, 168, 221–224, 226–227, 229–230, 232, 277, 279, 280, 283–286, 288, 290; Deborah S. Flynt.

**Library of Congress Cataloging-in-Publication Data**
Cooter, Robert B.
   The Flynt/Cooter Comprehensive Reading Inventory-2 : assessment of K-2 reading skills in English and Spanish / Robert B. Cooter, Jr., Bellarmine University, E. Sutton Flynt, The University of Memphis, Kathleen S. Cooter, Bellarmine University.—Second edition.
      pages cm
   Includes bibliographical references.
   ISBN 978-0-13-336252-7
1. Reading—Ability testing. 2. English language—Study and teaching. 3. English language—Study and teaching—Spanish speakers. I. Flynt, E. Sutton. II. Cooter, Kathleen Spencer, 1950- III. Title.
   LB1050.46.C684 2013
   372.48—dc23                                                         2013000759

6   17

ISBN 10:     0-13-336252-3
ISBN 13: 978-0-13-336252-7

**Robert B. Cooter, Jr.** currently serves as Dean of the Annsley Frazier Thornton School of Education and Ursuline Endowed Chair of Teacher Education at Bellarmine University in Louisville, Kentucky. The author of numerous books and articles on reading instruction, his primary research focuses on the improvement of literacy instruction for children living at the poverty level. From 2006–2011 Cooter was co-editor of *The Reading Teacher*, the world's largest-circulation refereed journal for literacy educators (International Reading Association). In the public schools, Dr. Cooter previously served as the first "Reading Czar" (associate superintendent) for the Dallas Independent School District (TX). In 2007, he and colleagues J. Helen Perkins and Kathleen Spencer Cooter received the national "Urban Impact Award" from the Council of Great City Schools. His latest work involves the implementation of a new Ph.D. program at Bellarmine University focused on developing "change agents" interested in improving education outcomes for children living in poverty circumstances.

**E. Sutton Flynt** currently serves as Professor of Literacy Education and Director of Teacher Education at the University of Memphis. Dr. Flynt has almost 40 years of teaching experience as a classroom teacher in the public schools, university professor, university department chairperson, and dean of a college of education. He has consulted with school districts in eight different states and served on state departments of education task forces in Louisiana, Kansas, and Tennessee.

Dr. Flynt has numerous professional publications in his areas of interest, primarily focusing on literacy assessment, pre-service teacher preparation, and content-area reading instruction. In 2007–2008 he coauthored a featured column on content literacy in *The Reading Teacher*. He has frequently presented scholarly works at such professional venues as the World Congress on Reading, the Annual Conference of the International Reading Association, the American Educational Research Association, and the Society for Research on Educational Effectiveness.

Professor Flynt's most recent research has focused on empirically determining the efficacy of Response to Intervention (RTI) Tier 2 commercial materials for the literacy achievement of K–2 students in urban and rural school districts.

**Dr. Kathleen Spencer Cooter** is Professor of Early Childhood/Special Education and School Leadership at Bellarmine University in Louisville, Kentucky. Prior to 2008, she was Associate Professor of Special Education at the University of Memphis. In addition, she served as outreach coordinator for the New Teacher Center, an exciting project working in conjunction with the Memphis City Schools to enhance teacher retention in urban schools. Professor Cooter also served as principal investigator for the Tennessee Early Intervention System (TEIS), serving the needs of children of over 3,000 families in western Tennessee.

Prior to joining the Special Education faculty at the University of Memphis, Dr. Cooter and a group of parents and committed community and university leaders raised some $3 million and founded the Texas Christian University (TCU) RISE School, now known as Kinderfrogs, a special school serving the needs of infants with Down syndrome. In October of 2001, Dr. Cooter received the "Employer of the Year Award" from the Fort Worth business community for her successes in employing

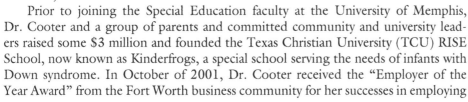

adults with Down syndrome as staff members at the TCU RISE School. Together with Starpoint School, a special school for students with learning disabilities, Cooter directed the teaching and research activities of both of TCU's laboratory schools. Upon her leaving in December 2003, TCU announced that a new wing would be added to Starpoint School as a gift from a grateful benefactor and named in her honor.

For two decades Professor Cooter worked as a teacher and administrator in both private and public schools serving children with special learning needs. As a teacher, Dr. Cooter worked primarily with special education students in preschool, elementary, and middle and high school settings. Kathy was honored as a Texas "Teacher of the Year" in her role as a special education professional.

For more than 15 years Kathleen Cooter has developed and served as the lead professor in a popular course for practicing school leaders known as the Principals' Fellowship in Texas, Tennessee, and Kentucky. This program has been credited with helping to turn around low-performing schools in the areas of reading and writing.

# CONTENTS

## SECTION III—The Comprehensive Reading Inventory–2 (CRI–2) Preliminary Assessments   29

FORM **A**

## Sentences for Initial Passage Selection   71

## Narrative Reading Passages   75

## Examiner's Assessment Protocols   99

FORM B

FORM C

FORM D

# PREFACE

For more than two decades, the Flynt/Cooter family of informal reading inventories has been the top choice of thousands of classroom teachers for quickly and reliably assessing the reading skills and needs of their students. Hundreds of education professors around the globe have seen the Flynt/Cooter as an essential tool in preparing the next generation of P–12 teachers serving native English speakers, and/or English learners via our CRI: Español version that is provided on our accompanying PDToolkit. The CRI's popularity has often been attributed to its innovative and easy-to-use subtests measuring the early/emergent reading skills of young learners; narrative and expository passages designed to assess oral reading, silent reading, and listening comprehension; as well as assessments of prior knowledge and language/vocabulary skills for students in grades 1–12. Likewise, the *Flynt/Cooter Comprehensive Reading Inventory–2 (CRI–2)* has been the choice of many reading and literacy researchers seeking an evidence-based and validated instrument for use in high-stakes research, such as the federally funded "Striving Readers" projects in the United States.

PD **PD** TOOLKIT™

for CRI–2

Click on CRI: Español
to see the Spanish
version of the *Flynt/Cooter
Comprehensive Reading Inventory–2.*

## NEW TO THIS EDITION

In the *Flynt/Cooter Comprehensive Reading Inventory–2 (CRI–2)* we have made a number of changes in response to suggestions made by teachers, researchers, and teacher education professionals. These changes are intended to make the *Flynt/Cooter CRI–2* even easier to use in real-world classrooms, make the analysis of data more efficient, and, above all, increase student learning. Additions and modifications made in this 2nd edition include:

- **Common Core standards** for the English Language Arts (see www .corestandards.org) are linked at each assessment level to help examiners easily chart student data and plan "next steps" in instruction.

- **Response to Intervention (RTI)** sections are included to help teachers plan Tier 1 and Tier 2 reading interventions.

- **Academic vocabulary lists** based on the Memphis Striving Readers research project led by the authors are included.

- **Expanded "IF–THEN" Charts** include more intervention suggestions matched to diagnostic data derived from the *Flynt/Cooter CRI–2.*

- **A quick-reference guide** for administering and scoring, based on suggestions of the eminent literacy researcher and CRI user Professor Michael Opitz, is included.

- **Fluency norms for grades 1–8** from the seminal research of Jan Hasbrouck and Gerald Tindal (2006) are included, as well as suggestions as to how these data might be used to plan instruction.

- **A Concepts of Print** test is included for determining the prior knowledge of early/emergent readers.

- **A Phonics Test** using real words replaces our previous test in order to improve assessment validity.

## CONTINUING FEATURES OF THE *FLYNT/COOTER CRI–2*

We continue to include in the CRI–2 most of the groundbreaking features that helped make the Flynt/Cooter the top choice of teachers and literacy coaches for many decades.

Click on Additional Resources, then select "Reliability and Validity: Technical Development of the CRI."

- **Reliability and validity data** developed by independent researchers make the *Flynt/Cooter CRI–2* an approved assessment instrument for adoption by most states and school districts as well as an appropriate instrument for funded literacy research. Extensive validation studies of the CRI (Forms A and B) were initially conducted during the 2004–2005 school year. In short, the CRI was found to be one of the most reliable and valid reading tests of its kind and compares quite favorably to other similar instruments available today. A complete summary of validity and reliability findings from the *CRI Validation Study* is presented in the accompanying PDToolkit.

- **High-interest narrative and expository passages (P–12)** are designed to more accurately assess students' true abilities in oral and silent reading comprehension, decoding abilities, vocabulary knowledge, reading fluency, and prior knowledge. These high-interest passages contrast sharply with the uninspiring passages used by other informal reading inventories that may lead to an underestimation of student abilities. All selections are representative of the materials found in core reading programs and core content-area textbooks.

- **Graded sentences for initial passage placement** are included (as opposed to the less valid graded word lists used by other informal reading inventories).

- Our exclusive **Miscue Analysis Grid system** allows for quickly analyzing students' oral reading errors for use in planning next steps in learning in real classroom situations.

- **Use of retelling** followed by strategic questioning to measure silent reading comprehension of narrative and expository passages speeds the assessment process and yields more reliable student data.

- **The Spanish version (CRI: Español) of the entire instrument for bilingual and/or English Language Learner assessment** is provided on the PDToolkit.

In the pages that follow you will find the complete Contents, Administration and Scoring Guidelines, and then the actual CRI–2 subtests and forms.

Accompanying *The Flynt/Cooter Comprehensive Reading Inventory: Assessment of K–12 Reading Skills in English and Spanish,* Second Edition, is an online resource site with media tools that, together with the text, provide you with the useful tools you need to administer classroom assessments.

To access the PDToolkit for CRI–2 for the first time, go to http://pdtoolkit .pearson.com and register using the following code: PDTOOL-BAZOO-OSMIC-VARNA-QUASH-ROVES.

Currently the following resources are available:

- Guidelines for Administering CRI–2

- CRI: Español

- Additional Resources

  - Expository passages for levels 10–12

  - Miscue tools and intervention strategies

  - Student Summary Form to record all assessment data from the CRI

  - And more

Thank you for choosing to use the CRI–2 and the CRI: Español. Please do not hesitate to contact us with your comments, questions, and suggestions as we work together to help all students become strong readers!

Robert B. Cooter, Jr. (e-mail: rcooter@bellarmine.edu)
E. Sutton Flynt (e-mail: esflynt@memphis.edu)
Kathleen Spencer Cooter (e-mail: kcooter@bellarmine.edu)

# ACKNOWLEDGMENTS

The authors are especially grateful to the eminent reading researcher and scholar, Professor Michael Opitz of the University of Northern Colorado, for providing us with his suggestions for improving the CRI–2 administration procedures. We also express our gratitude to Professors Ana María González and Joan Williams of Texas Lutheran University, and Professor Kathryn Prater of The University of North Carolina, Greensboro, for their significant contributions to the revision of the *Español Reading Inventory* included on the PDToolkit accompanying this text.

The authors would like to express their appreciation to the reviewers for this edition: Terra Barnes, Southwest Educational Development Center (SEDC); Judith Dunkerly, University of Nevada Las Vegas; Laurie Goodman, California State University, Fresno; Melissa Knapp, Robert E. Lillard Elementary Design Center; and Karen Zweben, Strath Haven Middle School. The authors would also like to express their appreciation to the reviewers of the CRI: Español for their thoughtful comments and insights, which guided its revision: Dora Alvarez, Southern Methodist University and University of Texas, Arlington; Zulmara Cline, California State University, San Marcos; Rosio Dresser, San Jose State University, East Bay; Denise Fleming, California State University, East Bay; Ana María González, Texas Lutheran University; Hilda Medrano, University of Texas, Pan American; Leslie Patterson, University of Houston; Maria G. Ramirez, University of Nevada, Las Vegas; RosaMaria Rojo; and Elizabeth Soriano, San Diego State University.

Finally, the authors are indebted to the authors of the original reading inventory translation for their foundational work: Kathy Escamilla, University of Colorado, Boulder; Sally Nathenson-Mejian, University of Colorado, Denver; Dora Alvarez, Southern Methodist University and University of Texas, Arlington; Patricia Garcia-Smith; and RosaMaria Rojo.

# SECTION I—OVERVIEW OF THE COMPREHENSIVE READING INVENTORY-2 (CRI-2) TESTS

Reading develops in a predictable progression that can be measured and monitored by a skilled classroom teacher or trained examiner. The *Flynt/Cooter Comprehensive Reading Inventory–2nd edition (CRI–2)* provides teachers with a practical assessment tool for everyday classroom assessment in real-world schools. Extensive field testing in urban, suburban, and rural classrooms with literally hundreds of teachers and reading specialists helped refine this easy-to-use instrument that can usually be administered in less than 15 minutes.

The CRI–2 focuses on the "Big Five" areas of reading examined by the National Reading Panel (2000) and in subsequent studies: phonemic awareness, phonics, comprehension, vocabulary, and fluency. In addition, the CRI–2 includes tests for other important areas of reading, including reading interests and attitudes, concepts of print, "alphabetics," and listening comprehension.

In this section we provide you with a brief overview of the various tests in the CRI–2, as well as a brief rationale drawn from evidence-based research for each. Later, we provide you with detailed instructions on the process for administering the CRI–2 and interpreting the data for making instructional decisions.

## INTEREST INVENTORY

One of the most important and often ignored aspects of reading assessment is the *affective* domain—that is, interest, attitude, and motivational factors related to reading success. To that end we include an **Interest Inventory** to assist examiners in learning more about students' background knowledge, interests, and motivations as related to reading. Information resulting from the **Interest Inventory** can be beneficial in such ways as helping teachers select reading materials that are appealing to students and matched to their background knowledge and vocabulary, and providing insights into study habits at home.

The **Interest Inventory** will not tell teachers *everything* they need to know about students' abilities, but it *can* help determine an informed departure point for quality reading instruction.

## READING ATTITUDE SURVEY— ELEMENTARY GRADES (K–5)

The **Reading Attitude Survey—Elementary Grades (K–5)** is based on the seminal research of Heathington and Alexander (1978), and McKenna and Kear (1990). This instrument helps teachers discover students' fundamental attitudes about reading at school, home, and for pleasure. Use this survey with students ranging from preschool to grade 5.

## CONCEPTS OF PRINT ASSESSMENT

Based on the work of Marie Clay (1972), the **Concepts of Print Assessment** is for preschool through grade 1 students and is intended to assess children's basic understanding of how books work in English. You will discover whether students understand basic print concepts and language such as *letter, word, sentence,* and *story,* as well as left-to-right and top-down progression, the difference between pictures and words, and punctuation.

# PHONEMIC AWARENESS AND OTHER "ALPHABETICS" ASSESSMENT TESTS

In this portion of the CRI–2 we provide several tests pertaining to early alphabet knowledge and letter recognition:

- The **Phonemic Awareness Tests (PATs)** consist of several subtests for examiners to use to discover how well students can discriminate sounds in spoken words, and how well they have learned three of the most fundamental aspects of phonemic awareness, an essential precursor to learning phonics.

  - The **Initial Consonant Sounds Test (ICST)** helps you to determine a student's ability to hear, segment, and produce beginning sounds (phonemes) in spoken words.

  - The **Phonemic Segmentation Test (PST)** measures a student's ability to hear whole spoken words, then segment the words into separate sounds (phonemes).

  - The **Blending Sounds Test (BST)** measures a student's ability to hear and blend spoken sounds (phonemes) to produce words.

- The **Letter Naming Test (LNT)** has students identify each of the 26 letters of the alphabet. Letters are presented in both upper- and lowercase forms randomly in Form 1, and separately in Forms 2 and 3.

# PHONICS AND DECODING TESTS

Phonics is assessed in two ways in the CRI–2: the **Phonics Test (PT)** and through the analysis of miscues following the oral reading of graded passages.

- The **Phonics Test (PT)** has students pronounce words representing the most common phonics patterns found in English. The **Phonics Test (PT) Analysis Grid** form helps you quickly and efficiently sort out any decoding problems a student might be having to help guide instruction.

- The **Oral Reading and Analysis of Miscues** section accompanies each and every graded passage (narrative and expository). Here the examiner notes oral reading miscues/errors. Using our exclusive **Miscue Grid** system, examiners are able to quickly and reliably analyze miscues to better understand which phonics and other decoding skills the student is using, or not using, in order to provide needed information for planning future instruction. The analysis of miscues is based on the research of Marie Clay (1985) that is commonly used by reading specialists and in Reading Recovery programs.

# VOCABULARY ASSESSMENT: THE HIGH-FREQUENCY WORD KNOWLEDGE SURVEY

Vocabulary knowledge is assessed using the **High-Frequency Word Knowledge Survey (HFWKS)**. Students simply read aloud a list of common words found in English text as the examiner flashes word cards (found on the PDToolkit). Additionally, some vocabulary questions are included following the oral reading selections. This can assist the examiner in understanding the level of a student's prior language knowledge and ability to use oral language skills upon demand.

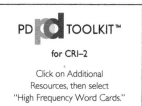

PD **TOOLKIT**™
for CRI–2
Click on Additional Resources, then select "High Frequency Word Cards."

## COMPREHENSION ASSESSMENT

The CRI–2 assesses various levels and types of reading comprehension. In grades 1 through 8, *silent reading comprehension* is assessed using both narrative (fiction) and expository (nonfiction) passages. In grades 9 through 12, nonfiction/expository passages are used that simulate the texts commonly used in core subject instruction. Examiners may also choose to measure *listening comprehension* for levels above a student's frustration level (some theorize that listening comprehension predicts a student's "potential reading level").

Silent reading comprehension is determined using a two-step assessment process. First, students orally retell what they recall from the passage just read while the examiner checks off comprehension questions answered during the retelling. After the oral retelling, examiners ask only those questions not addressed in the retelling. This process greatly reduces the time required for testing and is generally more thorough than questioning alone.

## FLUENCY ASSESSMENT

In the CRI–2 we focus on two aspects of fluency: (1) decoding and (2) reading rate (speed). Decoding is assessed through the **Phonics Test (PT)** and the **Oral Reading and Analysis of Miscues** discussed earlier.

Reading rate is measured quickly and easily using the student's oral reading of selected passages. The resulting score (words correct per minute, or **wcpm**) is then used to determine the student's fluency level using the research-based norms shown in Section II.

## AFTER TESTING, THEN WHAT?

Once the examiner has finished giving the CRI–2 tests, the next and all-important step is to analyze the resulting information so that it can be transformed into a data-driven classroom action plan.

In later sections we introduce you to our new **IF–THEN Charts** for grades K through 5 that will help you translate student data into classroom action plans. These charts were built using the **Common Core Standards** for the English Language Arts, and **end-of-year benchmarks** for each grade and skill level. With the help of the **IF–THEN Charts** you will be able to select appropriate teaching strategies, and plan Tier 1 and Tier 2 instruction for your students according to Response to Intervention (RtI) guidelines.

## REFERENCES

Clay, M. M. (1972). *The early detection of reading difficulties.* Portsmouth, NH: Heinemann.

Clay, M. M. (1985). *The early detection of reading difficulties* (3rd ed.). Portsmouth, NH: Heinemann.

Heathington, B. S., & Alexander, J. E. (1978). A child-based observation checklist to assess attitudes toward reading. *The Reading Teacher, 31*(7), 769–771.

McKenna, M., & Kear, D. J. (1990, May). Measuring attitude toward reading: A new tool for teachers. *The Reading Teacher, 43*(9), 626–639.

National Reading Panel. (2000). *Report of the National Reading Panel: Teaching children to read.* Washington, DC: National Institute of Child Health and Human Development.

# SECTION II—THE COMPREHENSIVE READING INVENTORY–2 (CRI–2) ADMINISTRATION PROCEDURES

## THE CRI–2 ASSESSMENT PROCESS

Figure 1 shows a process we recommend examiners follow in administering the various tests in the CRI–2. This four-step process begins with the gathering of information about student interests and reading attitudes and then moves on to the collection of specific information about the student's reading abilities. In the third step the examiner summarizes all data, analyzes the information using the IF–THEN Charts, then makes decisions about future instruction (i.e., Tier 1 and Tier 2 instruction). In the last step instruction is planned and delivered followed by reassessment to measure student progress and plan future instruction within the Response to Intervention (RTI) framework.

## USING THE PDTOOLKIT TO GET ACQUAINTED WITH THE CRI–2

for CRI–2

Click on Guidelines for Administering CRI–2 to hear audio information. Click on Additional Resources, then select "Tier 1 Interventions: Translating Assessment Data into Classroom Plans."

One component of the CRI–2 is a PDToolkit that provides an audio step-by-step guide for using the CRI–2 as well as ways of analyzing data and planning instruction. Before you administer your first set of tests, please listen to the Guidelines for Administering the CRI–2 on the PDToolkit.

## ADMINISTERING AND SCORING THE CRI–2

In the remainder of this section we provide step-by-step guidelines for administering the CRI–2. For the sake of brevity, we do not repeat here the instructions printed on each of the following subtests:

Interest Inventory

Reading Attitude Survey—Elementary Grades (K–5)

Alphabetics Assessments

Vocabulary Assessments

### Administration Procedures: Sentences for Initial Passage Selection

1. Begin by telling the student that you would like to hear him or her read some sentences.

2. Hand the student a copy of the **Graded Sentences for Initial Passage Selection** from the form (A, B, C, or D) you have chosen to use. (Note: For convenience, Dr. Opitz recommends that the Graded Sentences from each section be put together in a "Starter Sentences Booklet.") **Now, say something like, "Please read these sentences to me at just the right speed, not too fast and not too slow. Pretend like you are talking to me."**

3. As the student reads the sentences, make notes to yourself in the "Examiner's Notes" section of the **Examiner's Assessment Protocol** form.

   • Circle any omitted words.

AUTHORS' NOTE: *We are especially grateful to the eminent reading researcher and scholar Professor Michael Opitz of the University of Northern Colorado, for providing us with the tips and administration procedures he offers his undergraduate and graduate students in teaching them to use the CRI–2. Dr. Opitz's ideas are used throughout the sections that follow. Thanks, Michael!*

**Step 1: Starting Point Assessments**

- **Interest Inventory** (K–8)
- **Reading Attitude Survey** (elementary grades only, K–5)

**Step 2: Reading assessments for grades K–3 (Some older children will not need the alphabetics test.)**

1. Concepts of Print Assessment
2. Phonemic Awareness and Other "Alphabetics" Assessment Tests
   - Phonemic Awareness Tests (PATs): ICST, PST, BST, LNT
3. Phonics and Decoding Tests
   - Phonics Test (PT)
   - Oral Reading and Analysis of Miscues
4. Vocabulary Assessment: The High-Frequency Word Knowledge Survey (HFWKS)
5. Comprehension Assessment
6. Fluency Assessment
   - Graded sentences
   - Level A or B narrative reading passages: Assessments—Silent Reading Comprehension, Oral Reading and Analysis of Miscues, Miscue Analysis, Listening Comprehension
   - Level C or D expository reading passages: Assessments—Silent Reading Comprehension, Oral Reading and Analysis of Miscues, Miscue Analysis, Listening Comprehension

**Step 2: Reading assessments for grades 4 and up**

1. Vocabulary Assessment: The High-Frequency Word Knowledge Survey (HFWKS)
2. Comprehension Assessment
3. Fluency Assessment
   - Graded sentences
   - Level A or B narrative reading passages: Assessments—Silent Reading Comprehension, Oral Reading and Analysis of Miscues, Miscue Analysis, Listening Comprehension
   - Level C or D expository reading passages: Assessments—Silent Reading Comprehension, Oral Reading and Analysis of Miscues, Miscue Analysis, Listening Comprehension
   - Level E (Grades 10–12)

**Step 3: Complete *Student Summary Form* and analyze data (IF–THEN Thinking)**

**Step 4: Plan and Deliver Instruction (based on CRI–2 data), then reassess to measure student progress.**

**FIGURE 1  The CRI–2 Assessment Process**

- Insert a caret ^ and write the word if a word is inserted.
- If a student substitutes a word for the word used in the sentence, draw a line through the actual word and write the substituted word above it.
- Write any other notes that might be helpful in the future. For example, if the child came to an unknown word, what did he or she do?

4. Continue having the student read the Graded Sentences until he or she misses two words or more.

NOTE: *If students do not perform well on the Level 1 sentences you should administer the Preprimer and Primer passages. Following are the instructions for the Preprimer and Primer passages.*

## The Preprimer (PP) and Primer (P) Passages

Passages for emergent readers in Forms A and B of the CRI–2 have been given the conventional labels of *Preprimer (PP)* and *Primer (P),* but reflect a much more holistic view of early reading processes. At the Preprimer (PP) level, we provide a *wordless picture book* format. In each case the story is told using a series of four illustrations that tell a story when read or retold sequentially. Passages at the Primer (P) level also use the *four-illustration* format coupled with predictable text that tells the story. If a student seems unable to tell a story from the pictures, ask him or her to describe each picture. This may provide some insights into vocabulary knowledge, oral language skills, and whether a sense of story is developing. Further directions for administering the PP and P passages and completing accompanying checklists are included with the **Examiner's Assessment Protocol** forms (A and B) for each passage.

## Reading Passages: Narrative and Expository (Forms A–D)

### General Procedures

1. Select the passage(s) you want the student to read and the corresponding **Examiner's Assessment Protocol(s)**.

2. Present the student with a copy of the passage you want him or her to read.

### Specific Procedures

*Part I: Silent Reading Comprehension*

1. Read aloud the background statement shown on the **Examiner's Assessment Protocol** form you are using.

2. Provide enough time for the student to silently read the passage.

3. When the student has finished reading, ask him or her to retell the story or expository passage. Specific directions that tell you what to say and how to score responses are provided in the Teacher Directions section of the **Examiner's Assessment Protocol** form. This includes what is termed "unaided recall" (student retelling information) and "aided recall" (questions you ask pertaining to information the student did not mention in the retelling).

4. Count the total number of questions missed and write the number on the bottom of the **Examiner's Assessment Protocol** form. See Figure 2.

# PART I: SILENT READING COMPREHENSION

*Background Statement*

"This story is about how one group of boys feel about their athletic shoes. Read this story to find out how important special shoes are to playing sports. Read it carefully because I will ask you to tell me about it when you finish."

*Teacher Directions*

Once the student completes the silent reading, say, "Tell me about the story you just read." Answers to the questions below that the student provides during the retelling should be marked "ua" in the appropriate blank to indicate that this response was unaided. Ask all remaining questions not addressed during the retelling and mark those the student answers with an "a" to indicate the correct response was given after prompting by the teacher.

*Questions/Answers*

*Story Grammar Element/ Level of Comprehension*

___a___ 1. Where did the story take place?
(*Susan B. Anthony Elementary School or at a school*)

setting/literal
*at the Susan B. Anthony school*

_____ 2. Who were the two main characters in the story?
(*Jamie Lee and Josh Kidder*)

character-characterization/literal
*I don't remember*

_____ 3. What was the problem between Jamie and Josh?
(*Jamie didn't think Josh could be a good player because of his shoes, Josh didn't fit in, or other plausible responses*)

story problem(s)/inferential
*they had different kinds of shoes*

___a___ 4. How did Josh solve his problem with the other boys?
(*he outplayed all of them*)

problem resolution/inferential
*showing him his shoes still let him play basketball*

___a___ 5. What are two words that you could use to describe Jamie Lee?
(*conceited, stuck-up, or other plausible responses*)

character-characterization/ evaluative/expressive language
*a mean person*

_____ 6. What happened after the game?
(*the other boys gathered around and asked Josh his secret*)

problem resolution attempts/literal
*I don't remember*

___a___ 7. Why did everyone laugh when Josh said, "Two things—lots of practice and cheap shoes"?
(*because everything had happened because of his cheap shoes*)

problem resolution attempts/ inferential
*because he had lots of practice and cheap shoes*

___a___ 8. What lesson does this story teach?
(*responses will vary but should indicate a theme/moral related to "it's not what you wear that makes you good in a sport"*)

theme/evaluative
*shouldn't bully anyone just because of their shoes*

**FIGURE 2  Scored Student Example: Silent Reading Comprehension**

*Part II: Oral Reading and Analysis of Miscues*

1.  Using the directions under the heading "Part II: Oral Reading and Analysis of Miscues," instruct the student to read the passage aloud to you.

2.  As the student reads, follow along on the **Miscue Grid**, making notes as appropriate. Use the codes for marking and scoring miscues (reading errors) as shown later in this section.

3.  When the student has finished reading, count the total number of miscues and write this number on the bottom of the **Miscue Grid** form. (Note: We recommend recording the student so you can review the reading and make sure the miscues you recorded are accurate.)

4.  At this point you need to make a decision about whether to continue with another passage or stop with this one. Here's how you make this decision:

    • Locate the section called "E. Performance Summary" on the **Examiner's Assessment Protocol** form.

    • Place a checkmark next to the correct description for BOTH the silent reading and the oral reading accuracy categories.

    • If the student has reached "frustration level" in either category, STOP TESTING, and place a checkmark next to the "NO" where it states, "Continue to the next reading passage?"

5.  Begin instruction at the level just below the frustration-level passage.

*Miscue Grid: Error Types.*   Record the type(s) of miscues the student makes after the session is completed.

• **Mispronunciation**   Student incorrectly pronounces a word and substitutes a nonword. Write the incorrect pronunciation above the word on the *Examiner's Assessment Protocol* form.

Student: "*The deg ran away.*"

Notation: The ~~dog~~ *deg* ran away.

• **Substitutions**   Student substitutes a real word (or words) for a word in the text. Draw a line through the word and write what the student said above it.

Student: "*The tree was very high.*"

Notation: The ~~cloud~~ *tree* was very high.

• **Insertions**   A word is added that is *not* in the text. An insertion symbol (^) is recorded between the two appropriate words, and the inserted word is written above the insertion symbol.

Student: "*He'll want to have a look in the mirror.*"

Notation: He'll want to ^ *have a* look in the mirror.

• **Teacher Assists**   The student is "stuck" on a word and the teacher pronounces it. Record the incident as "TA" (teacher-assisted). This error is also counted when the student asks for help during silent reading.

Notation: automobile

- **Omissions**   If no word (or words) is given, the error is noted by circling the word(s) omitted on the *Examiner's Assessment Protocol* form.

   Notation: The cloud was (very) high.

*Miscue Grid: Error Totals.*   At this point in using the **Miscue Grid**, indicate the total of miscues for each line of text. You can cross-check the error total by totaling each vertical column corresponding to each error type. By totaling each vertical column, it is possible to determine which miscue type the student is making repeatedly. Note that self-corrections (described next) are not counted as miscues.

- **Self-Corrections**   The student corrects a miscue himself. Self-corrections are noted by writing "SC," but should not be counted as errors in the final tally, unless the student never correctly pronounces the word.

   Student: "*The money . . . the monkey was funny.*"

   Notation: "The monkey was funny."

*Miscue Grid: Analysis of Miscues.*   There are three important questions to ask yourself when analyzing each miscue:

- Does the miscue *make sense*? (Meaning, or M)
- Does the miscue sound right? (Syntax, or S)
- Does it resemble the printed word? (Visual, or V)

### *Here's how you do it:*

1.   Using the grid for the selected passage, take a look at **every** type of miscue.

2.   Ask yourself the three questions noted above for **every** miscue. If the answer is "yes," put a "1" in the appropriate column on the grid.

3.   Talley each column and note the totals in the appropriate spaces on the grid. (See Figure 3.)

4.   Go to *Part III: Miscue Analysis.* This section is divided into Parts A, B, C, D, and E. Go to Part C and write the total number of each type of miscue in the appropriate space. Provide one example for each type of miscue the student used when reading.

5.   Fill out the remaining section, *Part A: Fundamental Behaviors Observed* and *Part B: Word Attack Behaviors.* (See Figure 4.)

6.   Look for a *pattern* across all passages **except** for the passage where the student reached the frustration level. Which language cues does your student seem to use consistently? Which need to be developed further?

*Fluency: Determining Reading Rate.*   As noted earlier, you should record the student while he or she is reading aloud the selected passages. Then, after you have completed testing, use the recording of the *instructional-level* passage to determine the reading fluency rate in the following way:

**Step 1:** Following along on the **Miscue Grid** for the instructional-level passage read by the student, *circle the word reached after 30 seconds of reading the passage aloud.*

**Step 2:** Count the number of words read up to that point, then multiply the number of words read in 30 seconds by two (2). This is the number of words read by the student in 1 minute.

| Hot Shoes | Mis-pronun. | Sub-stitute | Inser-tions | Tchr. Assists | Omis-sions | Error Totals | Self-Correct. | Meaning (M) | Syntax (S) | Visual (V) |
|---|---|---|---|---|---|---|---|---|---|---|
| The guys at the Susan B. Anthony | | | | | | | | | | |
| Elementary School ~~loved~~ (lived) all the new sport | | 1 | | | | 1 | | | | |
| shoes. Some ~~were~~ (wear) the "Sky High" | | 1 | | | | 1 | | 1 | 1 | |
| ~~model~~ (mobil) by Leader. Others who | | 1 | | | | 1 | | | | |
| couldn't afford Sky High/ would settle (sc) | | | | | 2 | 2 | | 1 / 1 | 1 / 1 | |
| for a lesser shoe. Some liked the "Street (sc) | | | | | | | 1 | | | |
| Smarts" by Master, or the | | | | | | | | | | |
| "Uptown-Downtown" by Beebop. | | | | | | | | | | |
| The Anthony boys got to the point | | | | | | | | | | |
| with their shoes that they could | | | | | | | | | | |
| ~~identify~~ (in club.lee) their friends just by | 1 | | | | | 1 | | | | |
| looking at their feet. But the boy who | | | | | | | | | | |
| was the ~~envy~~ (enemy) of the entire fifth | | 1 | | | | 1 | | 1 | 1 | |
| grade was Jamie Lee. He had a | | | | | | | | | | |
| pair of "High Five Pump'em Ups" (sc) | | | | | | | 1 | | | |
| by ~~Superior~~. The ~~only~~ thing Anthony // (sooner) | 1 | | | | 1 | 2 | | 1 | 1 | |
| boys loved as much as their | | | | | | | | | | |
| shoes was basketball. | | | | | | | | | | |
| **TOTALS** | 2 | 4 | | | 3 | 9* | 2 | 5 | 5 | |

Summary of Reading Behaviors (Strengths and Needs)

**FIGURE 3  Scored Student Sample: Miscue Grid**

# PART III: MISCUE ANALYSIS

## Directions

Circle all reading behaviors you observed.

### A. Fundamental Behaviors Observed

(L → R Directionality)    (1-to-1 Matching)    (Searching for Clues)    Cross-Checking

### B. Word Attack Behaviors

No Attempt    (Mispronunciation (Invented Word Substitutions))    (Substitutes)

Skips/Reads On        Asks for Help        Repeats        (Attempts to Self-Correct)

"Sounds Out" (Segmenting)        Blends Sounds        Structural Analysis (Root Words, Affixes)

### C. Cueing Systems Used in Attempting Words

| CUEING TOOL | MISCUE EXAMPLES | ACTUAL TEXT |
|---|---|---|
| (M) Meaning | 5 of 9 miscues, M was used (wear, could enemy, etc) | |
| (S) Syntax | 5 of 9 miscues, S was used (wear, could enemy, etc) | |
| (V) Visual | In 0 of 9 miscues, no V was used. Need to check further. | |

### D. Fluency (word by word → fluent reading)

Word by Word _____    Mixed Phrasing __✓__    Fluent Reading __✓__    Fluency Rate in Seconds __84__

### E. Performance Summary

**Silent Reading Comprehension**

_____ 0–1 questions missed = Easy

_____ 2 questions missed = Adequate

__✓__ 3+ questions missed = Too hard

**Oral Reading Accuracy**

_____ 0–1 oral errors = Easy

_____ 2–5 oral errors = Adequate

__✓__ 6+ oral errors = Too hard

**Continue to the next reading passage?** _____ Yes  __✓__ No

FIGURE 4    Scored Student Example: Miscue Analysis

**TABLE 1  Oral Reading Fluency Norms for Grades 1–8: Words Correct per Minute (wcpm) at the Student's Instructional Reading Level**

| Grade Level | Words Correct per Minute (wcpm)—FALL* | Words Correct per Minute (wcpm)—SPRING* |
|---|---|---|
| Grade 1 | — | 53 |
| Grade 2 | 51 | 89 |
| Grade 3 | 71 | 107 |
| Grade 4 | 94 | 123 |
| Grade 5 | 110 | 139 |
| Grade 6 | 127 | 150 |
| Grade 7 | 128 | 150 |
| Grade 8 | 133 | 151 |

*Adapted from Hasbrouck, J., & Tindal, G. A. (2006). Oral reading fluency norms: A valuable assessment tool for reading teachers. *The Reading Teacher, 59*(7), 636–644.

**Step 3:** Using Table 1, compare the student's reading speed to that of other students at his or her grade level to determine whether the student is reading at an appropriate level of performance.

**Step 4:** Note the student's oral reading fluency rates in the space provided on the *Student Summary Form*.

*Part III: Miscue Analysis.*   This part of the CRI–2 provides a convenient checklist for quickly noting common miscue patterns and word attack behaviors used by students. This can be helpful for later reference when developing an intervention plan.

*Part IV: Listening Comprehension (Optional).*   Historically, some researchers (e.g., Carroll, 1997; Durrell, 1969) have posited that establishing a student's listening comprehension level provides an indication of a student's reading potential. The following explains how to establish a student's listening comprehension level using the *Flynt/Cooter CRI–2*.

1.  Begin by selecting a passage in an alternate form of the CRI–2 at which the student reached the frustration-level criterion. Tell the student that you are now going to read the passage to him or her and ask some questions afterward.

2.  Starting with the background statement for the passage, read aloud the passage.

3.  When you finish reading the passage, ask each of the questions provided for the passage.

4.  Continue reading higher-level passages to the student until he or she falls below the 75% criterion on the comprehension questions. The highest level at which the student can respond to 75% of the questions correctly is considered that student's listening comprehension level. (See Figure 5.)

## PART IV: LISTENING COMPREHENSION

### Directions

If you have decided not to continue to have the student read any other passages, then use this passage to begin assessing the student's listening comprehension. Begin by reading the background statement for this passage and then say, "I am going to read this story to you. Please listen carefully because I will be asking you some questions after I finish reading it to you." After reading the passage, ask the student the questions associated with the passage. If the student correctly answers more than six questions, you will need to move to the next level and repeat the procedure.

### Listening Comprehension

_____ 0–2 questions missed = move to the next passage level

\_\_✓\_\_ more than 2 questions missed = stop assessment or move down a level

Examiner's Notes

---

**FIGURE 5 Scored Student Sample: Listening Comprehension**

## COMPLETING THE STUDENT SUMMARY FORM

PD **TOOLKIT™**
for CRI-2
Click on Additional Resources, then select "Student Summary Form."

The purpose of the *Flynt/Cooter Comprehensive Reading Inventory–2nd Edition (CRI–2)* **Student Summary Form** is to help the examiner sort collected data, make determinations about where the student is in his or her reading development, and plan appropriate reading instruction. The **Student Summary Form** is laid out simply and follows the progression of tests found in the CRI–2. The next section discusses how the **Student Summary Form** is organized, along with a few special instructions.

### Part I. Student Interview

*CRI–2 Information Sources: Interest Inventory, Reading Attitude Survey*

In this section, summarize what has been learned about the student's home and school environment, reading attitudes, special interests that may be helpful in selecting reading materials for instruction, and the examiner's informal evaluation of the student's verbal skills.

### Part II. "Alphabetics" and Vocabulary Knowledge

*CRI–2 Information Sources: Phonemic Awareness Tests (PATs), Phonics Test (PT), High-Frequency Word Knowledge Survey (HFWKS)*

In this part of the **Student Summary Form** you will record what has been learned about the student's development in two key areas: "alphabetics" and vocabulary knowledge. *Alphabetics* was defined by the National Reading Panel (2000) as including phonemic awareness, alphabet knowledge, and phonics. Summarize what you have learned about the student's abilities in these three areas in this section of the **Student Summary Form**. Likewise, you should record any insights into the student's vocabulary knowledge after administering the **High-Frequency Word Knowledge Survey (HFWKS)**.

The examiner will note that for most of these skill areas we use a three-tier system for judging student development: emergent, developing, proficient. *Emergent* means that the student has little or no knowledge of the skill or how to use it. *Developing* means that the student has partly learned the skill(s), but is unable to demonstrate consistent competence. *Proficient* means that the student has mastered the skill and can consistently demonstrate that ability.

## Part III. Reading Comprehension, Fluency, and Oral Reading Assessments

*CRI–2 Information Sources: Reading Passages (Narrative and Expository Forms PP, P, and Levels 1–9): Silent Reading Comprehension, Reading Fluency Assessment (Optional), Oral Reading and Analysis of Miscues, Listening Comprehension (Optional)*

In this section of the **Student Summary Form**, summarize specific strengths and needs in the areas of reading comprehension (differentiate between narrative comprehension [Form A or B] and expository comprehension [Form C or D]), reading fluency (i.e., reading speed and oral reading prosody), and oral reading fluency according to your analysis of miscues.

Additionally, many of the questions in the selections are coded for vocabulary and/or expressive language. Summarize how well a child is able to use the context of the passage or his or her own prior knowledge to discern word or phrase meaning, describe adequately a character or a situation, and demonstrate understanding of figurative language.

Also provided are summary charts for overall reading (holistic) and miscues, cueing systems used, listening comprehension (optional), and reading fluency levels.

## Part IV. Student's Intervention History

In this section, examiners note the student's intervention history in terms of dates, descriptions of the intervention(s), and RTI. This is not only important information for possible recommendations involving Tier 2 and Tier 3 decisions, but is also sound teaching practice when planning instruction.

## Part V. Instructional Implications (IF–THEN Analyses)

In this section the examiner uses the data collected to plan "next steps" for instruction. For Response to Intervention (RTI) purposes, this will be the first step in planning the student's Tier 1 or Tier 2 interventions. Later, in the section titled "Tier I/II Interventions: Translating Assessment Data into Classroom Lesson Plans," we provide a full description of IF–THEN thinking and suggestions for making data-driven instructional decisions.

Figure 6 is a completed example of a **Student Summary Form** for Maria. On the PDToolkit you will find a blank copy of the **Student Summary Form** that can be printed for use in the classroom. The blank form can also be found in the Appendix at the back of this text.

PD **TOOLKIT™**

for CRI–2

Click on Additional Resources, then select "Student Summary Form."

## Pre- and Posttesting

The CRI–2 is especially useful as a universal screening tool, as it is specifically designed for pre- and posttesting purposes and may be used at the beginning of the school year, at mid-year, or upon initial placement in the program, as well as for annual reading progress reports at year's end. The same **Student Summary Form** can be used multiple times simply by varying the ink color for contrast and date identification (for example, black ink for the pretest and blue ink for the posttest).

# Student Summary Form

Student's name _____ *Maria Rizzo* _____ Age ___ *7* ___

School _____ *A. Maceo Smith* _____ Grade ___ *2* ___

Examiner _____ *Mr. Johnston* _____ Date _____ *2/7* _____

**Directions:** Record all significant summary information collected from the subtest administered.

## Part I. Student Interview

> **Background Knowledge, Reading Interests, Speaking Vocabulary**

*Student's interests and background knowledge* (These may be useful in making text selections):

*Informal evaluation of verbal skills* (If the student was interviewed one-on-one):

**FIGURE 6   Example of a Completed Student Summary Form**

# Part II. "Alphabetics" and Vocabulary Knowledge

> ### Phonemic Awareness Tests (PATs), Letter Naming, Phonics, Vocabulary

**Phonemic Awareness Tests** (Rate as one of these—Emergent, Developing, or Proficient—according to the criteria found in the instructions for each subtest.)

*Initial Consonant Sounds Test* (ICST)     ☐ Emergent          ☐ Developing          ☐ Proficient
Student needs:

*Phonemic Segmentation Test* (PST)     ☐ Emergent          ☐ Developing          ☐ Proficient
Student needs:

*Blending Sounds Test* (BST)     ☐ Emergent          ☐ Developing          ☐ Proficient
Student needs:

*Composite phonemic awareness skills*     ☐ **Emergent**          ☐ **Developing**          ☐ **Proficient**

---

**Letter Naming**

*Letter Naming Test* (LNT)     ☐ Emergent          ☐ Developing          ☐ Proficient
Student needs:

---

**Phonics**

*Phonics Test* (PT)     ☐ Emergent          ☐ Developing          ☐ Proficient
Student needs:

---

**Vocabulary Knowledge**

*High-Frequency Word Knowledge Survey* (HFWKS)—
Unknown words:

**FIGURE 6   Example of a Completed Student Summary Form** *(continued)*

## Part III. Reading Comprehension, Fluency, and Oral Reading Assessments

> **Reading Fluency and Reading Comprehension: Passages (Forms PP–9)**

### Overall Performance Levels on Reading Passages

|  | *Narrative passages* (A, B) | *Expository* (nonfiction) *passages* (C, D) |
|---|---|---|
| Easy (independent) | _____ | _____ |
| Adequate (instructional) | _____ | _____ |
| Too hard (frustration) | _____ | _____ |

### Miscue Summary Chart

**Directions:** *Enter total number of miscues from all passages into each block indicated.*

(Purpose: To identify patterns of miscues based on highest frequency of errors to inform instructional decisions.)

|  | Nonsense words | Substitutions | Insertions | Teacher Assists | Omissions |
|---|---|---|---|---|---|
| Total miscues from all passages |  |  |  |  |  |

### Error Analyses (Cueing Systems)

**Directions:** *Enter total number of times (all passages) the student used each of the cueing systems when a miscue was made.*

(Purpose: To determine the extent to which cueing systems are used to identify unknown words in print.)

Meaning cues (M) _____     Syntax cues (S) _____     Visual cues (V) _____

**Listening Comprehension** (highest level reached): _____

**Fluency** (Reading rate/wpm at "adequate" or instructional level)

_____ wpm for Narrative texts (Forms A or B); grade level (approximate) _____

_____ wpm for Expository texts (Forms C or D); grade level (approximate) _____

### Oral Language and Vocabulary Observations

*Maria was able to answer questions about vocabulary in the context of the stories with relative ease. She did have some trouble interpreting figurative language: example - Maria was not sure what "to cut back" or "secret weapon" meant in the stories.*

**FIGURE 6   Example of a Completed Student Summary Form** *(continued)*

## Part IV. Student's Intervention History for Tiers 1 and 2

Describe below the history of interventions attempted with this student and his or her responses to these interventions.

| | Date(s) | Description | Response to Intervention (RTI) |
|---|---|---|---|
| **Example** | 11/2013–5/2014 | Tutoring 1:1 after school | Grades in reading, spelling, and writing improved |
| | | | |
| | | | |

FIGURE 6   Example of a Completed Student Summary Form *(continued)*

## Part V. Instructional Implications (IF–THEN Analyses)

The CRI–2 uses findings from the National Reading Panel and other recent scientific research that identify the critical components of reading as *phonemic awareness, phonics, vocabulary, comprehension,* and *fluency,* as well as rapid letter naming. Performance for this student on the CRI–2 indicates the following:

*Strengths:*

____ Phonemic awareness

____ Rapid letter naming

____ Phonics

____ Vocabulary

____ Comprehension—narrative

____ Comprehension—expository

____ Comprehension—listening

____ Fluency—narrative

____ Fluency—expository

____ Vocabulary in context

____ Figurative language

*Weaknesses:*

____ Phonemic awareness

____ Rapid letter naming

____ Phonics

____ Vocabulary

____ Comprehension—narrative

____ Comprehension—expository

____ Comprehension—listening

____ Fluency—narrative

____ Fluency—expository

____ Vocabulary in context

____ Figurative language

*Teacher notes/intervention planning:*

## Overall Summary of Yearly Progress and Recommendations

Based on this student's current skill levels, strengths and weaknesses identified by the CRI–2, classroom performance, and responses to interventions, following are the priorities for the regular classroom reading instruction:

Teacher/Examiner _____ Date _____

**FIGURE 6** Example of a Completed Student Summary Form

# SETTING INTERVENTION GOALS IN TIERS

Tiers 1 and 2 interventions are easily derived from the data presented on the **Student Summary Form** for the area of need identified. For example, if the student has poor fluency with both narrative and expository texts, the teacher may create a learning "target" to increase fluency from the current grade level to the next grade level within 1 year using a variety of texts. If the child is markedly below grade-level expectations in, say, expository text fluency, the goal could focus on fluency gains specific to expository text typically found in content-area reading assignments.

## Classroom Accommodations

Looking at the pattern of errors can often help the teacher make reasonable classroom accommodations and modifications. For instance, if the child has poor listening comprehension, he may have trouble with lecture-type presentations and need classroom instructions repeated or recorded. If the child is markedly below grade-level expectations in, say, fluency, she may need more time than her classmates to read text, may need tests read orally, or may need a buddy to help her read difficult text.

- A reader with poor fluency, either expository or narrative, is typically a slow reader with regard to reading speed or rate. This reader needs more time than his or her peers to complete even the most basic reading task.

- Often a reader who has fluency issues in reading writes slowly or illegibly as well, thus necessitating more time for written assignments, decreased writing assignment length, and/or use of technology; he or she cannot copy from the board easily or quickly.

- A reader with poor vocabulary skills often has poor comprehension and may need explicit instruction in both vocabulary and comprehension skills.

- Poor listening comprehension will necessitate repetition of classroom instructions and preferential seating close to the teacher so as to reduce distractions.

# RESPONSE TO INTERVENTION (RTI) USING THE CRI–2

According to the practice guide *Assisting Students Struggling with Reading: Response to Intervention and Multi-Tier Intervention in the Primary Grades*, created by the U.S. Department of Education's (2009) Institute of Education Science (IES), a quality Response to Intervention (RTI) implementation has some universal characteristics, discussed next.

## IES Recommendations

**Recommendation 1.** *Screen all students for potential reading problems at the beginning of the year and again in the middle of the year.* Regularly monitor the progress of students who are at elevated risk for developing reading disabilities.

The CRI–2 is a valid and reliable easily administered universal screening tool. With its varying forms, it can be repeated as a posttest, thus giving teachers and parents specific information about the present level of a variety of reading skills as well as measuring reading progress. In addition, the inclusion of both narrative and expository text measures assists teachers to focus on particular text structures in their instruction with students.

**Recommendation 2.** *Provide differentiated reading instruction for all students based on assessments of students' current reading levels (Tier 1 instruction).*

The CRI–2 results help teachers determine the instructional level of each student as well as make distinctions between skills using the specific skill assessments provided and the inventory itself. Using the CRI–2 **IF–THEN Charts**, the teacher can make sound differentiated instructional decisions based on research and designed specifically to address students' identified areas of need.

**Recommendation 3.** *Provide intensive, systematic instruction on up to three foundational reading skills in small groups to students who score below the benchmark on universal screening. Typically these groups meet between three and five times a week for 20–40 minutes in addition to Tier 1 instruction (Tier 2 instruction).*

The CRI–2 provides student data that will help the teacher create classroom groupings specific to students' areas of concern. Students can be grouped using the CRI–2 data collected regarding their reading skill levels. Again, the **IF–THEN Charts** can be used by the teacher for making sound instructional decisions based on student need.

**Recommendation 4.** *Monitor the progress of Tier 2 students at least once a month. Use these data to determine whether students still require intervention.* For those still making insufficient progress, schoolwide teams should design a Tier 3 intervention plan.

The CRI–2 can be used as a progress-monitoring instrument, as it has equivalent forms. Thus, a teacher does not have to re-create an assessment to track student progress; using an equivalent form of the CRI–2 will provide sufficient feedback to the teacher about student growth and the efficacy of instruction. The teacher can give Form A as a universal screening, identify areas of concern, remediate, and then posttest student growth with Form B.

**Recommendation 5.** *Provide intensive instruction daily that promotes the development of various components of reading proficiency to students who show minimal progress after reasonable time in Tier 2 small group instruction (Tier 3).*

The CRI–2 can continue to be used as a progress-monitoring tool for students receiving Tier 3 instructional interventions. Its ease of use, variety of forms, and inclusion of both narrative and expository text make it a classroom-friendly and useful progress-monitoring/planning tool.

## Tier 1 Interventions: Translating Assessment Data into Classroom Lesson Plans

Evidence-based reading research has helped us to better understand the skills children must acquire to become fluent readers. With this knowledge, teachers can now track the progress of their students, plan next steps in teaching and learning for each student, and then reassess to measure how well learning is progressing as a result of planned instruction. Thus, knowing the stages of reading development provides teachers with a kind of reading roadmap for tracking and planning instruction.

The second key to success in reading education is assessing and tracking students in their reading development. Knowing where students are in their development helps teachers plan logical next steps based on what we know about reading development stages.

The third key to success is, in essence, the ability for teachers to analyze reading assessment data and translate this information to plan instruction to meet students' learning needs. We advocate using a method called *IF–THEN thinking* to analyze reading data, as described next.

## IF–THEN Thinking: Selecting Appropriate Intervention Strategies

*IF–THEN thinking* (Flynt & Cooter, 2004; Reutzel & Cooter, 2011) is a way of analyzing reading assessment data and linking this knowledge to appropriate classroom interventions. Thus, *if* you have identified specific learning needs for a student, *then* which teaching strategies are appropriate to offer the student next in your classroom instruction? Tables 2 through 8 provide some examples of IF–THEN Charts. These are adapted from Reutzel and Cooter's (2011) *Strategies for Reading Assessment and Instruction* which you might find helpful as a starting point for instruction. The Reutzel and Cooter text provides an even greater range of activities for your classroom. Another free resource for locating step-by-step lesson plans for many of these and other teaching strategies is **readwritethink,** found online at www.readwritethink.org, which is jointly sponsored by the International Reading Association and the National Council for Teachers of English.

### TABLE 2  IF–THEN Chart for Concepts of Print

| IF the student has this learning need . . . | THEN try using a teaching strategy such as . . . |
|---|---|
| Left-to-right directionality | • Interactive read-alouds<br>• Voice-point<br>• Shared reading |
| Voice–print matching | • Reading environmental print<br>• Interactive read-alouds<br>• Masking/highlighting |
| Concepts of words/letters | • Reading environmental print<br>• Language Experience Approach (LEA)<br>• Scrabble® letter tiles |
| Book handling | • Interactive read-alouds<br>• Shared reading |

### TABLE 3  IF–THEN Chart for Phonemic Awareness

| IF a student has this learning need . . . | THEN try using a strategy such as . . . |
|---|---|
| Initial sounds | • Word families (same/different beginning sounds)<br>• Songs and poetry<br>• Word rubber-banding<br>• Tongue twisters |
| Phonemic segmentation of spoken words | • Word rubber-banding<br>• Add/take a sound from spoken words<br>• Environmental print/logos<br>• Songs, chants, raps, poetry |
| Blending sounds into spoken words | • Add/take a sound<br>• Word rubber-banding<br>• Environmental print/logos<br>• Songs, chants, raps, poetry |
| Rhyming | • Odd-word out<br>• Songs, chants, raps, poetry<br>• Alphabet books<br>• Tongue twisters |

**TABLE 4   IF–THEN Chart for Phonics and Other Word Attack Skills**

| IF a student has this learning need . . . | THEN try using a strategy such as . . . |
| --- | --- |
| Letter sounds | • Explicit phonics instruction<br>• Word boxes<br>• Tongue twisters<br>• Letter sound cards<br>• Making words<br>• Decoding/sounding out nonsense words |
| "C" rule | • Explicit phonics instruction<br>• Word boxes<br>• Letter sound cards<br>• Making words<br>• Nonsense words |
| "G" rule | • Explicit phonics instruction<br>• Word boxes<br>• Letter sound cards<br>• Making words<br>• Nonsense words |
| CVC generalization | • Explicit phonics instruction<br>• Word boxes<br>• Letter sound cards<br>• Making words<br>• Nonsense words |
| Vowel digraphs | • Explicit phonics instruction<br>• Letter sound cards<br>• Making words<br>• Nonsense words |
| VCE (final E) generalization | • Explicit phonics instruction<br>• Nonsense words<br>• Word boxes<br>• Letter sound cards<br>• Making words |
| CV generalization | • Explicit phonics instruction<br>• Word boxes<br>• Letter sound cards<br>• Making words<br>• Nonsense words |
| *r*-controlled vowels | • Explicit phonics<br>• Nonsense words instruction<br>• Letter sound cards<br>• Making words<br>• Word boxes |
| Single consonant sounds | • Explicit phonics<br>• Nonsense words<br>• Letter sound cards<br>• Making words |

TABLE 4   Continued

| Consonant digraphs | • Explicit phonics instruction<br>• Making words<br>• Nonsense words |
|---|---|
| Consonant blends | • Explicit phonics instruction<br>• Letter sound cards<br>• Making words |
| Double consonants | • Explicit phonics instruction<br>• Letter sound cards<br>• Making words |
| Onset and rime | • Explicit instruction<br>• Making words<br>• Tongue twisters<br>• Word boxes<br>• Letter sound cards<br>• Nonsense words |
| Syllabication | • Explicit phonics instruction<br>• Letter sound cards<br>• Making words<br>• Nonsense words |
| Structural analysis | • Creating nonsense words<br>• Spelling in parts (SIP)<br>• Making words<br>• Analytic phonics (word families) |

**TABLE 5   IF–THEN Chart for Reading Comprehension (Narrative Text/Stories)**

| IF a student has this learning need . . . | THEN try using a strategy such as . . . |
|---|---|
| Parts of a story (story grammar) | • Interactive read-alouds<br>• Story grammar instruction<br>• Summary writing<br>• Graphic organizers |
| Sequence of events | • Story grammar instruction<br>• Summary writing<br>• Graphic organizers |
| Use of background knowledge | • Story schema lesson<br>• Click or clunk strategy<br>• Graphic organizers |
| Book selection skills (interest) | • Rule of thumb<br>• Interactive read-alouds<br>• Book talks<br>• Interest Inventory (CRI–2) |
| Self-monitoring of comprehension | • Click or clunk strategy<br>• Oral retelling to a partner |
| Main idea | • Story schema lesson<br>• Graphic organizers<br>• Question-Answer Relationships (QARs) |

**TABLE 6   IF–THEN Chart for Reading Comprehension (Expository/Nonfiction Text—Core Subject Areas)**

| IF the student has this learning need . . . | THEN try using a teaching strategy such as . . . |
|---|---|
| Background knowledge | • Picture walk/talk<br>• Think-Pair-Share |
| Academic vocabulary and concepts | • Direct instruction: written summaries<br>• Graphic organizers<br>• Electronic talking books<br>• Wiki writing<br>• Reciprocal teaching |
| Higher-order comprehension | • Direct instruction: written summaries<br>• Graphic organizers<br>• e-reading/e-responding<br>• Wiki writing<br>• Reciprocal teaching |
| Student-generated questions | • Direct instruction: written summaries<br>• Classroom blogs (with or without technology)<br>• Reciprocal teaching |
| Organizational skills | • Direct instruction: written summaries<br>• Graphic organizers<br>• Comprehension Windows Strategy (see www.jstor.org/pss/20204631) |

**TABLE 7   IF–THEN Chart for Reading Fluency**

| IF a student has this learning need . . . | THEN try using a strategy such as . . . |
|---|---|
| Reading rate | • Repeated readings<br>• Choral reading<br>• Buddy reading<br>• Reading of television captions |
| Reading accuracy/automaticity | • Oral recitation lesson<br>• Assisted reading<br>• Guided oral reading |
| Quality/prosody | • Repeated readings<br>• Choral reading<br>• Guided oral reading<br>• Oral recitation lesson |

**TABLE 8  IF–THEN Chart for Vocabulary**

| IF a student has this learning need . . . | THEN try using a strategy such as . . . |
|---|---|
| Sight words | • Making words<br>• Word searches (newspapers, books, online sources)<br>• Word walls<br>• Vocabulary BINGO!<br>• Personal word lists<br>• Word bank |
| Morphemic analysis | • Word walls (e.g., word family sorts, endings, prefixes)<br>• Direct instruction: structural analysis<br>• Peer teaching |
| Core subject-area words | • Academic word walls<br>• Wheel of Fortune/Who Wants to Be a Millionaire?<br>• Graphic organizers<br>• Frayer Model<br>• Peer teaching<br>• Personal word lists<br>• Semantic maps<br>• Word bank<br>• Comparison grid |

PD **TOOLKIT**™

**for CRI–2**

Click on CRI: Español to see the Spanish version of the Flynt/Cooter Comprehensive Reading Inventory.

# INSTRUCTIONS FOR USING THE CRI: ESPAÑOL

Located on the PDToolkit that accompanies this text is the CRI: Español version for assessing the reading development of students whose first language is Spanish. *Administration and scoring procedures for the CRI: Español subtests are identical to those for the CRI–2.*

# REFERENCES

Carroll, J. B. (1997). Developmental parameters of reading comprehension. In J. Guthrie (Ed.), *Cognition, curriculum, and comprehension*. Newark, DE: International Reading Association.

Durrell, D. D. (1969). Listening comprehension versus reading comprehension. *Journal of Reading, 12*, 455–460.

Flynt, E. S., & Cooter, R. B. (2004). *The Flynt/Cooter Reading Inventory for the Classroom* (5th ed.). Upper Saddle River, NJ: Merrill/Prentice-Hall.

National Reading Panel. (2000). *Report of the National Reading Panel: Teaching children to read*. Washington, DC: National Institute of Child Health and Human Development.

Reutzel, D. R., & Cooter, R. B. (2011). *Strategies for reading assessment and instruction* (4th ed.). Boston: Pearson.

U.S. Department of Education, Institute of Education Science. (2009). *Assisting students struggling with reading: Response to Intervention and multi-tier intervention in the primary grades*. Washington, DC: National Center for Education Evaluation and Regional Assistance.

# SECTION III—THE COMPREHENSIVE READING INVENTORY-2 (CRI-2) PRELIMINARY ASSESSMENTS

# INTEREST INVENTORY

Following is a copy of the **Interest Inventory** described on p. 2 in Section I of the CRI–2. Make a copy of this inventory and use it to begin your assessment of individual students in your classroom. Information gathered about students' background knowledge, interests, and motivations will assist teachers in aligning instructional materials to fit students' strengths, needs, and abilities. Directions for using the **Interest Inventory** are included on the form itself; they are repeated here to allow a review of its use in assessment planning.

> **Directions:** *Ask the student the following questions to discover more about his or her interests that may be useful in selecting texts of interest during instruction. Record responses and observations that seem useful for instructional planning.*
>
> **Alternative Directions:** *This inventory can also be group administered where students are capable of recording written responses. However, one-on-one interviews are preferable because nonverbal cues are often observed.*

# READING ATTITUDE SURVEY—ELEMENTARY GRADES (K–5)

Another aspect of the affective domain for which we offer an assessment tool at the elementary level is reading attitude. The **Reading Attitude Survey—Elementary Grades (K–5)** is based on the research of McKenna and Kear (1990), and Heathington and Alexander (1978). This instrument helps teachers discover students' fundamental attitudes about reading at school, home, and for pleasure. Following is a copy of the **Reading Attitude Survey—Elementary Grades (K–5)**. Directions for using this survey are placed here but are also found on the Reading Attitude Survey on page 34.

> **Directions:** *Ask students to answer each of the following questions by marking the face that best describes how they feel. If this is administered one-on-one, encourage students to explain how they feel and note any information you think may be helpful for planning instruction.*

# CONCEPTS OF PRINT ASSESSMENT

*Purpose.* This is a test for preschool through grade 1 students intended to assess children's basic understanding of how books work in English. You will discover whether students understand basic print concepts and the basic language of reading instruction such as *letter*, *word*, and *sentence*; left-to-right and top-down progression; the difference between pictures and words; punctuation; and much more.

*Materials Needed.* We recommend that you use an early level storybook for this assessment, similar to those used in the second semester of first grade, that has both illustrations and a fair number of sentences per page.

*Procedure.* Follow along with the directions provided in the protocol from that follows and note any issues you notice to inform future instruction.

# Interest Inventory

Student's Name _____ Age _____

Date _____ Grade _____ Examiner _____

---

**Directions:** *Ask the student the following questions to discover more about his or her interests that may be useful in selecting texts of interest during instruction. Record responses and observations that seem useful for instructional planning.*

**Alternative Directions:** *This inventory can also be group administered where students are capable of recording written responses. However, one-on-one interviews are preferable because nonverbal cues are often observed.*

---

## For Primary-Level Students (Grades PK–3)

1.  Where do you live? Do you know your address? What is it?

2.  Who lives in your house with you?

3.  What kinds of jobs do you have at home?

4.  What is one thing you really like to do at home? How about video games?

5.  Do you ever read at home? (If yes, ask the next questions.) *When* do you read? What was the last thing you read?

*(continued)*

6. Does anyone ever read to you? (Ask *who* and *how often.*)

7. Do you have a TV in your room? How much TV do you watch every day? What are your favorite shows?

## For Students of Any Level (Optional for Primary Students)

1. If you were to win one million dollars in a contest, how might you use the money?

2. Do you use e-mail? Would you like me to send you an e-mail message sometime?

3. What are your favorite classes/subjects at school? Why?

4. What kinds of jobs do you think you might like to have when you are older?

5. Do you like to use computers? What do you like best?

6. Who are some famous people that you like? Why?

7. What is your favorite movie(s)?

8. What are some magazines that you like?

*(continued)*

9. Name some of the best books you have read.

10. Do you ever read parts of the newspaper? Which parts? Do you like the comics section?

11. What kinds of books would you most like to read in the future?

12. Do you know how to use the Internet? If yes, what are some of your favorite websites?

13. Who is your favorite person in the world? Why?

14. Do you like sports? If so, which ones? Who are your favorite athletes?

15. What makes a person a good reader?

16. What causes a person to not be a good reader?

**Examiner's Notes:**

# Reading Attitude Survey—Elementary Grades (K–5)

Student's Name _____ Age _____

Date _____ Grade _____ Examiner _____

> **Directions:** Ask students to answer each of the following questions by marking the face that best describes how they feel. If this is administered one-on-one, encourage students to explain how they feel and note any information you think may be helpful for planning instruction.

1. How do you feel when you find a book you want to read?

2. How do you feel when you have free time at school to read anything you want?

3. How do you feel about reading books or magazines at home?

4. How do you feel when you get a book as a gift?

5. How do you feel about starting to read a new book?

(continued)

6. How do you feel about reading books in the summer when school is out?

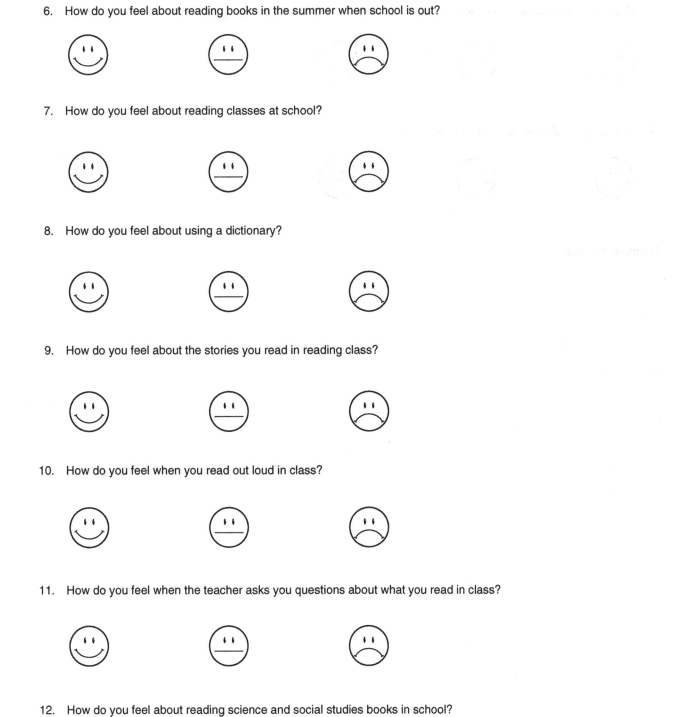

7. How do you feel about reading classes at school?

8. How do you feel about using a dictionary?

9. How do you feel about the stories you read in reading class?

10. How do you feel when you read out loud in class?

11. How do you feel when the teacher asks you questions about what you read in class?

12. How do you feel about reading science and social studies books in school?

*(continued)*

13. How do you feel when you are asked to complete worksheets and workbook pages at school?

14. How do you feel when you go to a bookstore?

**Examiner's Notes:**

*Sources:* Adapted from "Measuring Attitude Toward Reading: A New Tool for Teachers," by M. McKenna and D. J. Kear, May 1990, *The Reading Teacher, 43*(9), 626–639; "A Child-Based Observation Checklist to Assess Attitudes Toward Reading," by B. S. Heathington and J. E. Alexander, 1978, *The Reading Teacher, 31*(7), 769–771.

# Concepts of Print Assessment*

**Student's Name**_____ **Age** _____

**Date** _____ **Grade** _____

> **Directions:** *Use an early level trade book (storybook) for this assessment, similar to those used in the second semester of first grade, that has both illustrations and a fair number of sentences per page. If a book is not readily available you may use the Form A, Level 1 passage,* You Cannot Fly! *Follow the procedures for each task and note any observations as to how the child reacted in the far right-hand column.*

| Book Concepts | | |
|---|---|---|
| Cover of Book | Hand the child the book by the spine, and then ask the following questions. | |
| | Please show me how you hold a book. | |
| | Now show me the front of the book. | |
| | Please point to the name of the author; point to the name of the illustrator. | |
| | Show me the back of the book. | |
| | Please point to the book's title. | |
| | Can you show me the title page? | |
| **Directionality and Text Concepts** | | |
| Directionality | Which page do we read first? | |
| | Which page do we read last? | |
| Top to bottom of page; first word on a page | Show me where we start reading this book. | |
| | Where is the first word on this page? | |
| Left to right in sentence and return sweep | With your finger, show me which way we go when we are reading. | |
| Left-to-right page sequence | Where do we go next when we finish reading this page? | |
| Concept of a word | Can you point to a word? | |
| | How many words are in this sentence? | |
| Print is constant | Can you find two words that are the same? | |
| Last word in a sentence | Where is the last word on this page? | |
| Concept of a letter | Can you point to a letter? | |
| | Show me the first letter in this word. | |
| | Now show me the last letter in this word. | |
| Capital letters | Can you find a capital (or uppercase) letter? | |
| Lowercase letters | Can you show me a lowercase letter? | |

*This assessment was adapted from a similar tool we used as part of our Dallas Reading Academy Project. We very much appreciate the Lead Reading Teachers of the Dallas Independent School District for their professional insights and inspiration.

*(continued)*

| Punctuation Marks | | |
|---|---|---|
| Period | What is this mark called? | |
| | What do you do when you see it? | |
| Comma | What is this mark called? | |
| | What do you do when you see it? | |
| Question mark | What is this mark called? What does it mean? | |
| Exclamation mark | What is this mark called? What does it mean? | |
| Quotation marks | What are these marks called? What do they mean? | |

# ALPHABETICS ASSESSMENTS

Aimed at assessing what the National Reading Panel (2000) referred to as "Alphabetics," the following pages provide subtests for assessing phonemic awareness, alphabet knowledge, and phonics. Assessment protocols are described before each subtest series.

## Phonemic Awareness Tests (PATs)

### Initial Consonant Sounds Test (ICST): An Oddity Task

*Purpose.* The **Initial Consonant Sounds Test (ICST)** measures whether children have developed the awareness of beginning sounds in spoken words. Sometimes referred to in reading research as an "oddity task," this type of test requires that students identify the "odd word out" or, more specifically, the odd beginning sound from a list of spoken words. (Note: The beginning consonant sound in a one-syllable word is also known as the *onset*, and the remainder of the word as the *rime*.)

*Research.* This subtest was developed, field tested, and examined for concurrent validity as part of a comprehensive study at Vanderbilt University (Williams, 2003).

*Procedure.*
1.  Seat the child across from you at a table.

2.  Say, "We are going to play a word game. First, I will show you how this game is played. I am going to say three words slowly. Then, I will figure out which word has a different sound at the beginning."

3.  Next, say the words "**PAN, PIG, KITE**" slowly, emphasizing the beginning sound of each word just a little more than other sounds in the word. Say, "I will say the words one more time to see if I can tell which word has a different sound at the beginning—**PAN, PIG, KITE.**"

4.  Say, "The words **PAN** and **PIG** sound the same at the beginning, but **KITE** has a different beginning sound."

5.  Say, "Let me do one more for you—**COAT, BUS, BALL**. Did you notice that **COAT** has a different sound at the beginning than **BUS** and **BALL?** Now you try it."

6.  Ask the child now to decide which word is the odd word out. Say, "**RUN, ROPE, CALL.** Which word has a different sound at the beginning?" If the child has difficulty, you may repeat the words.

7.  If the student gives the correct answer, proceed to the **Initial Consonant Sounds Test (ICST)**: Form A. Forms B and C are equivalent forms of the ICST, and may be used for further testing, or for progress monitoring if instruction in phonemic awareness is needed.

NOTE: *You may say each row of words twice for the student.*

*Determining the Student's Developmental Level.* Developmental levels are an indication of the student's ability for a given skill. **Proficient** means that the student has attained relative mastery of the skill and does not require further instruction. **Developing** means that the student has some ability with the skill, but needs further instruction. **Emergent** essentially means that the student has little or no knowledge of the skill and requires instruction.

| DEVELOPMENTAL LEVEL | ITEMS CORRECT |
| --- | --- |
| Proficient | 8–10 |
| Developing | 4–7 |
| Emergent | 0–3 |

# Initial Consonant Sounds Test (ICST)

## Form A

| Soap | Six | Dog |
|------|------|------|
| Car | Man | Mop |
| Duck | Dog | Five |
| Pig | Pack | Fan |
| Fish | Fan | Leaf |
| Nest | Nut | Wheel |
| Cat | Cake | Nine |
| Sun | Tree | Tie |
| Clock | Bee | Bat |
| Sock | Feet | Fish |

# Initial Consonant Sounds Test (ICST)
## Form B

| Rope | Run | Dog |
|------|-----|-----|
| Can | More | Mop |
| Doll | Dark | Honey |
| Pore | Plan | Five |
| Fish | Four | Leaf |
| None | Nut | Wing |
| City | Celery | Note |
| Sing | Type | Tie |
| Get | Go | Bat |
| Very | Verse | Tree |

# Initial Consonant Sounds Test (ICST)

## Form C

| | | |
|---|---|---|
| Plane | Place | Log |
| Hill | Ran | Rope |
| Doll | Do | First |
| Port | Pretty | Lost |
| So | Sun | Boy |
| Neat | Never | Wing |
| Cut | Cake | Bird |
| Tongue | Top | Fish |
| Soap | Ball | Bake |
| Boat | Feet | Fork |

*Phonemic Segmentation Test (PST)*

*Purpose.* A child's ability to isolate individual sounds in spoken words, or *phonemes*, is an early indication as to whether he or she is ready for phonics instruction. In this subtest, students are asked to listen to spoken words pronounced by the examiner, and then isolate sounds in the initial, medial, and final positions in each word.

*Research.* This subtest was developed, field tested, and examined for concurrent validity as a part of a comprehensive study at Vanderbilt University (Williams, 2003).

*Procedures.* Begin by modeling for the student how phonemes heard in spoken words can be pronounced individually. Demonstrate using the "word rubber-banding" technique (i.e., hearing and saying each phoneme in a spoken word by stretching the word out slowly like a rubber band) and how you can hear the beginning or initial sound in words.

> *Say:* "Listen to how I can stretch a word like a rubber band and hear each sound in the word."

Using the words "look" and then "top," demonstrate word rubber-banding.

> *Say:* "Lllllllllllllooooooooooookkkkkkkk. When I say it that way and listen to the sound at the beginning of the word, I can hear the /l/ sound. Llllllllllll-looooooooookkk. Could you hear /l/ when I said 'top' that way?"

Repeat this modeling exercise using the word "look" and the student's own first or last name. Still another variation involves drawing out a sound or exaggerating the sound; for example, "MMMMMaaaaarrrryyyy had a little llllllllaaaaammmmmm" (Reutzel & Cooter, 2011a).

Next, let the child practice the word rubber-banding technique with the words we supply for this purpose, or choose some of your own. Make sure practice words you select have no more than three sounds or phonemes.

Next, explain to the child that you are going to play a quick game together. You will say a word, and then you will ask the child to tell you the sound he or she hears in a specific place in the word, such as beginning, middle, or end. For example, you may say, "slam." You would then say, "Say the sound at the end of the word 'slam.'" The child should respond correctly by articulating the sound /m/.

Now you may begin the **Phonemic Segmentation Test (PST)** with Form A. Forms B and C may be used, if needed, at other times in the school year to check for progress on phonemic segmentation learning as a result of your teaching. Record each response on the protocol form (these may be duplicated as much as you like for your classroom assessments).

*Determining the Student's Developmental Level.* Developmental levels are an indication of the student's ability for a given skill. *Proficient* means that the student has attained relative mastery of the skill and does not require further instruction. *Developing* means that the student has some ability with the skill, but needs further instruction. *Emergent* essentially means that the student has little or no knowledge of the skill and requires instruction.

On the PST, you can determine the student's developmental level by adding up the total number correct out of the 15 items from Parts 1–3 on Forms A, B, or C, then comparing the number correct to the following table.

| DEVELOPMENTAL LEVEL | ITEMS CORRECT |
|---------------------|---------------|
| Proficient          | 13–15         |
| Developing          | 9–12          |
| Emergent            | 0–8           |

# Phonemic Segmentation Test (PST)
# Form A

## Part 1. Beginning (Initial) Sounds in Spoken Words

*Examiner says:* "Please tell me the sound you hear at the beginning of each word as I say it. For example, if I say the word 'sit' you would say /s/. Do you have any questions?"

**Note:** If the child does not seem to understand, offer two or three other examples. After you pronounce each of the five target words below, note the student's response next to it on your protocol form in the space provided.

| Target Words and Phonemes | Student Responses |
| --- | --- |
| live /l/ | |
| big /b/ | |
| sat /s/ | |
| men /m/ | |
| not /n/ | |

**Score:** _____/5 words

## Part 2. Medial (Middle) Sounds in Spoken Words

*Examiner says:* "Now we are going to change our game just a little. Please tell me the sound you hear in the middle of each word as I say it. For example, if I say the word 'not' you would say /ŏ/. Do you have any questions?"

**Note:** If the child does not seem to understand, offer two or three other examples. After you pronounce each of the five target words below, note the student's response next to it on your protocol form in the space provided.

| Target Words and Phonemes | Student Responses |
| --- | --- |
| phone /ō/ | |
| rat /ă/ | |
| did /ĭ/ | |
| fine /ī/ | |
| these /ē/ | |

**Score:** _____/5 words

*(continued)*

# Phonemic Segmentation Test (PST)
# Form A

## Part 3. Final (Ending) Sounds in Spoken Words

*Examiner says:* "Now we will change the game just one more time. Please tell me the sound you hear at the end of each word as I say it. For example, if I say the word 'hot' you would say /t/. Do you have any questions?"

**Note:** If the child does not seem to understand, offer two or three other examples. After you pronounce each of the five target words below, note the student's response next to it on your protocol form in the space provided.

| Target Words and Phonemes | Student Responses |
|---|---|
| back /k/ | |
| say /ā/ | |
| not /t/ | |
| bun /n/ | |
| call /l/ | |

**Score:** _____/5 words

**Form A Total Score (Part 1 + Part 2 + Part 3) = _____/15 words**

# Phonemic Segmentation Test (PST)
# Form B

## Part 1. Beginning (Initial) Sounds in Spoken Words

*Examiner says:* "Please tell me the sound you hear at the beginning of each word as I say it. For example, if I say the word 'sit' you would say /s/. Do you have any questions?"

**Note:** If the child does not seem to understand, offer two or three other examples. After you pronounce each of the five target words below, note the student's response next to it on your protocol form in the space provided.

| Target Words and Phonemes | Student Responses |
| --- | --- |
| me /m/ | |
| can /k/ | |
| get /g/ | |
| have /h/ | |
| some /s/ | |

**Score:** _____/5 words

## Part 2. Medial (Middle) Sounds in Spoken Words

*Examiner says:* "Now we are going to change our game just a little. Please tell me the sound you hear in the middle of each word as I say it. For example, if I say the word 'not' you would say /ŏ/. Do you have any questions?"

**Note:** If the child does not seem to understand, offer two or three other examples. After you pronounce each of the five target words below, note the student's response next to it on your protocol form in the space provided.

| Target Words and Phonemes | Student Responses |
| --- | --- |
| tile / ī / | |
| date /ā / | |
| hush /e/ | |
| fun /ŭ / | |
| clock /ŏ / | |

**Score:** _____/5 words

*(continued)*

# Phonemic Segmentation Test (PST)
# Form B

## Part 3. Final (Ending) Sounds in Spoken Words

**Examiner says:** "Now we will change the game just one more time. Please tell me the sound you hear at the end of each word as I say it. For example, if I say the word 'cot' you would say /t/. Do you have any questions?"

**Note:** If the child does not seem to understand, offer two or three other examples. After you pronounce each of the five target words below, note the student's response next to it on your protocol form in the space provided.

| Target Words and Phonemes | Student Responses |
| --- | --- |
| cut /t/ | |
| fool /l/ | |
| loop /p/ | |
| rode /d/ | |
| home /m/ | |

**Score: _____/5 words**

## Form B Total Score (Part 1 + Part 2 + Part 3) = _____/15 words

# Phonemic Segmentation Test (PST)
# Form C

## Part 1. Beginning (Initial) Sounds in Spoken Words

*Examiner says:* "Please tell me the sound you hear at the beginning of each word as I say it. For example, if I say the word 'sit' you would say /s/. Do you have any questions?"

**Note:** If the child does not seem to understand, offer two or three other examples. After you pronounce each of the five target words below, note the student's response next to it on your protocol form in the space provided.

| Target Words and Phonemes | Student Responses |
|---|---|
| yard /y/ | |
| miss /m/ | |
| get /g/ | |
| rap /r/ | |
| bike /b/ | |

Score: _____/5 words

## Part 2. Medial (Middle) Sounds in Spoken Words

*Examiner says:* "Now we are going to change our game just a little. Please tell me the sound you hear in the middle of each word as I say it. For example, if I say the word 'not' you would say /ŏ/. Do you have any questions?"

**Note:** If the child does not seem to understand, offer two or three other examples. After you pronounce each of the five target words below, note the student's response next to it on your protocol form in the space provided.

| Target Words and Phonemes | Student Responses |
|---|---|
| mug / ə/ | |
| fat /ă/ | |
| did /ĭ/ | |
| mine /ī/ | |
| beat /ē/ | |

Score: _____/5 words

*(continued)*

# Phonemic Segmentation Test (PST)
# Form C

## Part 3. Final (Ending) Sounds in Spoken Words

*Examiner says:* "Now we will change the game just one more time. Please tell me the sound you hear at the end of each word as I say it. For example, if I say the word 'cot' you would say /t/. Do you have any questions?"

**Note:** If the child does not seem to understand, offer two or three other examples. After you pronounce each of the five target words below, note the student's response next to it on your protocol form in the space provided.

| Target Words and Phonemes | Student Responses |
| --- | --- |
| tack /k/ | |
| play /ā/ | |
| can /n/ | |
| rut /t/ | |
| some /m/ | |

**Score: _____/5 words**

**Form C Total Score (Part 1 + Part 2 + Part 3) = _____/15 words**

### Blending Sounds Test (BST)

*Purpose.* In the **Blending Sounds Test (BST)** students are asked to pronounce words by blending the spoken sounds of individual words stretched out verbally into *segmented* units (i.e., **sh-ip** or **f-a-n**). We call this "word rubber-banding." According to Griffith and Olson (1992), the ability to blend and pronounce a word from its segmented form demonstrates a slightly higher level of phonemic awareness than, say, recognizing rhyming sounds.

*Research.* This subtest was developed, field tested, and examined for concurrent validity as part of a comprehensive study at Vanderbilt University (Williams, 2003).

*Procedure.* The BST is divided into two parts. The **Blending Sounds Test BST—Part A: Onsets and Rime** is the simpler task and has students blend onsets and rimes. A *rime* is the vowel at the beginning of a syllable and the *onset* is the consonant or consonants that come just before the vowel (Opitz, 2000; Reutzel & Cooter, 2011b). For example, in the word "back," *b–* is the onset and *–ack* is the rime; in the word "blow," *bl–* is the onset and *–ow* is the rime.

In the **Blending Sounds Test BST—Part B: Blending Individual Sounds**, students perform a more advanced phonemic awareness performance task that has students blend individual sounds into words. For example, students may be asked to blend the sounds /s/ /ă/ /n/ /d/ into the whole word "sand."

If a student struggles with either task, then the teacher will need to plan instructional lessons that help the student(s) master that level of phonemic awareness before introducing the *alphabetic principle* and *phonics*.

*Determining the Student's Developmental Level.* Developmental levels are an indication of the student's ability for a given skill. *Proficient* means that the student has attained relative mastery of the skill and does not require further instruction. *Developing* means that the student has some ability with the skill, but needs further instruction. *Emergent* essentially means that the student has little or no knowledge of the skill and requires instruction.

For the BST, we have established the following developmental criteria based on research by Yopp (1988).

| DEVELOPMENTAL LEVEL | ITEMS CORRECT |
| --- | --- |
| Proficient | 20–30 |
| Developing | 16–19 |
| Emergent | 0–15 |

# Blending Sounds Test (BST)
# Part A: Onsets and Rime

*Procedures*

1. Explain to the student that you will be stretching words out like a rubber band and saying each sound.
2. Model the following stretched words for the child as well as pronouncing them as whole, blended words.

| Segmented Word/Sounds | Blended Word (Examiner Pronounces) |
|---|---|
| M -ug | Mug |
| L -ock | Lock |
| M -an | Man |

3. Next, as a practice for the student to check for understanding, stretch the following words and ask the child to tell you the word. Before you say each segmented word in rubber-banding style, you may ask (optional) "What am I saying?"

| Segmented Word/Sounds | Blended Word (Student Pronounces) |
|---|---|
| T -ack | Tack |
| H -at | Hat |
| Gl -ide | Glide |

4. Now you may begin administering Form A. Note each correct response with a checkmark (√ ). Total the number of correct responses to determine whether the mastery level (20+ correct responses) has been achieved.

# Blending Sounds Test (BST)
## Part A: Protocol Onsets and Rime

| Segmented Word/Sounds | Blended Word | Correct Response? (√) |
|---|---|---|
| M -ain | Main | |
| R -ate | Rate | |
| L -ight | Light | |
| C -oke | Coke | |
| M -ake | Make | |
| S -aw | Saw | |
| F -ill | Fill | |
| M -op | Mop | |
| B -ale | Bale | |
| W -ay | Way | |
| T -in | Tin | |
| F -or | For | |

*(continued)*

# Blending Sounds Test (BST)
## Part A: Protocol Onsets and Rime (Continued)

| Segmented Word/Sounds | Blended Word | Correct Response? (√) |
|---|---|---|
| M -all | Mall | |
| Tr -eat | Treat | |
| L -ine | Line | |
| St -ore | Store | |
| G -ame | Game | |
| B -ell | Bell | |
| S -ing | Sing | |
| L -uck | Luck | |
| B -est | Best | |
| Th -ink | Think | |
| T -ank | Tank | |
| M -ice | Mice | |

*(continued)*

# Blending Sounds Test (BST)

## Part A: Protocol Onsets and Rime (Continued)

| Segmented Word/Sounds | Blended Word | Correct Response? (√) |
|---|---|---|
| L -ip | Lip | |
| St -ump | Stump | |
| T -ap | Tap | |
| K -ick | Kick | |
| S -ir | Sir | |
| D -unk | Dunk | |
| Tr -ash | Trash | |

Total correct _____

# Blending Sounds Test (BST)
# Part B: Blending Individual Sounds

*Procedures*

1.  Explain to the student that you will be stretching words out like a rubber band and saying each sound.

2.  Model the following stretched words for the child as well as pronouncing them as whole, blended words.

| Segmented Word/Sounds | Blended Word (Examiner Pronounces) |
|---|---|
| S-i-t | Sit |
| F-a-n | Fan |
| T-o-p | Top |

3.  Next, as a practice for the student to check for understanding, stretch the following words and ask the child to tell you the word. Before you say each segmented word in rubber-banding style, you may ask (optional) "What am I saying?"

| Segmented Word/Sounds | Blended Word (Student Pronounces) |
|---|---|
| M-a-n | Man |
| C-a-p | Cap |

4.  Now you may begin administering Form B. Note each correct response with a checkmark (√). Total the number of correct responses to determine whether the mastery level (20+ correct responses) has been achieved.

# Blending Sounds Test (BST)
## Part B: Protocol Blending Individual Sounds

| Segmented Word/Sounds | Blended Word | Correct Response? (√) |
|---|---|---|
| S - i - t | Sit | |
| F - a - t | Fat | |
| F - i - n | Fin | |
| L - i - t | Lit | |
| B - ē - t | Beet | |
| H - a - s | Has | |
| S - ē | See | |
| G - o - t | Got | |
| S - e - t | Set | |
| S - ō | So | |
| L - a - p | Lap | |
| T - i - p | Tip | |

*(continued)*

# Blending Sounds Test (BST)

## Part B: Protocol Blending Individual Sounds (Continued)

| Segmented Word/Sounds | Blended Word | Correct Response? (√) |
|---|---|---|
| M - a - n | Man | |
| St - ā - te | State | |
| B - o - x | Box | |
| Sl - a - b | Slab | |
| R - u(ə) - g | Rug | |
| M - i - ce (ss) | Mice | |
| Sh - ē - t | Sheet | |
| F - r - o - g | Frog | |
| J - u - m - p | Jump | |
| T - ur - k - ē | Turkey | |
| M - ī - n - d | Mind | |
| W - ĭ - g | Wig | |

*(continued)*

# Blending Sounds Test (BST)

## Part B: Protocol Blending Individual Sounds (Continued)

| Segmented Word/Sounds | Blended Word | Correct Response? (√) |
|---|---|---|
| L - o - ck | Lock | |
| St - ĕ - m | Stem | |
| B - ē - k | Beak | |
| H - ī - de | Hide | |
| C - ă - sh | Cash | |
| D - ī - m | Dime | |

**Total correct** _____

# Letter Naming Test (LNT)

*Purpose.*   Based on the work of Marie Clay (1993), the **Letter Naming Test (LNT)** determines whether readers can identify letters of the alphabet in upper- and lowercase forms. Walsh, Price, and Gillingham (1988) found that letter naming was strongly related to early reading achievement for kindergarten children.

*Research.*   This subtest was developed, field tested, and examined for concurrent validity as part of a comprehensive study at Vanderbilt University (Williams, 2003).

*Procedure.*   Invite the student to be seated next to you and explain that you would like to find out which letters of the alphabet he or she can name as you point to them on a chart. Begin pointing at the top of **Student Form 1: Alphabet Letter Display (Mixed-Case Letters)**, working line by line and left to right to the bottom of the display, keeping letters below your line of focus covered. Using a photocopy of the student form(s) provided, mark which of the letters were correctly named. Ask the child to point to the letter you named in the display. Record this information. Most children, even readers with special learning needs, will be able to identify at least 50% of the letters requested (Reutzel & Cooter, 2011a).

If a student struggles with **Student Form 1: Alphabet Letter Display (Mixed-Case Letters)**, which uses a mix of upper- and lowercase letters, then try the same procedure using **Student Form 2: Alphabet Letter Display (All Uppercase Letters)**. This may help you discover whether the child has learned the alphabet in uppercase form only. Similarly, you may wish to try **Student Form 3: Alphabet Letter Display (All Lowercase Letters)** to discover learning gaps.

*Determining the Student's Developmental Level.*   Developmental levels are an indication of the student's ability for a given skill. *Proficient* means that the student has attained relative mastery of the skill and does not require further instruction. *Developing* means that the student has some ability with the skill, but needs further instruction. *Emergent* essentially means that the student has little or no knowledge of the skill and requires instruction.

On the LNT, we are interested in learning (1) whether the student can name all 26 letters of the alphabet in upper- and lowercase forms, and (2) how quickly the student can identify each letter (rapid letter naming). In letter naming you should note any unknown letters and whether upper- or lowercase form is an issue. Perfect letter identification is the goal, and this is reflected in the following developmental levels. Rapid letter naming has also been identified as desirable in reading research. Although research-based criteria in terms of "speed of letter identification" are unavailable at this time, we feel teachers should consider how long students take to identify each letter. A pause of more than, say, 5 seconds should be viewed as problematic and indicates more practice is in order for the student.

| DEVELOPMENTAL LEVEL | ITEMS CORRECT |
| --- | --- |
| Proficient | 26 |
| Developing | 20–25 |
| Emergent | 0–19 |

# Letter Naming Test (LNT)

## Student Form 1:
## Alphabet Letter Display (Mixed-Case Letters)

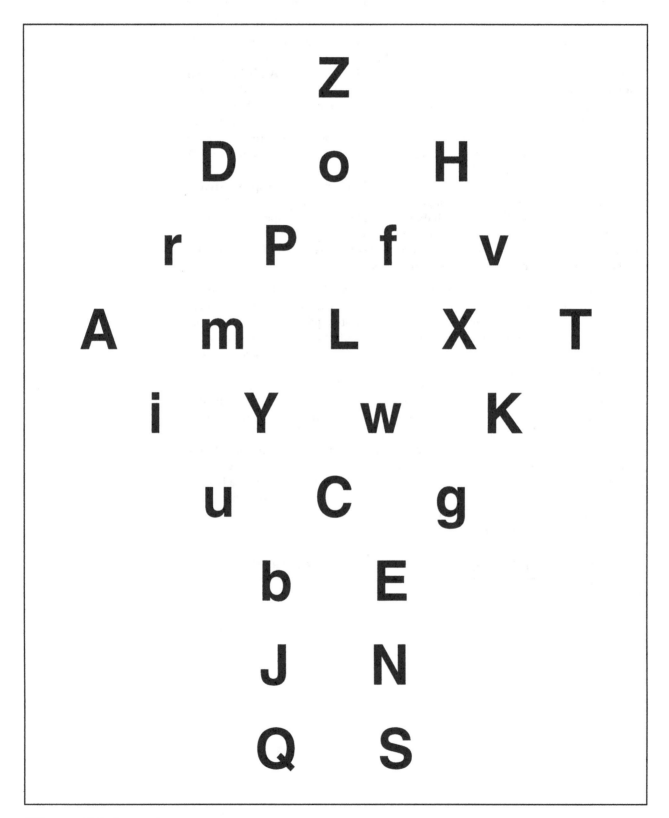

# Letter Naming Test (LNT)

## Student Form 2:
## Alphabet Letter Display (All Uppercase Letters)

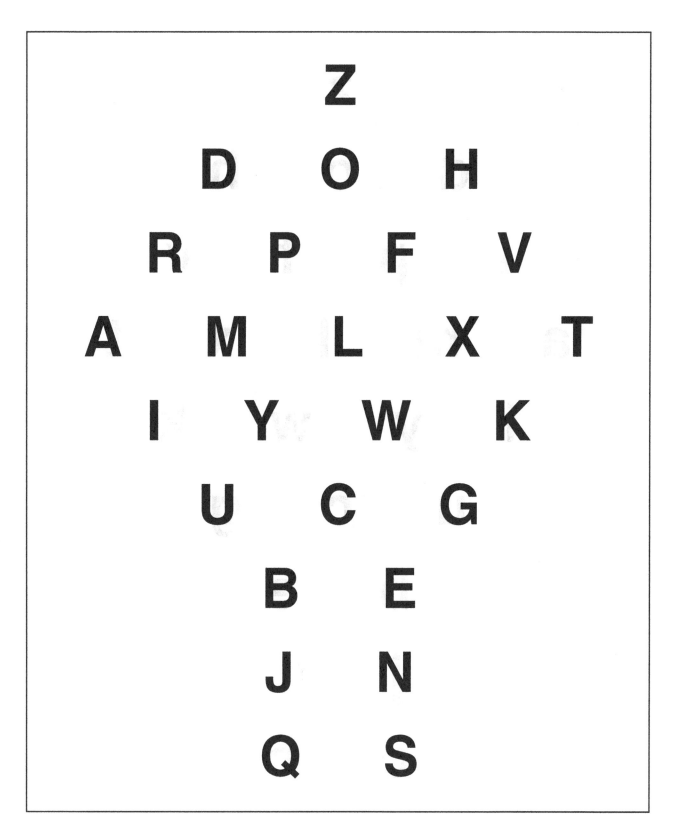

# Letter Naming Test (LNT)

## Student Form 3:
## Alphabet Letter Display (All Lowercase Letters)

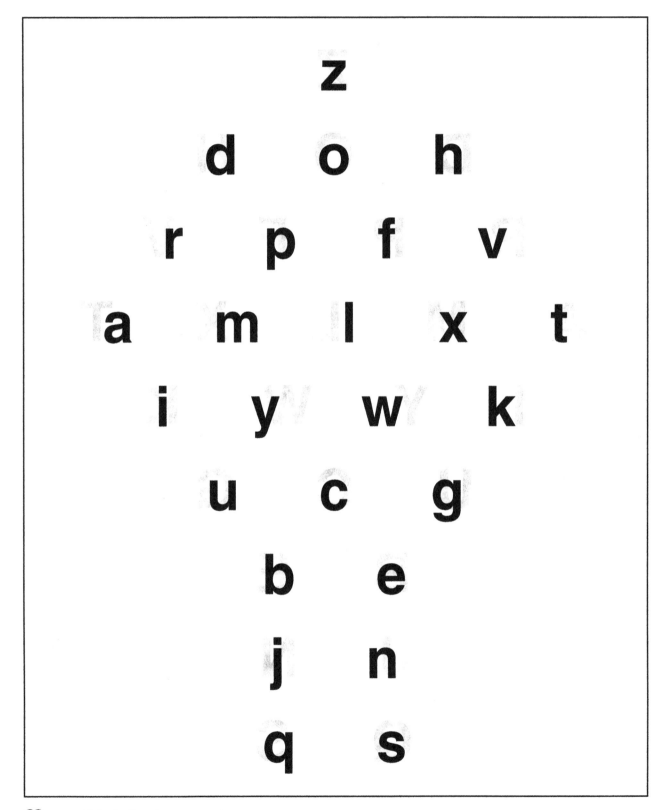

# Phonics Test (PT)

*Purpose.* The **Phonics Test (PT)** was designed for the CRI–2 as a quick assessment of phonics abilities for children in grades K–3. Areas of special focus include initial consonant sounds (onsets), correct pronunciation of common rimes, syllabication, affixes (prefixes and suffixes), and *r*-controlled vowels. These phonics areas are embedded within words that students are asked to read. Analysis of students' phonics abilities focuses on these fundamental areas.

*Research.* This subtest was developed, field tested, and examined for concurrent validity as part of a comprehensive study at Vanderbilt University (Williams, 2003).

*Instructions for Examiners.* Each row of the words for students to read aloud appears on the **Phonics Test (PT): Student Form**, and the form should be printed out by the examiner before testing. Alternatively, you may want to create word cards for testing purposes. You will also need to print a copy of the **Phonics Test (PT) Analysis Grid: Examiner's Protocol Form** for each student you assess. Finally, we recommend that you digitally record or video record students as they read each group of words so that you can check your analysis.

*Administration Procedure.* Seat the student at a table directly across from you. Turn on your digital recorder or video camera and say the student's name aloud and the date to mark the record, and then continue. Beginning with the first word, say to the student, "Please read the words in each row. Just pronounce them the way you think they would sound. For instance, this first word is 'dunk.' Go ahead and try to say the other words for me, reading the three words in each row until you finish reading all of the words."

As the student reads each word, make a notation to the right of each grouping of words on the **Phonics Test (PT) Analysis Grid** form indicating whether the child said the word correctly. Words pronounced correctly should be noted with a checkmark ($\sqrt{}$). Incorrect pronunciations should be written phonetically. For example, if a student mispronounced the word "jogging" (line 14), it might be written as "jigging" to the right of the word cluster on line 14 to reflect the way the student said it. Continue having the student read each cluster of words, marking any *miscues* (mispronounced words) in the blank area to the right of each word cluster on the **Phonics Test (PT) Analysis Grid** form.

*Analyzing the Miscues.* The PT is quick and easy to analyze. Analysis begins after the student has read all of the nonsense words. First, replay the student's recording to be sure that any miscues have been correctly recorded. Next, for each miscue noted, simply place a hash mark ("|") in the box indicating which phonics skill(s) the student seems to be lacking when trying to decode that particular nonsense word (i.e., beginning consonant sounds [onset], rimes, syllabication, affixes [common prefixes and suffixes], or *r*-controlled vowels). You should have at least one box marked for each miscue. If none of the phonics categories seems to be appropriate, which is possible, then make a note of the miscue at the bottom of the sheet in the area marked "Examiner's Notes," along with your interpretation of what the student may need to learn (e.g., CVC rule, hard *g* sound, vowel digraphs, etc.).

*Determining the Student's Developmental Level.* Developmental levels are an indication of the student's ability for a given skill. *Proficient* means that the student has attained relative mastery of the skill and does not require further instruction. *Developing* means that the student has some ability with the skill, but needs further instruction. *Emergent* essentially means that the student has little or no knowledge of the skill and requires instruction.

Add up the number of miscues in each column and record that number in the appropriate "Totals" box. In instances where the student has had two or more miscues in that category (i.e., beginning sounds/onset, rimes, syllabication, affixes, or *r*-controlled vowels), you should consider further informal classroom assessments to confirm the area of need before developing explicit instructional plans to teach the skill. See the following chart for determining developmental levels for each miscue category.

| DEVELOPMENTAL LEVEL | MISCUES BY CATEGORY |
| --- | --- |
| Proficient | 0–1 |
| Developing | 2–3 |
| Emergent | 4 or more |

# Phonics Test (PT)
## Student Form

| | | | |
|---|---|---|---|
| 1. | dunk | zip | born |
| 2. | fight | claw | pining |
| 3. | sunk | quench | batting |
| 4. | bashed | soup | lads |
| 5. | viper | yapping | cod |
| 6. | fur | note | leg |
| 7. | holly | winter | boat |
| 8. | taper | police | labor |

| 9.  | car    | veal    | relay    |
| 10. | nice   | sub     | wisp     |
| 11. | drop   | font    | butter   |
| 12. | babble | sheet   | leek     |
| 13. | home   | catnip  | shade    |
| 14. | fade   | jogging | chapel   |
| 15. | windy  | fishes  | waist    |
| 16. | chain  | number  | discover |

# Phonics Test (PT) Analysis Grid
## Examiner's Protocol Form

**Directions:** *Create a copy of this form to record students' responses. Record the students' answers so you can review any you miss. Look for patterns in the miscues students make.*

| | | | | Initial Sound | Rime | Syllab. | Affixes | *r*-control. V. |
|------|--------|---------|----------|------|------|---------|---------|------------------|
| 1. | dunk | zip | born | | | | | |
| 2. | fight | claw | pining | | | | | |
| 3. | sunk | quench | batting | | | | | |
| 4. | bashed | soup | lads | | | | | |
| 5. | viper | yapping | cod | | | | | |
| 6. | fur | note | leg | | | | | |
| 7. | holly | winter | boat | | | | | |
| 8. | taper | police | labor | | | | | |
| 9. | car | veal | relay | | | | | |
| 10. | nice | sub | wisp | | | | | |
| 11. | drop | font | butter | | | | | |
| 12. | babble | sheet | leek | | | | | |
| 13. | home | catnip | shade | | | | | |
| 14. | fade | jogging | chapel | | | | | |
| 15. | windy | fishes | waist | | | | | |
| 16. | chain | number | discover | | | | | |
| **Totals:** | | | | | | | | |

**Examiner's Notes:**

# VOCABULARY ASSESSMENTS

Vocabulary knowledge is assessed in the CRI–2 using the **High-Frequency Word Knowledge Survey (HFWKS)**. This is a quick and easy test to administer that has students simply read aloud common words found in English text that are presented using the HFWKS word cards found on the PDToolkit. The student is allowed up to *5 seconds* to name each of the words. If a word is not known the examiner should go on to the next word card after marking the unknown word on the **Student Record Form**. Following is a brief description of the purpose and research related to this test, as well as instructions for administering the HFWKS.

## High-Frequency Word Knowledge Survey (HFWKS)

*Purpose.* *High-frequency words* occur repeatedly and account for a majority of written words. Understanding text relies in part on the immediate recognition of these high-frequency words. Studies of print have found that just 109 words account for more than 50% of all words in student textbooks, and a total of only 5,000 words accounts for about 90% of the words in student texts (Adams, 1990; Carroll, Davies, & Richman, 1971). Knowledge of high-frequency sight words, logically, can help readers manage text in a more fluent way.

The HFWKS is a simple and quick assessment of a student's ability to recognize some of the highest-utility words in print. Based on Fry's (1980) research in which a word list of the 300 most common words in print was described, students are asked to pronounce individually words in a list.

*Procedure.* Ask the student to be seated across from you and explain that you would like to find out which words he or she can name on the word cards. Begin with card 1 and continue through all 100 cards. Note on a copy of the **Student Record Form** that follows any words that are not known. Allow students no more than 5 seconds to call each word. After 5 seconds any unknown words should be placed in the stack with other unknown words.

Any unknown words should be taught to the student because these words appear regularly in English-language texts.

*Preparing for Your First Assessment.* Print the word cards from the PDToolkit for the HFWKS. Cut the word cards apart and put them in numerical order. You may wish to print each of the word card sheets on heavy stock paper and laminate them so that they can be reused indefinitely.

As previously noted, record unknown words for each student tested using the **Student Record Form** that follows. (This form may be duplicated as often as you wish.)

# High-Frequency Word Knowledge Survey (HFWKS)
## Student Record Form

**Student's Name** _____

**Date Tested** _____

**Directions:** *Circle any words the student does* not *know.*

| | | | | | |
|---|---|---|---|---|---|
| the | of | and | a | to | in |
| is | you | that | it | he | was |
| for | on | are | as | with | his |
| they | I | at | be | this | have |
| from | or | one | had | by | words |
| but | not | what | all | were | we |
| when | your | can | said | there | use |
| an | each | which | she | do | how |
| their | if | will | up | other | about |
| out | many | then | them | these | so |
| some | her | would | make | like | him |
| into | time | has | look | two | more |
| write | go | see | number | no | way |
| could | people | my | than | first | water |
| been | called | who | oil | its | now |
| find | long | down | day | did | get |
| come | made | may | part | | |

# REFERENCES

Adams, M. J. (1990). *Beginning to read: Thinking and learning about print.* Cambridge, MA: MIT Press.

Carroll, J. B., Davies, P., & Richman, B. (1971). *Word frequency book.* Boston: Houghton Mifflin.

Clay, M. M. (1993). *An observation survey for early literacy achievement.* Portsmouth, NH: Heinemann.

Fry, E. (1980). The new instant word list. *The Reading Teacher, 34,* 284–289.

Griffith, P. L., & Olson, M. W. (1992). Phonemic awareness helps beginning readers break the code. *The Reading Teacher, 45,* 516–523.

Heathington, B. S., & Alexander, J. E. (1978). A child-based observation checklist to assess attitudes toward reading. *The Reading Teacher, 31*(7), 769–771.

McKenna, M., & Kear, D. J. (1990, May). Measuring attitude toward reading: A new tool for teachers. *The Reading Teacher, 43*(9), 626–639.

National Reading Panel. (2000). *Report of the National Reading Panel: Teaching children to read.* Washington, DC: National Institute of Child Health and Human Development.

Opitz, M. (2000). *Rhymes and reasons: Literature & language play for phonological awareness.* Portsmouth, NH: Heinemann.

Reutzel, D. R., & Cooter, R. B. (2011a). *Strategies for reading assessment and instruction: Helping every child succeed* (4th ed.). Boston: Pearson.

Reutzel D. R., & Cooter, R. B. (2011b). *Teaching children to read: The teacher makes the difference* (6th ed.). Boston: Allyn & Bacon/Pearson.

Walsh, D. J., Price, G. G., & Gillingham, M. G. (1988). The critical but transitory importance of letter naming. *Reading Research Quarterly, 23,* 108–122.

Williams, S. G. (2003). The Starpoint Phonics Test. Unpublished manuscript.

Yopp, H. K. (1988). The validity and reliability of phonemic awareness tests. *Reading Research Quarterly, 23,* 159–177.

# SENTENCES FOR INITIAL PASSAGE SELECTION

## FORM A

## FORM A: LEVEL 1

1. He wanted to fly.

2. The family got together.

3. The boy was jumping.

## FORM A: LEVEL 2

1. I was walking fast to town.

2. She cried about going home.

3. I was pulled out of the hole.

## FORM A: LEVEL 3

1. The forest was something to see.

2. I was enjoying sleeping when my mom called.

3. I had to go to bed early last night.

## FORM A: LEVEL 4

1. I dislike being the youngest.

2. I'm always getting into trouble.

3. They insisted on watching the show daily.

## FORM A: LEVEL 5

1. Athletic shoes come in all kinds of colors.

2. Serious players manage to practice a lot.

3. A cheap pair of shoes doesn't last very long.

## FORM A: LEVEL 6

1. He was searching for the evidence.

2. She realized the rock formation was too high.

3. The conservationist hoped to reforest the mountain.

## FORM A: LEVEL 7

1. Unfortunately she was confused about the next activity.

2. The submerged rocks were dangerous.

3. She disappeared around the bend at a rapid rate.

## FORM A: LEVEL 8

1. Ascending the mountain was rigorous and hazardous.

2. The cliff provided a panoramic view of the valley.

3. The incubation period lasted two weeks.

## FORM A: LEVEL 9

1. The abduction made everyone suspicious.

2. The detective was besieged by the community.

3. Her pasty complexion made her look older.

# NARRATIVE READING PASSAGES

# The Accident

# Let's Go Swimming

I went swimming.

My dog jumped in the pool.

**3**

My friends came over and jumped in the pool too.

**4**

We had a great time swimming.

## You Cannot Fly!

Once a boy named Sam wanted to fly.

His mother and father said, "You cannot fly."

His sister said, "You cannot fly."

Sam tried jumping off a box.

He tried jumping off his bed.

He fell down each time.

Sam tried hard but he still could not fly.

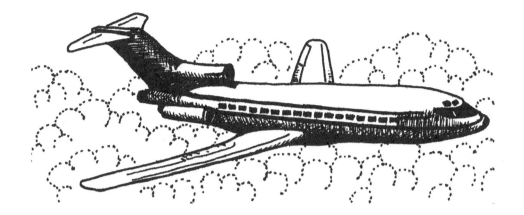

Then one day a letter came for Sam.

The letter said, "Come and see me, Sam, on the next airplane."

It was from his grandfather.

Sam went to his family and read the letter.

Sam said, "Now I can fly."

Sam and his family all laughed together.

## The Pig and the Snake

One day Mr. Pig was walking to town.

He saw a big hole in the road.

A big snake was in the hole.

"Help me," said the snake, "and I will be your friend."

"No, no," said Mr. Pig. "If I help you get out, you will bite me. You are a snake!"

The snake cried and cried.

So Mr. Pig pulled the snake out of the hole.

Then the snake said, "Now I am going to bite you, Mr. Pig."

"How can you bite me after I helped you out of the hole?" said Mr. Pig.

The snake said, "You knew I was a snake when you pulled me out!"

### The Big Bad Wolf

One day Mr. Wolf was walking through the forest. He was enjoying an afternoon walk and not bothering anyone. All of a sudden it started to rain and he became wet and cold.

Just when Mr. Wolf was about to freeze to death, he saw a small house in the woods. Smoke was coming from the chimney, so he knocked on the door. No one was home, but a note on the door said:

*Come in and make yourself warm. I'll be back about 2:00 p.m.*

*Love,*

*Granny*

The poor wet wolf came in and began to warm himself by the fire. He saw one of Granny's nightgowns on the bed, so he decided to put it on instead of his wet clothes. Since he was still very, very cold, he decided to get into Granny's bed. Soon he was fast asleep.

Mr. Wolf fell into a deep sleep. When he awoke, Mr. Wolf found an old woman, a little girl wearing a red coat, and a woodcutter standing around the bed. The woodcutter was yelling at Mr. Wolf and saying something about how he was going to kill him with his axe. Mr. Wolf jumped out of the bed and ran for his life.

Later that day, Mr. Wolf was finally safe at home. His wife said, "Just you wait, those humans will make up a story about how big and bad *you* were."

### New Clothes

Bobby was the youngest member of his family. He didn't like being the youngest because he couldn't stay up late and watch television. Most of all, he disliked having to wear hand-me-down clothes from his brother.

One day Bobby went to his mother and said, "Mom, I'm tired of wearing Brad's clothes. Why can't I have some more new clothes this school year?"

His mother replied, "Bobby, you know we can't afford to buy even more new clothes. You should be happy with the new clothes we have already bought. Besides, most of Brad's clothes are just like new."

As Bobby walked away, his mother said, "Bobby, if you can find a way to earn some money, I'll see what I can do to help you get what you want."

Bobby thought and thought. Finally, an idea hit him. Brad and his sister, Sara, had part-time jobs, and they didn't always have time to do their work around the house. What if he did some of their work for a small fee?

Bobby approached Brad and Sara about his idea. They liked his idea and agreed to pay Bobby for cleaning their rooms and making their beds.

As Bobby turned to leave the room, Sara said, "Bobby, do a good job or we will have to cut back how much we pay you."

Bobby took care of his brother's and sister's rooms for four weeks. Finally on the last Saturday before school started, Bobby's mom took him to the mall. Bobby got to pick out a cool pair of baggy jeans and a new shirt. On the first day of school, Bobby felt proud of his new clothes that he had worked so hard to buy. His mother was even prouder.

## Hot Shoes

The guys at the Susan B. Anthony Elementary School loved all the new sport shoes. Some wore the "Sky High" model by Leader. Others who couldn't afford Sky Highs would settle for a lesser shoe. Some liked the "Street Smarts" by Master, or the "Uptown-Downtown" by Beebop. The Anthony boys got to the point with their shoes that they could identify their friends just by looking at their feet. But the boy who was the envy of the entire fifth grade was Jamie Lee. He had a pair of "High Five Pump'em Ups" by Superior. The only thing Anthony boys loved as much as their shoes was basketball. They would lace up their fancy athletic shoes and play basketball all afternoon. Everyone was sure that the shoes helped them jump higher and run faster.

One day a new student showed up on the playground. His name was Josh Kidder, and no one knew him. He lived in the poor part of town and wore a cheap pair of black hightop tennis shoes. They were made by an old-fashioned company called White Dot. When Jamie Lee saw Josh's White Dot shoes, he said, "No serious basketball player wears White Dots. Where have you been, Kidder?" Josh said, "Well, I may not have a pair of shoes like yours but I would like to play basketball with you and the other guys."

Jamie Lee and the other boys kind of chuckled and said, "Sure kid, no problem." What happened next is a matter of history now at Susan B. Anthony School. Josh ran faster, jumped higher, and scored more points (35 points to be exact) than anybody else that day. Jamie Lee, whom Josh guarded, managed only two points.

When it was all over the boys gathered around Josh. He was the hero of the day. "What's your secret weapon?" asked Randy. Josh just smiled and said, "Two things—lots of practice and cheap shoes." Everyone laughed.

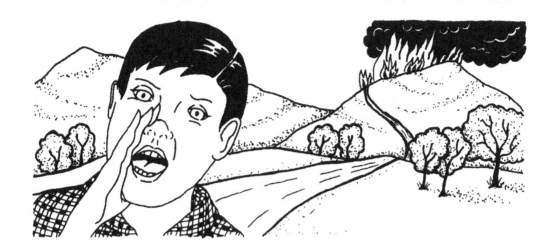

## Mountain Fire

One August afternoon Brad and Kevin went tracking with their fathers on Mount Holyoak. Brad's father was a conservationist for the Forest Service and was searching for evidence of cougars. Many people feared that the cougars were extinct on Mount Holyoak. The boys became excited when they found what appeared to be a partial cougar track near a stream. But as the day wore on, no new tracks were found.

After lunch Brad's father sent the boys upstream while he circled west. He told the boys to return to the lunch site in an hour. After about forty-five minutes, the boys found the stream's source and could follow it no more. They decided to search close to the stream before starting back. They saw interesting rock formations, eagles' nests on high ledges and, finally, two fresh cougar footprints. Both boys were very excited until they realized that they no longer could hear the stream. They were lost.

The boys searched an hour or more for the mountain stream, but without success. They were tired, dirty, and getting worried. Brad decided to start a small fire in hopes of his father seeing the smoke. Kevin reminded Brad of the danger of forest fires but finally agreed to help collect the twigs, branches, and brush. The moment Brad struck a match in the extra-dry mountain air and stuck it to the dry tinder, the fire exploded into a large fireball.

In a matter of minutes, trees all around the boys burst into flames. The fire spread quickly up the mountainside. The boys ran downhill as fast as they could.

Before the day was out, hotshot crews, airplanes carrying fire retardants, and bucket-loaded helicopters were on the scene trying to contain the fire. The fire raged for days, however, and by the time it was put out, more than 45,000 acres of timber had been consumed.

For several years Brad and Kevin spent every spare moment helping to reforest the mountain. One day the forest ranger commented, "Well, boys, it looks like things are about back to normal." Brad looked down at his feet and sadly replied, "Maybe, but no new cougar tracks have been seen since the fire."

## The Canoe Trip

Katherine and her family like to spend their vacation camping out. Frequently they go to either Great Smoky Mountains National Park or Yellowstone National Park. Since they have camped out for many years, they have become quite accomplished. Katherine is able to start a fire with flint and steel, build a lean-to for shelter, and find food in the forest on which to live.

Katherine's favorite outdoor activity is canoeing. Although she is quite a good canoer, there is one canoe trip that she'll never forget. It was a canoe trip she took with her family and her friend Amy down the Madison River near West Yellowstone.

Katherine and Amy were in a canoe together following her parents down the river. The early going was fine, and they didn't have any major problems. The girls did get confused once or twice in their steering, and the boat would go sideways. But after about thirty minutes on the river, Katherine and Amy felt secure about their ability to navigate. Unfortunately their canoe could not keep up with Katherine's parents' canoe because they were carrying all the rations in two coolers. Slowly the lead canoe disappeared around a bend.

When the girls' canoe rounded a bend, not only could they not see the lead canoe but they were heading directly into some rough white water. The rough water was swift and there were a lot of rocks submerged below the surface. The swiftness and rocks were causing problems for the jittery canoe and the two inexperienced girls.

Just as the canoe was about to clear the rough water, it struck a large boulder just beneath the surface. Before the girls knew what had happened, the canoe had capsized, sending them into the icy cold river. Naturally they had on life jackets so they were not in much danger. But the two coolers full of food and the canoe started floating away from them at a rapid rate.

Katherine managed to grab hold of the canoe and one paddle. Amy swam over to the shore. After much effort both girls managed to pull in the canoe, empty the water, and start downstream after the lost coolers. But since they had only one paddle they limped along, unable to catch up to the now disappeared coolers.

Some forty-five minutes later, feeling cold and upset, the girls rounded a sharp bend in the river. To their surprise they saw the rest of the family sitting on the south-side shore of the river. Katherine's dad had built a fire and was roasting hot dogs. Katherine's mother and little brother were sitting on the two coolers eating a hot dog and munching on potato chips. Dad said, "What took you two so long? We didn't know you were going to stop and take a swim, but thanks for sending the food on ahead." As cold as they were, Katherine and Amy couldn't help but laugh.

## The Eagle

There exists an old Native American legend about an eagle who thought he was a chicken. It seems that a Hopi farmer and his only son decided to climb a nearby mountain to observe an eagle's nest. The trip would take them all day, so they brought along some rations and water for the trek. The man and the boy crossed the enormous fields of maize and beans into the foothills. Soon thereafter they were ascending the mountain, and the climb became rigorous and hazardous. They occasionally looked back toward their home and at the panoramic view of the entire valley.

Finally the farmer and son reached the mountain's summit. Perched on the highest point on a ledge was the eagle's nest. The farmer reached his hand into the nest after realizing that the mother had gone in search of food. He brought out a most precious prize, an eagle's egg. He tucked it into his tunic and the two descended the mount.

The egg was placed in the nest of a chicken for incubation. It soon hatched. The eaglet grew with the baby chicks and adopted their habits for gathering food in the barnyard—namely, scratching for feed the farmer threw out.

Sometime later an Anasazi brave passed through the area and saw this enormous brown eagle scratching and walking about in the barnyard. He dismounted from his horse and went to the farmer. "Why do you have an eagle acting as a chicken? It is not right," queried the noble brave.

"That's no eagle, it's a chicken," retorted the farmer. "Can't you see that it scratches for food with the other chickens? No, it is indeed a chicken," exclaimed the farmer.

"I will show you that this is an eagle," said the brave.

The brave took the eagle on his arm and climbed to the top of the barn. Then saying, "You are an eagle, the most noble of birds. Fly and soar as you were destined!" he threw the eagle from the barn. But the startled eagle fluttered to the ground and began pecking for food.

"See," said the farmer. "Told you it is a chicken."

The brave replied, "I'll show you this is an eagle. It is clear what I must do."

Again the brave took the eagle on his arm and began walking toward the mountain. He climbed all day until he reached a high bluff overlooking the valley. Then the brave, with outstretched arm, held the bird out and said, "You are an eagle, the most noble of birds. Fly and soar as you were destined to."

Just then a mountain breeze washed across the eagle. His eyes brightened as he caught the wild scent of freedom. In a moment the eagle stretched his mighty wings and let out a magnificent screech. Leaping from the brave's arm, he flew high into the western sky.

The eagle saw more of the world in that one great moment than his barnyard friends would discover in a lifetime.

### The Case of Angela Violet

Angela Violet was an elderly lady in our neighborhood who some people thought suspicious. She was rarely seen outside her spacious Victorian-styled home, and then only to retrieve the daily mail. Her pasty complexion and ancient dress made her appear like an apparition. Small children in the neighborhood speculated that she might be some sort of witch. It appeared that Miss Violet had no contact with the outside world.

One autumn day news spread through the community that a high school cheerleader, Katrina Bowers, had disappeared. The police feared that Katrina had been abducted. State and local police joined forces with the Federal Bureau of Investigation in the massive search effort. In spite of all the best efforts in the constabulary, no trace of Katrina Bowers was uncovered. After ten days of suspense and worry, the search was called off.

Three weeks after Katrina's apparent abduction a break in the case occurred. An anonymous telephone caller informed the police that Miss Angela Violet had kidnapped Katrina. It was alleged that Miss Violet was holding her captive in her basement. Because of Miss Violet's unusual lifestyle, the police were inclined to give some credence to the tip. A search warrant was issued and the police converged on her house.

Detective Donna Jordan knocked on the shabby door of Miss Violet's residence. Two other officers attended Detective Jordan. Miss Violet showed surprise but welcomed the police into her home graciously. She consented to having her home searched.

By the time the police had completed their search, two television news trucks had taken position outside her home. When the detectives came out of the house without Miss Violet, the anxious newspeople besieged them with queries.

Detective Jordan stepped forward and calmly said, "What we found was a kindly lady who is caring night and day for her ailing mother. There is no evidence whatsoever that Miss Violet has any involvement in the Katrina Bowers case."

People in the community began to reach out to Miss Violet and her mother from then on. They took food and sat with Miss Violet's mother so she could get out more. As for Katrina Bowers, she was located safe and sound in California with relatives. She had been a runaway case.

# EXAMINER'S ASSESSMENT PROTOCOLS

# PREPRIMER (PP) LEVEL ASSESSMENT PROTOCOLS

The Accident (Wordless picture story)

## PART I: WORDLESS PICTURE STORY READING

### Background Statement

"These pictures tell a story about a girl and something that happened to her. Look at each picture as I show it to you and think about the story the pictures tell. Later, I will want you to tell me the story using the pictures."

### Teacher Directions

Refer the student to each picture slowly and in order as numbered. Do not comment on the pictures. Then repeat the procedure, asking the student to tell the story in the student's own words. Record the student's reading using a tape recorder, and transcribe the reading as it is being dictated. Replay the recording later to make sure that your transcription is accurate and complete.

## PART II: EMERGENT READING BEHAVIOR CHECKLIST

### Directions

Following are emergent reading behaviors identified through research and grouped according to broad developmental stages. Check all behaviors you have observed. *If the student progresses to Stage 3 or 4, continue your assessment using the Primer (P) Level passage.*

**Stage 1: Early Connections to Reading—Describing Pictures**

_____ Attends to and describes (labels) pictures in books

_____ Has a limited sense of story

_____ Follows verbal directions for this activity

_____ Uses oral vocabulary appropriate for age/grade level

_____ Displays attention span appropriate for age/grade level

_____ Responds to questions in an appropriate manner

_____ Appears to connect pictures (sees as being interrelated)

**Stage 2: Connecting Pictures to Form a Story**

_____ Attends to pictures and develops oral stories

_____ Uses only childlike or descriptive (storyteller) language to tell the story, rather than book language (e.g., "Once upon a time . . ."; "There once was a little boy . . .")

**Stage 3: Transitional Picture Reading**

_____ Attends to pictures as a connected story

_____ Mixes storyteller language with book language

### Stage 4: Advanced Picture Reading

_____ Attends to pictures and develops oral stories

_____ Speaks as though reading the story (uses book language)

## Examiner's Notes

# PRIMER (P) LEVEL ASSESSMENT PROTOCOLS

Let's Go Swimming (25 words)

## PART I: PICTURE STORY READING—ORAL READING AND ANALYSIS OF MISCUES

### Background Statement

"This is a story about a child having fun. Let's look at each picture first. Now, read the story to yourself. Later, I will want you to read the story to me."

### Teacher Directions

Refer the student to each frame of the story slowly and in order as numbered. Do not read the story or comment on the pictures. After the student has read the story silently, ask the student to read the story aloud. Record the student's reading using a tape recorder, and mark any miscues on the Miscue Grid provided. Following the oral reading, complete the Emergent Reading Behavior Checklist. Assessment information obtained from both the Miscue Grid and the Emergent Reading Behavior Checklist will help you determine whether to continue your assessment. If the student is unable to read the passage independently the first time, read it aloud, then ask the student to try to read the story again. This will help you understand whether the student is able to memorize and repeat text, an important developmental milestone. The assessment should stop after this activity, if the child is unable to read the text independently. (Note: The Miscue Grid should be completed after the assessment session has been concluded in order to minimize stress for the student.)

## ERROR TYPES

| | Mis-pronun. | Sub-stitute | Inser-tions | Tchr. Assists | Omis-sions | Error Totals | Self-Correct. |
|---|---|---|---|---|---|---|---|
| **Let's Go Swimming** | | | | | | | |
| I went swimming. | | | | | | | |
| My dog jumped in the pool. | | | | | | | |
| My friends came over and | | | | | | | |
| jumped in the pool too. | | | | | | | |
| We had a great time swimming. // | | | | | | | |
| **TOTALS** | | | | | | | |

## ERROR ANALYSIS

| Meaning (M) | Syntax (S) | Visual (V) |
|---|---|---|
| | | |
| | | |
| | | |
| | | |
| | | |
| | | |
| | | |

Summary of Reading Behaviors (Strengths and Needs)

# PART II: EMERGENT READING BEHAVIOR CHECKLIST

## Directions

Following are emergent reading behaviors identified through research and grouped according to broad developmental stages. After the student has completed the oral reading, check each behavior observed below to help determine development level and whether to continue the assessment. *If the student seems to be at Stage 6 or 7 and the oral reading scored at an Easy or Adequate level, continue the assessment using the Level 1 passage.*

### Stage 5: Early Print Reading

_____ Tells a story using the pictures

_____ Knows print moves from left to right, top to bottom

_____ Creates part of the text using book language and knows some words on sight

### Stage 6: Early Strategic Reading

_____ Uses context to guess at some unknown words (guesses make sense)

_____ Notices beginning sounds in words and uses them in guessing unknown words

_____ Seems to sometimes use syntax to help identify words in print

_____ Recognizes some word parts, such as root words and affixes

### Stage 7: Moderate Strategic Reading

_____ Sometimes uses context and word parts to decode words

_____ Self-corrects when making an oral reading miscue

_____ Retells the passage easily and may embellish the story line

_____ Shows some awareness of vowel sounds

Examiner's Notes

## PART III: DEVELOPMENTAL/PERFORMANCE SUMMARY

Oral Reading Accuracy

_____ 0–1  oral errors = Easy

_____ 2–5  oral errors = Adequate

_____ 6+   oral errors = Too hard

**Continue to the next assessment level passage?** _____ Yes  _____ No

Examiner's Notes

# LEVEL 1 ASSESSMENT PROTOCOLS

You Cannot Fly! (95 words)

## PART I: SILENT READING COMPREHENSION

### Background Statement

"Have you ever wished you could fly? A boy named Sam in this story wants to fly. Read this story to find out if Sam gets to fly. Read it carefully because when you're through I'm going to ask you to tell me about the story."

### Teacher Directions

Once the student completes the silent reading, say, "Tell me about the story you just read." Answers to the questions below that the student provides during the retelling should be marked "ua" in the appropriate blank to indicate that this response was unaided. Ask all remaining questions not addressed during the retelling and mark those that the student answers with an "a" to indicate that the correct response was given after prompting by the teacher.

| Questions/Answers | Story Grammar Element/ Level of Comprehension |
|---|---|
| _____ 1. What was the name of the boy in the story? (Sam) | character-characterization/literal |
| _____ 2. What did Sam really want to do? (Sam wanted to fly, but couldn't) | story problem(s)/literal |
| _____ 3. What were two ways Sam tried to fly? (jumping off his bed and a box) | problem resolution attempts/literal |
| _____ 4. How was Sam's problem finally solved? (Sam got to ride on an airplane) | problem resolution/inferential |
| _____ 5. The story says that Sam "tried hard." What does it mean to "try hard"? (to try things over and over; really make an effort; not give up easily) | inferential/figurative language/ expressive language |
| _____ 6. Where did the story take place? (Sam's house) | setting/inferential |
| _____ 7. What did Sam learn about being able to fly? (people can't fly except in airplanes) | theme/evaluative |
| _____ 8. What words would you use to tell someone what kind of boy Sam was? (responses will vary; accept plausible ones) | character-characterization/evaluative |

## ERROR TYPES          ERROR ANALYSIS

**You Cannot Fly!**

| | Mis-pronun. | Sub-stitute | Inser-tions | Tchr. Assists | Omis-sions | Error Totals | Self-Correct. | Meaning (M) | Syntax (S) | Visual (V) |
|---|---|---|---|---|---|---|---|---|---|---|
| Once a boy named Sam wanted to | | | | | | | | | | |
| fly. His mother and father said, | | | | | | | | | | |
| "You cannot fly." His sister said, | | | | | | | | | | |
| "You cannot fly." Sam tried jumping | | | | | | | | | | |
| off a box. He tried jumping off | | | | | | | | | | |
| his bed. He fell down each time. | | | | | | | | | | |
| Sam tried hard but he still | | | | | | | | | | |
| could not fly. Then one day | | | | | | | | | | |
| a letter came for Sam. The letter | | | | | | | | | | |
| said, "Come and see me, Sam, on | | | | | | | | | | |
| the next airplane." It was from | | | | | | | | | | |
| his grandfather. Sam went to his | | | | | | | | | | |
| family and read the letter. Sam | | | | | | | | | | |
| said, "Now I can fly." Sam and his | | | | | | | | | | |
| family all laughed together.// | | | | | | | | | | |
| **TOTALS** | | | | | | | | | | |

Summary of Reading Behaviors (Strengths and Needs)

# PART II: ORAL READING AND ANALYSIS OF MISCUES

## Directions

Say, "Now I would like to hear you read this story out loud. Please start at the beginning and keep reading until I tell you to stop." *Have the student read orally until the oral reading stop-marker ( / / ) is reached.* Follow along on the Miscue Grid, marking any oral reading errors as appropriate. Then complete the Performance Summary to determine whether to continue the assessment. (*Note:* The Miscue Grid should be completed *after* the assessment session has been concluded in order to minimize stress for the student.)

# PART III: MISCUE ANALYSIS

## Directions

Circle all reading behaviors you observed.

## A. Fundamental Behaviors Observed

L → R Directionality      1-to-1 Matching      Searching for Clues      Cross-Checking

## B. Word Attack Behaviors

No Attempt      Mispronunciation (Invented Word Substitutions)      Substitutes

Skips/Reads On      Asks for Help      Repeats      Attempts to Self-Correct

"Sounds Out" (Segmenting)      Blends Sounds      Structural Analysis (Root Words, Affixes)

## C. Cueing Systems Used in Attempting Words

| CUEING TOOL | MISCUE EXAMPLES | ACTUAL TEXT |
|---|---|---|
| (M) Meaning | | |
| (S) Syntax | | |
| (V) Visual | | |

## D. Fluency (word by word → fluent reading)

Word by Word _____      Mixed Phrasing _____      Fluent Reading _____      Fluency Rate in Seconds _____

## E. Performance Summary

### Silent Reading Comprehension

_____ 0–1 questions missed = Easy

_____ 2 questions missed = Adequate

_____ 3+ questions missed = Too hard

### Oral Reading Accuracy

_____ 0–1 oral errors = Easy

_____ 2–5 oral errors = Adequate

_____ 6+ oral errors = Too hard

Continue to the next reading passage? _____ Yes _____ No

# PART IV: LISTENING COMPREHENSION

## Directions

If you have decided not to continue to have the student read any other passages, then use this passage to begin assessing the student's listening comprehension. Begin by reading the background statement for this passage and then say, "I am going to read this story to you. Please listen carefully because I will be asking you some questions after I finish reading it to you." After reading the passage, ask the student the questions associated with the passage. If the student correctly answers more than six questions, you will need to move to the next level and repeat the procedure.

## Listening Comprehension

_____ 0–2 questions missed = move to the next passage level

_____ more than 2 questions missed = stop assessment or move down a level

## Examiner's Notes

# LEVEL 2 ASSESSMENT PROTOCOLS

The Pig and the Snake (111 words)

## PART I: SILENT READING COMPREHENSION

### Background Statement

"Read this story to find out what happened to Mr. Pig when he tried to help a snake in trouble. Be sure to read it carefully because I'm going to ask you to tell me about the story."

### Teacher Directions

Once the student completes the silent reading, say, "Tell me about the story you just read." Answers to the questions below that the student provides during the retelling should be marked "ua" in the appropriate blank to indicate that this response was unaided. Ask all remaining questions not addressed during the retelling and mark those that the student answers with an "a" to indicate that the correct response was given after prompting by the teacher.

| *Questions/Answers* | *Story Grammar Element/ Level of Comprehension* |
|---|---|
| _____ 1. Where did the story take place?<br>*(on the road to town)* | setting/literal |
| _____ 2. Who were the animals in the story?<br>*(Mr. Pig and a snake)* | character-characterization/literal |
| _____ 3. What was the snake's problem?<br>*(he was stuck in a hole and wanted help getting out)* | story problem(s)/literal |
| _____ 4. How did the snake solve his problem?<br>*(by getting the pig to help him by promising not to hurt him)* | problem resolution/inferential |
| _____ 5. What words would you use to describe the snake?<br>*(sneaky, liar, or any other plausible response)* | character-characterization/ evaluative/vocabulary/expressive vocabulary |
| _____ 6. What lesson did Mr. Pig learn?<br>*(responses will vary but should indicate a theme/moral related to "you can't always trust what someone says")* | theme/evaluative |
| _____ 7. How did Mr. Pig feel after he helped pull the snake out of the hole?<br>*(surprised, upset, etc.)* | character-characterization/inferential |
| _____ 8. What was one thing the snake did to get Mr. Pig to help him out of the hole?<br>*(cried or said he would be his friend)* | problem resolution attempts/literal |

## ERROR TYPES | ERROR ANALYSIS

| The Pig and the Snake | Mis-pronun. | Sub-stitute | Inser-tions | Tchr. Assists | Omis-sions | Error Totals | Self-Correct. | Meaning (M) | Syntax (S) | Visual (V) |
|---|---|---|---|---|---|---|---|---|---|---|
| One day Mr. Pig was walking to | | | | | | | | | | |
| town. He saw a big hole in the | | | | | | | | | | |
| road. A big snake was in the | | | | | | | | | | |
| hole. "Help me," said the snake, | | | | | | | | | | |
| "and I will be your friend." "No, no," | | | | | | | | | | |
| said Mr. Pig. "If I help you get | | | | | | | | | | |
| out, you will bite me. You are | | | | | | | | | | |
| a snake!" The snake cried and | | | | | | | | | | |
| cried. So Mr. Pig pulled the | | | | | | | | | | |
| snake out of the hole. | | | | | | | | | | |
| Then the snake said, "Now I am | | | | | | | | | | |
| going to bite you, Mr. Pig." | | | | | | | | | | |
| "How can you bite me after | | | | | | | | | | |
| I helped you out of the hole?" | | | | | | | | | | |
| said Mr. Pig. The snake said, // | | | | | | | | | | |
| "You knew I was a snake | | | | | | | | | | |
| when you pulled me out." | | | | | | | | | | |
| **TOTALS** | | | | | | | | | | |

Summary of Reading Behaviors (Strengths and Needs)

# PART II: ORAL READING AND ANALYSIS OF MISCUES

## Directions

Say, "Now I would like to hear you read this story out loud." Have the student read orally until the 100-word sample is completed. Follow along on the Miscue Grid, marking any oral reading errors as appropriate. *Remember to count miscues only up to the point in the story containing the oral reading stop-marker (//).* Then complete the Performance Summary to determine whether to continue the assessment. (*Note:* The Miscue Grid should be completed *after* the assessment session has been concluded in order to minimize stress for the student.)

# PART III: MISCUE ANALYSIS

## Directions

Circle all reading behaviors you observed.

## A. Fundamental Behaviors Observed

L → R Directionality        1-to 1-Matching        Searching for Clues        Cross-Checking

## B. Word Attack Behaviors

No Attempt        Mispronunciation (Invented Word Substitutions)        Substitutes

Skips/Reads On        Asks for Help        Repeats        Attempts to Self-Correct

"Sounds Out" (Segmenting)        Blends Sounds        Structural Analysis (Root Words, Affixes)

## C. Cueing Systems Used in Attempting Words

| CUEING TOOL | MISCUE EXAMPLES | ACTUAL TEXT |
|---|---|---|
| (M) Meaning | | |
| (S) Syntax | | |
| (V) Visual | | |

## D. Fluency (word by word → fluent reading)

Word by Word _____        Mixed Phrasing _____        Fluent Reading _____        Fluency Rate in Seconds _____

## E. Performance Summary

| *Silent Reading Comprehension* | *Oral Reading Accuracy* |
|---|---|
| _____ 0–1 questions missed = Easy | 0–1 oral errors = Easy |
| _____ 2 questions missed = Adequate | 2–5 oral errors = Adequate |
| _____ 3+ questions missed = Too hard | 6+ oral errors = Too hard |

**Continue to the next reading passage?** _____ Yes        _____ No

# PART IV: LISTENING COMPREHENSION

## Directions

If you have decided not to continue to have the student read any other passages, then use this passage to begin assessing the student's listening comprehension. Begin by reading the background statement for this passage and then say, "I am going to read this story to you. Please listen carefully because I will be asking you some questions after I finish reading it to you." After reading the passage, ask the student the questions associated with the passage. If the student correctly answers more than six questions, you will need to move to the next level and repeat the procedure.

## Listening Comprehension

\_\_\_\_\_ 0–2 questions missed = move to the next passage level

\_\_\_\_\_ more than 2 questions missed = stop assessment or move down a level

Examiner's Notes

# LEVEL 3 ASSESSMENT PROTOCOLS
## The Big Bad Wolf (235 words)

## PART I: SILENT READING COMPREHENSION

### Background Statement

"Have you ever had someone say something about you that wasn't true? Mr. Wolf thinks he has. Read and find out what really happened. Read it carefully because I'm going to ask you to tell me about the story."

### Teacher Directions

Once the student completes the silent reading, say "Tell me about the story you just read." Answers to the questions below that the student provides during the retelling should be marked "ua" in the appropriate blank to indicate that this response was unaided. Ask all remaining questions not addressed during the retelling and mark those that the student answers with an "a" to indicate that the correct response was given after prompting by the teacher.

| Questions/Answers | Story Grammar Element/ Level of Comprehension |
|---|---|
| _____ 1. Who was the story about? <br> *(Mr. Wolf, Granny, little girl, woodcutter)* | character-characterization/literal |
| _____ 2. Where was Mr. Wolf when he saw the house? <br> *(in the forest)* | setting/literal |
| _____ 3. Why did Mr. Wolf need to get into the house? <br> *(he was wet and freezing)* | story problem(s)/literal |
| _____ 4. What made Mr. Wolf think it was OK to go into the house? <br> *(the note on the door)* | problem resolution attempts/ inferential |
| _____ 5. What did Mr. Wolf do after entering the house? <br> *(began to warm himself and changed into a nightgown)* | problem resolution attempts/literal |
| _____ 6. Why did Mr. Wolf have to run for his life? <br> *(woodcutter was going to kill him)* | problem resolution attempts/literal |
| _____ 7. What lesson did Mr. Wolf learn? <br> *(responses will vary but should indicate a theme/moral related to not doing things without permission)* | theme/evaluative |
| _____ 8. What did Mrs. Wolf say that told you she did not trust humans? <br> *(she said the humans would make up a story about her husband)* | character-characterization/ inferential/language |

## ERROR TYPES / ERROR ANALYSIS

**The Big Bad Wolf**

| | Mis-pronun. | Sub-stitute | Inser-tions | Tchr. Assists | Omis-sions | Error Totals | Self-Correct. | Meaning (M) | Syntax (S) | Visual (V) |
|---|---|---|---|---|---|---|---|---|---|---|
| One day Mr. Wolf was walking | | | | | | | | | | |
| through the forest. He was enjoying | | | | | | | | | | |
| an afternoon walk and not bothering | | | | | | | | | | |
| anyone. All of a sudden it started | | | | | | | | | | |
| to rain and he became wet and cold. | | | | | | | | | | |
| Just when Mr. Wolf was about | | | | | | | | | | |
| to freeze to death, he saw a small | | | | | | | | | | |
| house in the woods. Smoke was | | | | | | | | | | |
| coming from the chimney, so he | | | | | | | | | | |
| knocked on the door. No one was | | | | | | | | | | |
| home, but a note on the door said: | | | | | | | | | | |
| *Come in and make yourself warm. I'll be back about 2:00 p.m.* | | | | | | | | | | |
| *Love,* | | | | | | | | | | |
| *Granny* | | | | | | | | | | |
| The poor wet wolf came in and | | | | | | | | | | |
| began to warm himself by // *the* | | | | | | | | | | |
| *fire.* | | | | | | | | | | |
| **TOTALS** | | | | | | | | | | |

**Summary of Reading Behaviors (Strengths and Needs)**

# PART II: ORAL READING AND ANALYSIS OF MISCUES

## Directions

Say, "Now I would like to hear you read this story out loud." Have the student read orally until the 100-word sample is completed. Follow along on the Miscue Grid, marking any oral reading errors as appropriate. *Remember to count miscues only up to the point in the story containing the oral reading stop-marker (//).* Then complete the Performance Summary to determine whether to continue the assessment. (*Note:* The Miscue Grid should be completed *after* the assessment session has been concluded in order to minimize stress for the student.)

# PART III: MISCUE ANALYSIS

## Directions

Circle all reading behaviors you observed.

## A. Fundamental Behaviors Observed

L → R Directionality          1-to-1 Matching          Searching for Clues          Cross-Checking

## B. Word Attack Behaviors

No Attempt          Mispronunciation (Invented Word Substitutions)          Substitutes

Skips/Reads On          Asks for Help          Repeats          Attempts to Self-Correct

"Sounds Out" (Segmenting)          Blends Sounds          Structural Analysis (Root Words, Affixes)

## C. Cueing Systems Used in Attempting Words

| CUEING TOOL | MISCUE EXAMPLES | ACTUAL TEXT |
|---|---|---|
| (M) Meaning | | |
| (S) Syntax | | |
| (V) Visual | | |

## D. Oral Reading Fluency (word by word → fluent reading)

Word by Word _____          Mixed Phrasing _____          Fluent Reading _____          Fluency Rate in Seconds _____

## E. Performance Summary

| *Silent Reading Comprehension* | *Oral Reading Accuracy* |
|---|---|
| _____ 0–1 questions missed = Easy | _____ 0–1 oral errors = Easy |
| _____ 2 questions missed = Adequate | _____ 2–5 oral errors = Adequate |
| _____ 3+ questions missed = Too hard | _____ 6+ oral errors = Too hard |

**Continue to the next reading passage?** _____ Yes          _____ No

# PART IV: LISTENING COMPREHENSION

## *Directions*

If you have decided not to continue to have the student read any other passages, then use this passage to begin assessing the student's listening comprehension. Begin by reading the background statement for this passage and then say, "I am going to read this story to you. Please listen carefully because I will be asking you some questions after I finish reading it to you." After reading the passage, ask the student the questions associated with the passage. If the student correctly answers more than six questions, you will need to move to the next level and repeat the procedure.

## Listening Comprehension

_____ 0–2 questions missed = move to the next passage level

_____ more than 2 questions missed = stop assessment or move down a level

Examiner's Notes

# LEVEL 4 ASSESSMENT PROTOCOLS

New Clothes (294 words)

## PART I: SILENT READING COMPREHENSION

*Background Statement*

"Read this story to find out what happens when Bobby decides he wants some new clothes. Be sure to read it carefully because I'm going to ask you to tell me about the story when you finish."

*Teacher Directions*

Once the student completes the silent reading, say, "Tell me about the story you just read." Answers to the questions below that the student provides during the retelling should be marked "ua" in the appropriate blank to indicate that this response was unaided. Ask all remaining questions not addressed during the retelling and mark those that the student answers with an "a" to indicate that the correct response was given after prompting by the teacher.

| *Questions/Answers* | *Story Grammar Element/ Level of Comprehension* |
|---|---|
| _____ 1. Who are the characters in this story? <br> *(Bobby, Mom, Sara, and Brad)* | character-characterization/literal |
| _____ 2. Where does the story mainly take place? <br> *(Bobby's home)* | setting/literal |
| _____ 3. Besides being the youngest, what is Bobby's big problem in the story? <br> *(earning money to buy new clothes)* | story problem(s)/literal |
| _____ 4. What did Bobby do to earn money? <br> *(he cleaned his brother's and sister's rooms)* | problem resolution/literal |
| _____ 5. Besides hand-me-down clothes, what was one other thing that Bobby disliked about being the youngest? <br> *(couldn't stay up late and watch TV)* | story problem(s)/literal |
| _____ 6. What does Bobby do at the end of the story? <br> *(buys some new clothes)* | problem resolution/literal |
| _____ 7. Can you think of some words, other than "proud," that would describe how Bobby felt on the first day of school? <br> *("happy," "cool," other plausible responses)* | character-characterization/ evaluative/language |
| _____ 8. Why do you think Bobby's mother was "even prouder"? <br> *(responses should indicate that Bobby's mother was proud that her son had worked hard and found a way to earn money)* | character-characterization |

## ERROR ANALYSIS

## ERROR TYPES

| | Mis-pronun. | Sub-stitute | Inser-tions | Tchr. Assists | Omis-sions | Error Totals | Self-Correct. | Meaning (M) | Syntax (S) | Visual (V) |
|---|---|---|---|---|---|---|---|---|---|---|
| **New Clothes** | | | | | | | | | | |
| Bobby was the youngest member | | | | | | | | | | |
| of his family. He didn't like being | | | | | | | | | | |
| the youngest because he couldn't | | | | | | | | | | |
| stay up late and watch television. | | | | | | | | | | |
| Most of all, he disliked having to | | | | | | | | | | |
| wear hand-me-down clothes from | | | | | | | | | | |
| his brother. One day Bobby went | | | | | | | | | | |
| to his mother and said, "Mom, | | | | | | | | | | |
| I'm tired of wearing Brad's | | | | | | | | | | |
| clothes. Why can't I have | | | | | | | | | | |
| some more new clothes this | | | | | | | | | | |
| school year?" His mother replied, | | | | | | | | | | |
| "Bobby, you know we can't | | | | | | | | | | |
| afford to buy even more new clothes. | | | | | | | | | | |
| You should be happy with the new | | | | | | | | | | |
| clothes we have already bought. | | | | | | | | | | |
| Besides, most of Brad's clothes | | | | | | | | | | |
| are just like // *new*." | | | | | | | | | | |
| **TOTALS** | | | | | | | | | | |

**Summary of Reading Behaviors (Strengths and Needs)**

# PART II: ORAL READING AND ANALYSIS OF MISCUES

## Directions

Say, "Now I would like to hear you read some of this story out loud." Have the student read orally until the 100-word sample is completed. Follow along on the Miscue Grid, marking any oral reading errors as appropriate. *Remember to count miscues only up to the point in the story containing the oral reading stop-marker (//).* Then complete the Performance Summary to determine whether to continue the assessment. (*Note:* The Miscue Grid should be completed *after* the assessment session has been concluded in order to minimize stress for the student.)

# PART III: MISCUE ANALYSIS

## Directions

Circle all reading behaviors you observed.

## A. Fundamental Behaviors Observed

L → R Directionality        1-to-1 Matching        Searching for Clues        Cross-Checking

## B. Word Attack Behaviors

No Attempt        Mispronunciation (Invented Word Substitutions)        Substitutes

Skips/Reads On        Asks for Help        Repeats        Attempts to Self-Correct

"Sounds Out" (Segmenting)        Blends Sounds        Structural Analysis (Root Words, Affixes)

## C. Cueing Systems Used in Attempting Words

| CUEING TOOL | MISCUE EXAMPLES | ACTUAL TEXT |
|---|---|---|
| (M) Meaning | | |
| (S) Syntax | | |
| (V) Visual | | |

## D. Fluency (word by word → fluent reading)

Word by Word _____        Mixed Phrasing _____        Fluent Reading _____        Fluency Rate in Seconds _____

## E. Performance Summary

| *Silent Reading Comprehension* | *Oral Reading Accuracy* |
|---|---|
| _____ 0–1 questions missed = Easy | _____ 0–1 oral errors = Easy |
| _____ 2 questions missed = Adequate | _____ 2–5 oral errors = Adequate |
| _____ 3+ questions missed = Too hard | _____ 6+ oral errors = Too hard |

**Continue to the next reading passage?** _____ Yes _____ No

# PART IV: LISTENING COMPREHENSION

## *Directions*

If you have decided not to continue to have the student read any other passages, then use this passage to begin assessing the student's listening comprehension. Begin by reading the background statement for this passage and then say, "I am going to read this story to you. Please listen carefully because I will be asking you some questions after I finish reading it to you." After reading the passage, ask the student the questions associated with the passage. If the student correctly answers more than six questions, you will need to move to the next level and repeat the procedure.

## Listening Comprehension

\_\_\_\_\_ 0–2 questions missed = move to the next passage level

\_\_\_\_\_ more than 2 questions missed = stop assessment or move down a level

Examiner's Notes

# LEVEL 5 ASSESSMENT PROTOCOLS

Hot Shoes (327 words)

## PART I: SILENT READING COMPREHENSION

### Background Statement

"This story is about how one group of boys feels about their athletic shoes. Read this story to find out how important special shoes are to playing sports. Read it carefully because I will ask you to tell me about it when you finish."

### Teacher Directions

Once the student completes the silent reading, say, "Tell me about the story you just read." Answers to the questions below that the student provides during the retelling should be marked "ua" in the appropriate blank to indicate that this response was unaided. Ask all remaining questions not addressed during the retelling and mark those that the student answers with an "a" to indicate the correct response was given after prompting by the teacher.

| Questions/Answers | Story Grammar Element/ Level of Comprehension |
|---|---|
| _____ 1. Where did the story take place? *(Susan B. Anthony Elementary School or at a school)* | setting/literal |
| _____ 2. Who were the two main characters in the story? *(Jamie Lee and Josh Kidder)* | character-characterization/literal |
| _____ 3. What was the problem between Jamie and Josh? *(Jamie didn't think Josh could be a good player because of his shoes, Josh didn't fit in, or other plausible responses)* | story problem(s)/inferential |
| _____ 4. How did Josh solve his problem with the other boys? *(he outplayed all of them)* | problem resolution/inferential |
| _____ 5. What are two words that you could use to describe Jamie Lee? *(conceited, stuck-up, or other plausible responses)* | character-characterization/ evaluative/expressive language |
| _____ 6. What happened after the game? *(the other boys gathered around and asked Josh his secret)* | problem resolution attempts/literal |
| _____ 7. Why did everyone laugh when Josh said, "Two things—lots of practice and cheap shoes"? *(because everything had happened because of his cheap shoes)* | problem resolution attempts/ inferential |
| _____ 8. What lesson does this story teach? *(responses will vary but should indicate a theme/moral related to "it's not what you wear that makes you good in a sport")* | theme/evaluative |

## ERROR TYPES | ERROR ANALYSIS

| | Mis-pronun. | Sub-stitute | Inser-tions | Tchr. Assists | Omis-sions | Error Totals | Self-Correct. | Meaning (M) | Syntax (S) | Visual (V) |
|---|---|---|---|---|---|---|---|---|---|---|
| **Hot Shoes** | | | | | | | | | | |
| The guys at the Susan B. Anthony | | | | | | | | | | |
| Elementary School loved all the new sport | | | | | | | | | | |
| shoes. Some wore the "Sky High" | | | | | | | | | | |
| model by Leader. Others who | | | | | | | | | | |
| couldn't afford Sky Highs would settle | | | | | | | | | | |
| for a lesser shoe. Some liked the "Street | | | | | | | | | | |
| Smarts" by Master, or the | | | | | | | | | | |
| "Uptown-Downtown" by Beebop. | | | | | | | | | | |
| The Anthony boys got to the point | | | | | | | | | | |
| with their shoes that they could | | | | | | | | | | |
| identify their friends just by | | | | | | | | | | |
| looking at their feet. But the boy who | | | | | | | | | | |
| was the envy of the entire fifth | | | | | | | | | | |
| grade was Jamie Lee. He had a | | | | | | | | | | |
| pair of "High Five Pump'em Ups" | | | | | | | | | | |
| by Superior. The only thing Anthony // | | | | | | | | | | |
| *boys loved as much as their* | | | | | | | | | | |
| *shoes was basketball.* | | | | | | | | | | |
| **TOTALS** | | | | | | | | | | |

Summary of Reading Behaviors (Strengths and Needs)

# PART II: ORAL READING AND ANALYSIS OF MISCUES

## Directions

Say, "Now I would like to hear you read this story out loud." Have the student read orally until the 100-word sample is completed. Follow along on the Miscue Grid, marking any oral reading errors as appropriate. *Remember to count miscues only up to the point in the story containing the oral reading stop-marker (//).* Then complete the Performance Summary to determine whether to continue the assessment. (*Note:* The Miscue Grid should be completed *after* the assessment session has been concluded in order to minimize stress for the student.)

# PART III: MISCUE ANALYSIS

## Directions

Circle all reading behaviors you observed.

## A. Fundamental Behaviors Observed

L → R Directionality      1-to-1 Matching      Searching for Clues      Cross-Checking

## B. Word Attack Behaviors

No Attempt      Mispronunciation (Invented Word Substitutions)      Substitutes

Skips/Reads On      Asks for Help      Repeats      Attempts to Self-Correct

"Sounds Out" (Segmenting)      Blends Sounds      Structural Analysis (Root Words, Affixes)

## C. Cueing Systems Used in Attempting Words

| CUEING TOOL | MISCUE EXAMPLES | ACTUAL TEXT |
|-------------|-----------------|-------------|
| (M) Meaning |                 |             |
| (S) Syntax  |                 |             |
| (V) Visual  |                 |             |

## D. Fluency (word by word → fluent reading)

Word by Word _____      Mixed Phrasing _____      Fluent Reading _____      Fluency Rate in Seconds _____

## E. Performance Summary

*Silent Reading Comprehension*

_____ 0–1 questions missed = Easy

_____ 2 questions missed = Adequate

_____ 3+ questions missed = Too hard

*Oral Reading Accuracy*

_____ 0–1 oral errors = Easy

_____ 2–5 oral errors = Adequate

_____ 6+ oral errors = Too hard

**Continue to the next reading passage?** _____ Yes _____ No

# PART IV: LISTENING COMPREHENSION

## *Directions*

If you have decided not to continue to have the student read any other passages, then use this passage to begin assessing the student's listening comprehension. Begin by reading the background statement for this passage and then say, "I am going to read this story to you. Please listen carefully because I will be asking you some questions after I finish reading it to you." After reading the passage, ask the student the questions associated with the passage. If the student correctly answers more than six questions, you will need to move to the next level and repeat the procedure.

## Listening Comprehension

_____ 0–2 questions missed = move to the next passage level

_____ more than 2 questions missed = stop assessment or move down a level

Examiner's Notes

# LEVEL 6 ASSESSMENT PROTOCOLS

Mountain Fire (369 words)

## PART I: SILENT READING COMPREHENSION

### Background Statement

"This story is about two boys who are lost on a mountain. Read the story to find out what they did to find their way home and what the results were of their problem resolution attempts. Read it carefully because I will ask you to tell me about what you read."

### Teacher Directions

Once the student completes the silent reading, say, "Tell me about the story you just read." Answers to the questions below that the student provides during the retelling should be marked "ua" in the appropriate blank to indicate that this response was unaided. Ask all remaining questions not addressed during the retelling and mark those that the student answers with an "a" to indicate that the correct response was given after prompting by the teacher.

| Questions/Answers | Story Grammar Element/ Level of Comprehension |
|---|---|
| _____ 1. Where did the story take place?<br>  (*Mount Holyoak*) | setting/literal |
| _____ 2. Who were the two boys in the story?<br>  (*Brad, Kevin*) | character-characterization/literal |
| _____ 3. Why were the boys sent upstream by Brad's father?<br>  (*to look for cougar tracks*) | problem resolution attempts/ inferential |
| _____ 4. What was Brad's and Kevin's problem after going upstream?<br>  (*they became lost*) | story problem(s)/literal |
| _____ 5. What did the boys do to be found?<br>  (*they started a fire*) | problem resolution/literal |
| _____ 6. What happened after their fire got out of hand?<br>  (*people came and put the fire out; other specifics related to this question are acceptable*) | problem resolution attempts/literal |
| _____ 7. In the story, the boys saw "interesting rock formations." In your own words, what would make an interesting rock formation?<br>  (*rocks that are unusually shaped or similar*) | vocabulary/expressive language |
| _____ 8. What new problem resulted from the forest fire?<br>  (*cougars were no longer in the area*) | story problem(s)/inferential |

## ERROR TYPES / ERROR ANALYSIS

| | Mis-pronun. | Sub-stitute | Inser-tions | Tchr. Assists | Omis-sions | Error Totals | Self-Correct. | Meaning (M) | Syntax (S) | Visual (V) |
|---|---|---|---|---|---|---|---|---|---|---|
| **Mountain Fire** | | | | | | | | | | |
| One August afternoon Brad and Kevin | | | | | | | | | | |
| went tracking with their fathers on | | | | | | | | | | |
| Mount Holyoak. Brad's father was a | | | | | | | | | | |
| conservationist for the Forest Service | | | | | | | | | | |
| and was searching for evidence of | | | | | | | | | | |
| cougars. Many people feared that the | | | | | | | | | | |
| cougars were extinct on Mount Holyoak. | | | | | | | | | | |
| The boys became excited when they | | | | | | | | | | |
| found what appeared to be a partial | | | | | | | | | | |
| cougar track near a stream. But as | | | | | | | | | | |
| the day wore on, no new tracks were | | | | | | | | | | |
| found. After lunch Brad's father sent | | | | | | | | | | |
| the boys upstream while he circled | | | | | | | | | | |
| west. He told the boys to return to the lunch site | | | | | | | | | | |
| in an hour. After about forty-five minutes,// | | | | | | | | | | |
| *the boys found the stream's* | | | | | | | | | | |
| *source and could follow it no more.* | | | | | | | | | | |
| **TOTALS** | | | | | | | | | | |

**Summary of Reading Behaviors (Strengths and Needs)**

# PART II: ORAL READING AND ANALYSIS OF MISCUES

## Directions

Say, "Now I would like to hear you read this story out loud." Have the student read orally until the 100-word sample is completed. Follow along on the Miscue Grid, marking any oral reading errors as appropriate. *Remember to count miscues only up to the point in the story containing the oral reading stop-marker (//).* Then complete the Performance Summary to determine whether to continue the assessment. (*Note:* The Miscue Grid should be completed *after* the assessment session has been concluded in order to minimize stress for the student.)

# PART III: MISCUE ANALYSIS

## Directions

Circle all reading behaviors you observed.

## A. Fundamental Behaviors Observed

L → R Directionality     1-to 1-Matching     Searching for Clues     Cross-Checking

## B. Word Attack Behaviors

No Attempt     Mispronunciation (Invented Word Substitutions)     Substitutes

Skips/Reads On     Asks for Help     Repeats     Attempts to Self-Correct

"Sounds Out" (Segmenting)     Blends Sounds     Structural Analysis (Root Words, Affixes)

## C. Cueing Systems Used in Attempting Words

| CUEING TOOL | MISCUE EXAMPLES | ACTUAL TEXT |
|---|---|---|
| (M) Meaning | | |
| (S) Syntax | | |
| (V) Visual | | |

## D. Fluency (word by word → fluent reading)

Word by Word _____     Mixed Phrasing _____     Fluent Reading _____     Fluency Rate in Seconds _____

## E. Performance Summary

### Silent Reading Comprehension

_____ 0–1 questions missed = Easy

_____ 2 questions missed = Adequate

_____ 3+ questions missed = Too hard

### Oral Reading Accuracy

_____ 0–1 oral errors = Easy

_____ 2–5 oral errors = Adequate

_____ 6+ oral errors = Too hard

**Continue to the next reading passage?** _____ Yes _____ No

# PART IV: LISTENING COMPREHENSION

## *Directions*

If you have decided not to continue to have the student read any other passages, then use this passage to begin assessing the student's listening comprehension. Begin by reading the background statement for this passage and then say, "I am going to read this story to you. Please listen carefully because I will be asking you some questions after I finish reading it to you." After reading the passage, ask the student the questions associated with the passage. If the student correctly answers more than six questions, you will need to move to the next level and repeat the procedure.

## Listening Comprehension

\_\_\_\_\_ 0–2 questions missed = move to the next passage level

\_\_\_\_\_ more than 2 questions missed = stop assessment or move down a level

Examiner's Notes

# LEVEL 7 ASSESSMENT PROTOCOLS

## The Canoe Trip (491 words)

### Part I: Silent Reading Comprehension

*Background Statement*

"The story is about two girls who take a canoe trip. Read the story and find out what happens to the girls while canoeing. Read it carefully because I'm going to ask you to tell me about it when you finish."

*Teacher Directions*

Once the student completes the silent reading, say, "Tell me about the story you just read." Answers to the questions below that the student provides during the retelling should be marked "ua" in the appropriate blank to indicate that this response was unaided. Ask all remaining questions not addressed during the retelling and mark those that the student answers with an "a" to indicate that the correct response was given after prompting by the teacher.

| *Questions/Answers* | *Story Grammar Element/ Level of Comprehension* |
|---|---|
| _____ 1. Where did this story take place? <br> *(West Yellowstone)* | setting/literal |
| _____ 2. Who was the story mainly about? <br> *(Katherine and Amy)* | character-characterization/literal |
| _____ 3. What was the girls' problem? <br> *(they capsized their canoe)* | story problem(s)/literal |
| _____ 4. In the story, Katherine and Amy felt secure about their "ability to navigate." What does the word "navigate" mean? <br> *(to plan to move in a chosen direction or path)* | vocabulary/inferential |
| _____ 5. Why couldn't the girls catch up with the floating coolers? <br> *(because of the time it took to empty the canoe and the swiftness of the water)* | problem resolution attempts/ inferential |
| _____ 6. How did the problem of the lost food turn out? <br> *(Katherine's parents caught the floating coolers)* | story solution/literal |
| _____ 7. How did Katherine and Amy feel after reaching Katherine's parents? <br> *(relieved, embarrassed, or other plausible responses)* | character-characterization/evaluative |
| _____ 8. Why is "all's well that ends well" a good theme for this story? <br> *(responses will vary but should reflect the fact that the girls didn't give up and everything turned out fine when they reached Katherine's parents)* | theme/evaluative |

## ERROR ANALYSIS

## ERROR TYPES

| | Mis-pronun. | Sub-stitute | Inser-tions | Tchr. Assists | Omis-sions | Error Totals | Self-Correct. | Meaning (M) | Syntax (S) | Visual (V) |
|---|---|---|---|---|---|---|---|---|---|---|
| **The Canoe Trip** | | | | | | | | | | |
| Katherine and her family like to spend their | | | | | | | | | | |
| vacation camping out. Frequently they | | | | | | | | | | |
| go to either Great Smoky | | | | | | | | | | |
| Mountains National Park or Yellowstone | | | | | | | | | | |
| National Park. Since they have | | | | | | | | | | |
| camped out for many years, | | | | | | | | | | |
| they have become quite accomplished. | | | | | | | | | | |
| Katherine is able to start a fire with flint | | | | | | | | | | |
| and steel, build a lean-to for shelter, | | | | | | | | | | |
| and find food in the forest on which to live. | | | | | | | | | | |
| Katherine's favorite outdoor activity is canoeing. | | | | | | | | | | |
| Although she is quite a good canoer, there is | | | | | | | | | | |
| one canoe trip that she'll never forget. | | | | | | | | | | |
| It was a canoe trip she took with her family | | | | | | | | | | |
| and her friend // *Amy down the Madison* | | | | | | | | | | |
| *River near West Yellowstone.* | | | | | | | | | | |
| **TOTALS** | | | | | | | | | | |

**Summary of Reading Behaviors (Strengths and Needs)**

# PART II: ORAL READING AND ANALYSIS OF MISCUES

## Directions

Say, "Now I would like to hear you read this story out loud." Have the student read orally until the 100-word sample is completed. Follow along on the Miscue Grid, marking any oral reading errors as appropriate. *Remember to count miscues only up to the point in the story containing the oral reading stop-marker (//).* Then complete the Performance Summary to determine whether to continue the assessment. (*Note:* The Miscue Grid should be completed *after* the assessment session has been concluded in order to minimize stress for the student.)

# PART III: MISCUE ANALYSIS

## Directions

Circle all reading behaviors you observed.

## A. Fundamental Behaviors Observed

L → R Directionality          1-to-1 Matching          Searching for Clues          Cross-Checking

## B. Word Attack Behaviors

No Attempt          Mispronunciation (Invented Word Substitutions)          Substitutes

Skips/Reads On          Asks for Help          Repeats          Attempts to Self-Correct

"Sounds Out" (Segmenting)          Blends Sounds          Structural Analysis (Root Words, Affixes)

## C. Cueing Systems Used in Attempting Words

| CUEING TOOL | MISCUE EXAMPLES | ACTUAL TEXT |
|---|---|---|
| (M) Meaning | | |
| (S) Syntax | | |
| (V) Visual | | |

## D. Fluency (word by word → fluent reading)

Word by Word _____          Mixed Phrasing _____          Fluent Reading _____          Fluency Rate in Seconds _____

## E. Performance Summary

*Silent Reading Comprehension*

_____ 0–1 questions missed = Easy

_____ 2 questions missed = Adequate

_____ 3+ questions missed = Too hard

*Oral Reading Accuracy*

_____ 0–1 oral errors = Easy

_____ 2–5 oral errors = Adequate

_____ 6+ oral errors = Too hard

**Continue to the next reading passage?** _____ Yes _____ No

# PART IV: LISTENING COMPREHENSION

## Directions

If you have decided not to continue to have the student read any other passages, then use this passage to begin assessing the student's listening comprehension. Begin by reading the background statement for this passage and then say, "I am going to read this story to you. Please listen carefully because I will be asking you some questions after I finish reading it to you." After reading the passage, ask the student the questions associated with the passage. If the student correctly answers more than six questions, you will need to move to the next level and repeat the procedure.

## Listening Comprehension

_____ 0–2 questions missed = move to the next passage level

_____ more than 2 questions missed = stop assessment or move down a level

Examiner's Notes

# LEVEL 8 ASSESSMENT PROTOCOLS

The Eagle (501 words)

## PART I: SILENT READING COMPREHENSION

### Background Statement

"This story is an old Native American tale about an eagle. Read the passage and try to identify the message the story tells. Read it carefully because I'm going to ask you to tell me about it when you finish."

### Teacher Directions

Once the student completes the silent reading, say, "Tell me about the story you just read." Answers to the questions below that the student provides during the retelling should be marked "ua" in the appropriate blank to indicate that this response was unaided. Ask all remaining questions not addressed during the retelling and mark those the student answers with an "a" to indicate that the correct response was given after prompting by the teacher.

| Questions/Answers | Story Grammar Element/ Level of Comprehension |
|---|---|
| _____ 1. Where does the story take place? <br> *(mountain and farm)* | setting/literal |
| _____ 2. Who were the people in the story? <br> *(Hopi farmer, his son, and Anasazi brave)* | character-characterization/literal |
| _____ 3. What was the problem presented in the story? <br> *(convincing the eagle that he wasn't a chicken)* | story problem(s)/inferential |
| _____ 4. What did the eagle do that was like a chicken? <br> *(scratching, pecking at food, wouldn't fly)* | problem resolution attempts/literal |
| _____ 5. What was the brave's first attempt to convince the bird it was an eagle? <br> *(tried to get it to fly from barn)* | problem resolution attempts/literal |
| _____ 6. How did the brave finally get the bird to recognize it could fly? <br> *(by taking it up to a high bluff so that it could see the valley and sense freedom)* | problem resolution/literal |
| _____ 7. What words would you use to describe the farmer? <br> *(responses will vary but should relate to the farmer being deceitful, uncaring, or a liar)* | vocabulary/ character-characterization/evaluative |
| _____ 8. What lesson does this story teach? <br> *(responses will vary but should indicate a theme/moral related to "you are what you think you are")* | theme/evaluative |

## ERROR ANALYSIS

| | Meaning (M) | Syntax (S) | Visual (V) |
|---|---|---|---|

## ERROR TYPES

| | Mis-pronun. | Sub-stitute | Inser-tions | Tchr. Assists | Omis-sions | Error Totals | Self-Correct. |
|---|---|---|---|---|---|---|---|

**The Eagle**

There exists an old Native American legend

about an eagle who thought he was a

chicken. It seems that a Hopi farmer

and his only son decided to climb

a nearby mountain to observe an

eagle's nest. The trip would take them all day,

so they brought along some rations and water

for the trek. The man and the boy crossed the

enormous fields of maize and beans

into the foothills. Soon thereafter

they were ascending the mountain,

and the climb became rigorous

and hazardous. They occasionally

looked back toward their home and

at the panoramic view of the entire //

*valley. Finally the farmer and son*

*reached the mountain's summit.*

**TOTALS**

**Summary of Reading Behaviors (Strengths and Needs)**

# PART II: ORAL READING AND ANALYSIS OF MISCUES

## Directions

Say, "Now I would like to hear you read this story out loud." Have the student read orally until the 100-word sample is completed. Follow along on the Miscue Grid, marking any oral reading errors as appropriate. *Remember to count miscues only up to the point in the story containing the oral reading stop-marker (//).* Then complete the Performance Summary to determine whether to continue the assessment. (*Note:* The Miscue Grid should be completed *after* the assessment session has been concluded in order to minimize stress for the student.)

# PART III: MISCUE ANALYSIS

## Directions

Circle all reading behaviors you observed.

## A. Fundamental Behaviors Observed

L → R Directionality      1-to-1 Matching      Searching for Clues      Cross-Checking

## B. Word Attack Behaviors

No Attempt      Mispronunciation (Invented Word Substitutions)      Substitutes

Skips/Reads On      Asks for Help      Repeats      Attempts to Self-Correct

"Sounds Out" (Segmenting)      Blends Sounds      Structural Analysis (Root Words, Affixes)

## C. Cueing Systems Used in Attempting Words

| CUEING TOOL | MISCUE EXAMPLES | ACTUAL TEXT |
|---|---|---|
| (M) Meaning | | |
| (S) Syntax | | |
| (V) Visual | | |

## D. Fluency (word by word → fluent reading)

Word by Word _____      Mixed Phrasing _____      Fluent Reading _____      Fluency Rate in Seconds _____

## E. Performance Summary

### Silent Reading Comprehension

_____ 0–1 questions missed = Easy

_____ 2 questions missed = Adequate

_____ 3+ questions missed = Too hard

### Oral Reading Accuracy

_____ 0–1 oral errors = Easy

_____ 2–5 oral errors = Adequate

_____ 6+ oral errors = Too hard

Continue to the next reading passage? _____ Yes _____ No

## PART IV: LISTENING COMPREHENSION

### Directions

If you have decided not to continue to have the student read any other passages, then use this passage to begin assessing the student's listening comprehension. Begin by reading the background statement for this passage and then say, "I am going to read this story to you. Please listen carefully because I will be asking you some questions after I finish reading it to you." After reading the passage, ask the student the questions associated with the passage. If the student correctly answers more than six questions, you will need to move to the next level and repeat the procedure.

### Listening Comprehension

\_\_\_\_\_ 0–2 questions missed = move to the next passage level

\_\_\_\_\_ more than 2 questions missed = stop assessment or move down a level

Examiner's Notes

# LEVEL 9 ASSESSMENT PROTOCOLS

The Case of Angela Violet (375 words)

## PART I: SILENT READING COMPREHENSION

### Background Statement

"This story is about a young girl's disappearance. Read the story carefully because I will ask you to tell me about it when you finish."

### Teacher Directions

Once the student completes the silent reading, say, "Tell me about the story you just read." Answers to the questions below that the student provides during the retelling should be marked "ua" in the appropriate blank to indicate that this response was unaided. Ask all remaining questions not addressed during the retelling and mark those that the student answers with an "a" to indicate that the correct response was given after prompting by the teacher.

| Questions/Answers | Story Grammar Element/ Level of Comprehension |
|---|---|
| _____ 1. What time of year did the story take place? *(autumn)* | setting/literal |
| _____ 2. What was the main problem in the story? *(Katrina Bowers had disappeared)* | story problem(s)/inferential |
| _____ 3. What problem resolution attempts did the authorities take when they received the telephone tip? *(they got a search warrant and went to Miss Violet's house)* | problem resolution attempts/literal |
| _____ 4. How was Katrina's case finally solved? *(she was found in California)* | problem resolution/literal |
| _____ 5. What was Miss Violet's reaction to the police wanting to search her house? *(she didn't mind, she welcomed the search)* | problem resolution attempts/literal |
| _____ 6. Describe two characteristics of Miss Violet. *(responses will vary but should suggest kind, caring, gentle, lonely)* | vocabulary/character-characterization/ inferential/expressive language |
| _____ 7. What did the people in the community do after Miss Violet was proved innocent? *(began to do things for and with her)* | problem resolution attempts/literal |
| _____ 8. What is the lesson of this story? *(responses will vary but should indicate a theme/ moral related to "you can't judge a book by its cover")* | theme/evaluative |

## ERROR ANALYSIS

## ERROR TYPES

| | Mis-pronun. | Sub-stitute | Inser-tions | Tchr. Assists | Omis-sions | Error Totals | Self-Correct. | Meaning (M) | Syntax (S) | Visual (V) |
|---|---|---|---|---|---|---|---|---|---|---|
| **The Case of Angela Violet** | | | | | | | | | | |
| Angela Violet was an elderly lady in our | | | | | | | | | | |
| neighborhood who some people thought | | | | | | | | | | |
| suspicious. She was rarely seen outside her | | | | | | | | | | |
| spacious Victorian-styled home, and then only | | | | | | | | | | |
| to retrieve the daily mail. Her pasty complexion | | | | | | | | | | |
| and ancient dress made her appear like an | | | | | | | | | | |
| apparition. Small children in the neighborhood | | | | | | | | | | |
| speculated that she might be some sort of witch. | | | | | | | | | | |
| It appeared that Miss Violet had no contact with | | | | | | | | | | |
| the outside world. One autumn day news spread | | | | | | | | | | |
| through the community that a high school | | | | | | | | | | |
| cheerleader, Katrina Bowers, had disappeared. | | | | | | | | | | |
| The police feared that Katrina had been | | | | | | | | | | |
| abducted. State and local police joined // forces | | | | | | | | | | |
| *with the Federal Bureau of Investigation in the* | | | | | | | | | | |
| *massive search effort.* | | | | | | | | | | |
| **TOTALS** | | | | | | | | | | |

**Summary of Reading Behaviors (Strengths and Needs)**

# PART II: ORAL READING AND ANALYSIS OF MISCUES

## Directions

Say, "Now I would like to hear you read this story out loud." Have the student read orally until the 100-word sample is completed. Follow along on the Miscue Grid, marking any oral reading errors as appropriate. *Remember to count miscues only up to the point in the story containing the oral reading stop-marker (//).* Then complete the Performance Summary to determine whether to continue the assessment. (*Note:* The Miscue Grid should be completed *after* the assessment session has been concluded in order to minimize stress for the student.)

# PART III: MISCUE ANALYSIS

## Directions

Circle all reading behaviors you observed.

## A. Fundamental Behaviors Observed

L → R Directionality        1-to-1 Matching        Searching for Clues        Cross-Checking

## B. Word Attack Behaviors

No Attempt        Mispronunciation (Invented Word Substitutions)        Substitutes

Skips/Reads On        Asks for Help        Repeats        Attempts to Self-Correct

"Sounds Out" (Segmenting)        Blends Sounds        Structural Analysis (Root Words, Affixes)

## C. Cueing Systems Used in Attempting Words

| CUEING TOOL | MISCUE EXAMPLES | ACTUAL TEXT |
|---|---|---|
| (M) Meaning | | |
| (S) Syntax | | |
| (V) Visual | | |

## D. Fluency (word by word → fluent reading)

Word by Word _____        Mixed Phrasing _____        Fluent Reading _____        Fluency Rate in Seconds _____

## E. Performance Summary

### Silent Reading Comprehension

_____ 0–1 questions missed = Easy

_____ 2 questions missed = Adequate

_____ 3+ questions missed = Too hard

### Oral Reading Accuracy

_____ 0–1 oral errors = Easy

_____ 2–5 oral errors = Adequate

_____ 6+ oral errors = Too hard

## PART IV: LISTENING COMPREHENSION

### Directions

If you have decided not to continue to have the student read any other passages, then use this passage to begin assessing the student's listening comprehension. Begin by reading the background statement for this passage and then say, "I am going to read this story to you. Please listen carefully because I will be asking you some questions after I finish reading it to you." After reading the passage, ask the student the questions associated with the passage. If the student correctly answers more than six questions, you will need to move to the next level and repeat the procedure.

### Listening Comprehension

\_\_\_\_\_ 0–2 questions missed = move to the next passage level

\_\_\_\_\_ more than 2 questions missed = stop assessment or move down a level

### Examiner's Notes

# SENTENCES FOR INITIAL PASSAGE SELECTION

## FORM B

## FORM B: LEVEL 1

1. Today is my birthday.

2. I wanted to have a party.

3. She stopped at the trees.

## FORM B: LEVEL 2

1. We have extra leaves to rake.

2. I need some extra money.

3. She heard me in the kitchen.

## FORM B: LEVEL 3

1. I was beginning to get afraid.

2. He could hear the voice get closer.

3. Tomorrow I will finish my work.

## FORM B: LEVEL 4

1. She walked carefully into the darkness.

2. I know it is important to eat vegetables.

3. He slipped as he reached up into the oak tree.

## FORM B: LEVEL 5

1. The tree withered away after the storm.

2. The neighborhood was shaken after the fire.

3. I was frightened by my dream.

## FORM B: LEVEL 6

1. By not participating, he was barely passing in school.

2. I allowed the gifted students extra time.

3. Especially high achievement is a result of good instruction.

## FORM B: LEVEL 7

1. I made an appointment to purchase the bike.

2. The plastic covering the application form was especially thick.

3. His robust legs made a difference in his overall physical strength.

## FORM B: LEVEL 8

1. He was provoked because he was small in stature.

2. The familiar mockery led to the fight.

3. His bruised ego never really recovered.

## FORM B: LEVEL 9

1. Her nontraditional dress improved her appearance.

2. The anonymous letter wasn't taken seriously.

3. He was a formidable-looking person, even wearing a sleazy coat.

# NARRATIVE READING PASSAGES

# Eyes in My Closet

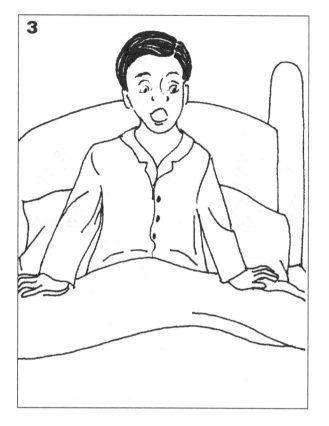

# The T-Ball Game

I like to play T-ball at school.

On Friday we played the big game.

**3**

I got a hit at the end of the game.

**4**

I made it home and won the game.

## Birthday at the Zoo

It was Sunday.

I got out of bed and went to eat.

Mom said, "Today is your birthday, Pat. What do you want to do?"

I wanted a party but I did not tell Mom.

I said, "I just want to play."

Mom said, "Come take a ride with me."

I got in the car and soon we were in the city.

The car stopped. We got out.

We walked past some trees and I saw a sign that said "City Zoo."

All my friends were at the gate.

I was all smiles. Mom had planned a party for me.

It was the best birthday ever.

## Mary's New Bike

Mary wanted a new bike. She helped around the house to make money. She had even helped her father rake leaves for extra money. But she still didn't have the money for the new ten-speed bike.

One day her Aunt Deb came to visit Mary's family. Aunt Deb heard that Mary wanted a new bike. She told Mary that she had some work for her. Mary walked over to Aunt Deb's house the very next day.

Aunt Deb had Mary mop her kitchen floor. Mary cleaned out the flower beds. Mary swept out the carport. Finally Aunt Deb asked Mary to fold her clean clothes. Mary was tired by the end of the day. But when Aunt Deb paid Mary her money, Mary smiled and hugged Aunt Deb. She hurried home to tell her parents the good news. They smiled and told her how proud they were.

The next day Mary went to the store.

### Bedtime

The sun was going down. The air was hot and Wild Willie was afraid. Never had he been in such a dry, hot place. His horse, Wizard, was trying to find a few blades of grass. Wild Willie was beginning to fall asleep from staying awake so long. Then he heard the sound again—the same sound he had been hearing for days. What could it be? Why was it following him? How could he find out what or who it was?

Slowly Wizard turned around. Willie stood up in the stirrups to see over the sand dune. He saw no one. Again he heard the sound. This time it came from behind. It was a slow rumbling sound. He got off his horse. He took his gun and got ready. Slowly the sound came closer and closer. Willie raised his gun. . . .

Then the TV went off and a voice said, "Beth, it's time to go to bed. Tomorrow is a school day and it's getting late." "Aw, Mom, can't I finish seeing the show?" I asked. "No, you can watch it another time," my mother replied.

As I went slowly upstairs to bed, I wondered what Wild Willie had seen. Maybe it had been some kind of animal or just a person in a wagon. But it was probably the Ghost of the Sand Wind. Yeah, that had to be it. Other people had claimed to have seen it. But I won't know until the reruns.

## A Different Time

Marlo lived in a different time and a different place. He lived in a time of darkness and gloom. Marlo lived in a small hut with his poor parents. He didn't have nice clothes and he didn't have much to eat. But neither of these things bothered Marlo. There was only one thing he wanted. But he couldn't have it because the ruler would not let any of his people have it. This most important thing was to be able to read. Today this may seem like a dumb wish, but to Marlo it wasn't.

One day Marlo's father sent him to the castle with a cart of vegetables. On the way Marlo met an old man who had strange eyes. The old man's head was hooded, but his eyes were deep blue and sparkled. The old man asked Marlo if he could please have a few vegetables to eat. Marlo agreed even though he knew he would get into trouble. When the old man finished, he said, "Come to the old oak tree tonight and the future will be yours." Marlo walked away wondering what the old man meant.

That night Marlo slipped out of the hut. He ran up the road until he reached the old oak tree. There he found the old man sitting on the ground.

The old man stood up and handed Marlo a box. He said, "Marlo, inside this box is what you want. Your life will never be the same."

Marlo took the box, looked down for a second, and then the old man was nowhere to be seen. Marlo rushed home. He carefully opened the box. And there in the light of his one candle Marlo saw what was in the box. It was a book.

### Afternoon Walk

One day Allison was walking in the woods behind her house. Some of the other children in the neighborhood liked to tease her by saying that the woods were haunted. "There's an old, withered, witch-like woman in those woods who comes out at two o'clock every day to catch children," they'd say. "She makes them do housework and things like that. Then she sells them to a grim- looking dwarf from far away when they are too tired to work. Once captured they are never seen again." Allison knew her friends were only telling stories, but it still frightened her sometimes when she went into the woods.

On this particular morning, Allison thought she would take a short stroll to find wild flowers for her mother. After walking for an hour or so, she stopped to rest under an elm tree. Unfortunately she fell fast asleep. The next thing she knew, Allison was being shaken by a terribly ugly old woman dressed all in black. Startled, Allison looked at her watch. It was two o'clock. The old woman took Allison to a run-down old hut.

For what seemed like hours, Allison had to wash dishes, clean out a doghouse, and scrub floors. While cleaning out the doghouse, she found a dog tag that read "Spirit." She tucked it into her pocket thinking she would give it to the woman later. The old woman checked on Allison every few minutes. She always asked Allison if she were tired. Allison always said that she wasn't tired because she remembered the story of the dwarf.

It was just after Allison finished the doghouse that her chance to escape occurred. The old woman went into a back room calling for Spirit so Allison quickly ran out the door. Allison ran and ran until she finally couldn't run any farther. She lay down under an elm tree and fell asleep.

Allison was awakened by her brother who said, "Mom says it's getting late and you'd better come home quick." Allison said, "Oh, boy, what an awful dream I just had." She told her brother all about her dream on the way home. All he said was, "Get serious."

That night when Allison undressed to take her bath, a small metal tag fell from her pocket that had "Spirit" printed on it.

### Laser Boy

My name is Bob and I'm a teacher. Several years ago I knew a student that I'd like to tell you about.

Matthew was a 13-year-old who never seemed to do well in school. Some say that he was a misfit, someone who doesn't quite fit in with the other kids his age. Not only that, Matthew had trouble in school nearly his whole life. He failed to complete his homework even when it was an easy assignment. By not participating in class, not turning in homework, and only doing a fair job on tests, Matthew always seemed to be just barely passing.

One day when Matthew was in seventh grade, his teacher decided to find out what Matthew's problem was in school. The teacher had him tested and found out from the special education teacher that Matthew was gifted in the areas of science and mathematics! The special education teacher said, "Oh, yes, sometimes students who do poorly in school are quite gifted. They just haven't been allowed to show what they can do. Also, some gifted students are not especially strong in some school subjects. But they are excellent in music, working with mechanical objects, or even athletics."

After Matthew's discovery was made, he was asked what he was interested in studying. Matthew answered that he wanted to study lasers. For the rest of that year, Matthew read everything he could find in the library at the university having to do with lasers. Later, a professor in California was found who was an expert on laser technology. The professor agreed to talk with Matthew on a regular basis to help answer questions or solve any problems Matthew had.

During the last part of seventh grade, Matthew worked on a special science project. He built a model laser. It was fantastic! Matthew's model was accurate to the last detail. Everyone was very impressed with his project. All the kids at school began calling him "laser boy." He found new friends and his life at school and home greatly improved.

Since that very special year when I got to know "laser boy," I've looked at students who are experiencing trouble in a new way. I'm convinced that everyone has special talents. We only need to discover what they are.

## The Paper Route

Scott had a chance to earn his own money for the first time. Answering an advertisement for newspaper carriers, he set up an appointment with Mr. Miley, the distribution manager. Mr. Miley was a rather short and stocky man who spoke with a loud voice.

After reviewing Scott's application, Mr. Miley said, "You look like a dependable young man to me. Do your parents approve of your becoming a paper carrier?" "Yes, sir," replied Scott, "and I have a letter from my dad saying it's OK with him."

"You can have the job, Scott," said Mr. Miley. "However, I want you to realize that this is a long route and you will have to get up very early. You will also have to have robust legs and a good bike," warned Mr. Miley.

Getting started was not easy. Scott had to be out of bed by 4:30 a.m. Next he had to pick up the papers and roll them up for placement in a plastic bag. He would usually finish that much by 5:30 a.m. Then it was time to deliver the papers.

Most days Scott could deliver all his newspapers in just two trips. His father had purchased a new bike for Scott and attached an enormous basket to it. The really hard days were Thursday and Sunday. Newspapers were especially large on those days. Scott would have to make as many as five trips to get the papers delivered on those days.

The good part of the job was, of course, the money. Scott found that he was making about 250 dollars a month. He was also developing his physical strength.

But the negative side of the job was bad weather and cranky customers. When it rained, Scott got drenched. When it snowed, Scott froze. Scott's biggest complaint was his cranky customers, particularly Mr. Gripper. Mr. Gripper insisted on his paper being put in his mailbox, rain or shine. If Scott failed to do this, Mr. Gripper always called the newspaper office and complained. But Scott avoided most complaints by going out of his way to please his customers.

After one year on the job, Scott was called into Mr. Miley's office for an end-of-year conference. During the year Scott had managed to save 1,300 dollars and pay back his father for the bike. So when Mr. Miley asked him if he wanted to continue working for the paper, Scott said, "Yes." But he added, "It was a lot more work than I counted on and I could live without the Mr. Grippers of the world. But I really like the work."

## Riley and Leonard

At times Leonard felt like the most unpopular boy in school. No matter what he did, he was constantly ridiculed by his classmates. Maybe it was because he was small in stature and wore thick bifocals. Or maybe it was because he didn't like sports. Possibly it was because he couldn't afford the designer clothes the other kids seemed to live for. Regardless, Leonard felt like a loser and was unhappy with his situation.

One day, while putting his books in his locker, the familiar mockery began. A small covey of classmates formed a semicircle around Leonard. Each began to taunt him and call him names. Most joined in after Riley McClure made Leonard drop his books. They all laughed and called him *bozo, nerd,* and *dweeb.* But Leonard tried not to be provoked—that is, until Riley made horrible slurs about Leonard's family and particularly Leonard's mother. Leonard couldn't resist. He lunged at Riley but Riley was much bigger and Leonard's attack ended in disaster. Riley slammed him into the lockers, grabbed Leonard by the throat, and made Leonard holler "calf rope," a sign of total submission.

As the group disbanded, so they wouldn't be late for their next class, Lorrie Warner approached Leonard. She apologized for the group's behavior and tried to comfort Leonard's hurt pride. She said, "What goes around comes around." But her consoling didn't help Leonard's bruised ego.

Twenty years later Leonard found himself president of the largest bank in town. He was well respected in the community and was quite generous when it came to civic projects. Although he had never married, he had recently begun dating Lorrie Warner, his old classmate.

One Friday evening Leonard and Lorrie were eating at a fancy restaurant. They had finished their meal and were heading out the door when a beggar approached. The beggar requested money to buy food. There was something curious about the beggar that Leonard could not place. But being generous, Leonard gave the man ten dollars. The beggar was so surprised by the large amount that he shook Leonard's hand vigorously before quickly backing away into the street. Lorrie screamed a word of caution but it was too late. The beggar had stepped into the path of a truck and was struck broadside. Leonard and Lorrie waited for the ambulance to carry the man away.

The next morning the headlines carried the story of the beggar. He had died from internal injuries early that morning. As Leonard read the details, he suddenly dropped the paper and turned pale. The beggar's name was Riley McClure.

### The Long Night

I arrived late at the New Orleans International Airport because of delays in St. Louis. The night was descending on the Crescent City as I entered the cab for the short ride to city center. As the cab headed toward the city, the cabbie engaged me in an informative conversation about the Crescent City. She had an island accent and her multicolored dress was very nontraditional. After I told her I wanted to go to Rampart in the French Quarter, she abruptly turned left and headed southwest.

Fifteen minutes later, without a word, I got out of the cab and proceeded up Rampart. I had gone only two blocks when I noticed that a bleak little man was following me. I say bleak because when I saw his silhouette under a fluorescent street light, he looked as if something mean and cruel had happened in his early life. You know, he had a kind of woebegone appearance. Every time I stopped, he stopped. If I sped up my pace, his pace quickened. Finally, I slipped into an anonymous doorway. As he approached I swiftly reached out and grabbed him by his grimy coat. I asked him why he was following me but all he did was whimper and hand me a crumpled-up note. As my eyes fell on the note, he slipped out of my grasp and ran into the eerily approaching fog.

The note contained the following message: "Your death is behind you. Run if you value your life." I didn't think, I ran.

As I rounded the corner of Rampart and Royal, I ran straight into a police officer. I felt relief. I told him my story. He chuckled and didn't take me seriously. As he walked away I saw a set of eyes from behind a refuse container in an alleyway. I ran again.

As I cut through an alley I was accosted by two large, burly men. They said they had been sent by Nero. They asked me where I had put the package. I told them I had no idea of what they were referring to. They gathered me up and forced me into a dingy building.

As soon as my eyes adjusted to the glow of the incandescent lights, I saw a large, rotund man at a table. He looked formidable. I was forced to sit across the table from the man. He leaned forward and I could see his face. A face of evil. He studied me carefully, and then he looked at my assailants. "This isn't Mouser, you idiots. Get him out of here." They blindfolded me and walked me out of the building a different way. An hour later I found myself on a deserted street.

Two days later I left the Crescent City. I never told anyone about my experience, and I've never been back.

# EXAMINER'S ASSESSMENT PROTOCOLS

# PREPRIMER (PP) LEVEL ASSESSMENT PROTOCOLS

Eyes in My Closet (Wordless picture story)

## PART I: WORDLESS PICTURE STORY READING

### Background Statement

"These pictures tell a story about a child who is going to bed. Look at each picture as I show it to you and think about the story the pictures tell. Later, I will want you to tell me the story using the pictures."

### Teacher Directions

Refer the student to each picture slowly and in order as numbered. Do not comment on the pictures. Then repeat the procedure, asking the student to tell the story in the student's own words. Record the student's reading using a tape recorder, and transcribe the reading as it is being dictated. Replay the recording later to make sure that your transcription is accurate and complete.

## PART II: EMERGENT READING BEHAVIOR CHECKLIST

### Directions

Following are emergent reading behaviors identified through research and grouped according to broad developmental stages. Check all behaviors you have observed. *If the student progresses to Stage 3 or 4, continue your assessment using the Primer (P) Level passage.*

**Stage 1: Early Connections to Reading—Describing Pictures**

_____ Attends to and describes (labels) pictures in books

_____ Has a limited sense of story

_____ Follows verbal directions for this activity

_____ Uses oral vocabulary appropriate for age/grade level

_____ Displays attention span appropriate for age/grade level

_____ Responds to questions in an appropriate manner

_____ Appears to connect pictures (sees as being interrelated)

**Stage 2: Connecting Pictures to Form a Story**

_____ Attends to pictures and develops oral stories

_____ Uses only childlike or descriptive (storyteller) language to tell the story, rather than book language (e.g., "Once upon a time . . ."; "There once was a little boy . . .")

**Stage 3: Transitional Picture Reading**

_____ Attends to pictures as a connected story

_____ Mixes storyteller language with book language

### Stage 4: Advanced Picture Reading

_____ Attends to pictures and develops oral stories

_____ Speaks as though reading the story (uses book language)

Examiner's Notes

# PRIMER (P) LEVEL ASSESSMENT PROTOCOLS

The T-Ball Game (32 words)

## PART I: PICTURE STORY READING—ORAL READING AND ANALYSIS OF MISCUES

### Background Statement

"This is a story about a child who is playing a game. Let's look at each picture first. Now, read the story to yourself. Later, I will want you to read the story to me."

### Teacher Directions

Refer the student to each frame of the story slowly and in order as numbered. Do not read the story or comment on the pictures. After the student has read the story silently, ask the student to read the story aloud. Record the student's reading using a tape recorder, and mark any miscues on the Miscue Grid provided. Following the oral reading, complete the Emergent Reading Behavior Checklist. Assessment information obtained from both the Miscue Grid and the Emergent Reading Behavior Checklist will help you determine whether to continue your assessment. If the student is unable to read the passage independently the first time, read it aloud, then ask the student to try to read the story again. This will help you understand whether the student is able to memorize and repeat text, an important developmental milestone. The assessment should stop after this activity if the child is unable to read the text independently. (*Note:* The Miscue Grid should be completed *after* the assessment session has been concluded in order to minimize stress for the student.)

## ERROR TYPES

## ERROR ANALYSIS

| The T-Ball Game | Mis-pronun. | Sub-stitute | Inser-tions | Tchr. Assists | Omis-sions | Error Totals | Self-Correct. | Meaning (M) | Syntax (S) | Visual (V) |
|---|---|---|---|---|---|---|---|---|---|---|
| I like to play T-ball | | | | | | | | | | |
| at school. On Friday we | | | | | | | | | | |
| played the big game. I | | | | | | | | | | |
| got a hit at the end of | | | | | | | | | | |
| the game. I made it | | | | | | | | | | |
| home and won the game. // | | | | | | | | | | |
| TOTALS | | | | | | | | | | |

Summary of Reading Behaviors (Strengths and Needs)

# PART II: EMERGENT READING BEHAVIOR CHECKLIST

## Directions

Following are emergent reading behaviors identified through research and grouped according to broad developmental stages. After the student has completed the oral reading, check each behavior observed below to help determine development level and whether to continue the assessment. *If the student seems to be at Stage 6 or 7 and the oral reading scored at an Easy or Adequate level, continue the assessment using the Level 1 passage.*

### Stage 5: Early Print Reading

_____ Tells a story using the pictures

_____ Knows print moves from left to right, top to bottom

_____ Creates part of the text using book language and knows some words on sight

### Stage 6: Early Strategic Reading

_____ Uses context to guess at some unknown words (guesses make sense)

_____ Notices beginning sounds in words and uses them in guessing unknown words

_____ Seems to sometimes use syntax to help identify words in print

_____ Recognizes some word parts, such as root words and affixes

### Stage 7: Moderate Strategic Reading

_____ Sometimes uses context and word parts to decode words

_____ Self-corrects when making an oral reading miscue

_____ Retells the passage easily and may embellish the story line

_____ Shows some awareness of vowel sounds

Examiner's Notes

# PART III: DEVELOPMENTAL/PERFORMANCE SUMMARY

Oral Reading Accuracy

_____ 0–1 oral errors = Easy

_____ 2 oral errors = Adequate

_____ 6+ oral errors = Too hard

**Continue to the next assessment level passage?** _____ Yes _____ No

Examiner's Notes

# LEVEL 1 ASSESSMENT PROTOCOLS

Birthday at the Zoo (106 words)

## PART I: SILENT READING COMPREHENSION

### Background Statement

"What do you like to do on your birthday? Read this story carefully to find out what special thing a girl wanted for her birthday. I'm going to ask you to tell me about the story when you're through reading it."

### Teacher Directions

Once the student completes the silent reading, say, "Tell me about the story you just read." Answers to the questions below that the student provides during the retelling should be marked "ua" in the appropriate blank to indicate that this response was unaided. Ask all remaining questions not addressed during the retelling and mark those that the student answers with an "a" to indicate that the correct response was given after prompting by the teacher.

| Questions/Answers | Story Grammar Element/ Level of Comprehension |
|---|---|
| _____ 1. Who were the people in the story? <br> *(Pat and her mom)* | character-characterization/literal |
| _____ 2. What was Pat's wish? <br> *(Pat wanted to have a party)* | story problem(s)/literal |
| _____ 3. What did Pat say she wanted to do for her birthday? <br> *(just play)* | problem resolution attempts/literal |
| _____ 4. Did Pat get her wish? How do you know? <br> *(yes, she had a surprise party at the zoo)* | problem resolution/literal |
| _____ 5. How did Pat and Mom get to the zoo? <br> *(drove in by car)* | problem resolution attempts/literal |
| _____ 6. What words would you use to describe how Pat felt at the zoo? <br> *(surprised, happy, etc.)* | character-characterization/ inferential vocabulary |
| _____ 7. Where was Pat when the story began? <br> *(in her bedroom or house)* | setting/inferential |
| _____ 8. When did Pat first know that she was going to have a birthday party? <br> *(when she got to the zoo and saw her friends)* | problem resolution attempts/ inferential |

## ERROR TYPES

## ERROR ANALYSIS

| Birthday at the Zoo | Mis-pronun. | Sub-stitute | Inser-tions | Tchr. Assists | Omis-sions | Error Totals | Self-Correct. | Meaning (M) | Syntax (S) | Visual (V) |
|---|---|---|---|---|---|---|---|---|---|---|
| It was Sunday. I got out of bed | | | | | | | | | | |
| and went to eat. Mom said, "Today | | | | | | | | | | |
| is your birthday, Pat. What do you | | | | | | | | | | |
| want to do?" I wanted a party but I | | | | | | | | | | |
| did not tell Mom. I said, "I just want | | | | | | | | | | |
| to play." Mom said, "Come take | | | | | | | | | | |
| a ride with me." I got in the car and | | | | | | | | | | |
| soon we were in the city. The car | | | | | | | | | | |
| stopped. We got out. We walked | | | | | | | | | | |
| past some trees and I saw a sign | | | | | | | | | | |
| that said "City Zoo." All my friends | | | | | | | | | | |
| were at the gate. I was all smiles. | | | | | | | | | | |
| Mom had planned a party for me. // | | | | | | | | | | |
| It was the best birthday ever. | | | | | | | | | | |
| TOTALS | | | | | | | | | | |

Summary of Reading Behaviors (Strengths and Needs)

# PART II: ORAL READING AND ANALYSIS OF MISCUES

*Directions*

Say, "Now I would like to hear you read this story out loud." Have the student read orally until the 100-word sample is completed. Follow along on the Miscue Grid, marking any oral reading errors as appropriate. *Remember to count miscues only up to the point in the story containing the oral reading stop-marker (//).* Then complete the Performance Summary to determine whether to continue the assessment. (*Note:* The Miscue Grid should be completed *after* the assessment session has been concluded in order to minimize stress for the student.)

# PART III: MISCUE ANALYSIS

*Directions*

Circle all reading behaviors you observed.

## A. Fundamental Behaviors Observed

L → R Directionality     1-to-1 Matching     Searching for Clues     Cross-Checking

## B. Word Attack Behaviors

No Attempt     Mispronunciation (Invented Word Substitutions)     Substitutes

Skips/Reads On     Asks for Help     Repeats     Attempts to Self-Correct

"Sounds Out" (Segmenting)     Blends Sounds     Structural Analysis (Root Words, Affixes)

## C. Cueing Systems Used in Attempting Words

| CUEING TOOL | MISCUE EXAMPLES | ACTUAL TEXT |
|---|---|---|
| (M) Meaning | | |
| (S) Syntax | | |
| (V) Visual | | |

## D. Fluency (word by word → fluent reading)

Word by Word _____     Mixed Phrasing _____     Fluent Reading _____     Fluency Rate in Seconds _____

## E. Performance Summary

*Silent Reading Comprehension*

_____ 0–1 questions missed = Easy

_____ 2 questions missed = Adequate

_____ 3+ questions missed = Too hard

*Oral Reading Accuracy*

_____ 0–1 oral errors = Easy

_____ 2–5 oral errors = Adequate

_____ 6+ oral errors = Too hard

**Continue to the next reading passage?** _____ **Yes** _____ **No**

# PART IV: LISTENING COMPREHENSION

## *Directions*

If you have decided not to continue to have the student read any other passages, then use this passage to begin assessing the student's listening comprehension. Begin by reading the background statement for this passage and then say, "I am going to read this story to you. Please listen carefully because I will be asking you some questions after I finish reading it to you." After reading the passage, ask the student the questions associated with the passage. If the student correctly answers more than six questions, you will need to move to the next level and repeat the procedure.

## Listening Comprehension

_____ 0–2 questions missed = move to the next passage level

_____ more than 2 questions missed = stop assessment or move down a level

Examiner's Notes

# LEVEL 2 ASSESSMENT PROTOCOLS

Mary's New Bike (156 words)

## PART I: SILENT READING COMPREHENSION

### Background Statement

"Have you ever tried to earn money for something special? Read this story to find out how Mary was able to earn something special. Read it carefully because I am going to ask you to tell me about the story when you finish."

### Teacher Directions

Once the student completes the silent reading, say, "Tell me about the story you just read." Answers to the questions below that the student provides during the retelling should be marked "ua" in the appropriate blank to indicate that this response was unaided. Ask all remaining questions not addressed during the retelling and mark those that the student answers with an "a" to indicate that the correct response was given after prompting by the teacher.

| Questions/Answers | Story Grammar Element/ Level of Comprehension |
|---|---|
| _____ 1. Who was this story about? <br> (*Mary*) | character-characterization/literal |
| _____ 2. What was Mary's problem in the story? <br> (*she wanted a new bike but she didn't have enough money*) | story problem(s)/literal |
| _____ 3. What had Mary done to earn money in the past? <br> (*rake leaves and help around the house*) | problem resolution attempts/literal |
| _____ 4. Besides Mary, who were the people in the story? <br> (*Aunt Deb, Mary's family*) | character-characterization/literal |
| _____ 5. How did Mary finally solve her problem? <br> (*worked hard for Aunt Deb and earned enough money*) | problem resolution/inferential |
| _____ 6. What were two things Mary did for Aunt Deb? <br> (*mopped floor, swept carport, cleaned out flower beds*) | problem resolution attempts/literal |
| _____ 7. What lesson did Mary learn about getting something you really want? <br> (*it takes time and hard work*) | theme/evaluative |
| _____ 8. Why did Mary go to the store the next day? <br> (*to buy her bike*) | problem resolution attempts/ inferential |

## ERROR TYPES / ERROR ANALYSIS

| Mary's New Bike | Mis-pronun. | Sub-stitute | Inser-tions | Tchr. Assists | Omis-sions | Error Totals | Self-Correct. | Meaning (M) | Syntax (S) | Visual (V) |
|---|---|---|---|---|---|---|---|---|---|---|
| Mary wanted a new bike. She helped | | | | | | | | | | |
| around the house to make money. She had | | | | | | | | | | |
| even helped her father rake leaves for extra | | | | | | | | | | |
| money. But she still didn't have the money | | | | | | | | | | |
| for the new ten-speed bike. One day her | | | | | | | | | | |
| Aunt Deb came to visit Mary's family. | | | | | | | | | | |
| Aunt Deb heard that Mary wanted a new | | | | | | | | | | |
| bike. She told Mary that she had some work | | | | | | | | | | |
| for her. Mary walked over to Aunt Deb's | | | | | | | | | | |
| house the very next day. Aunt Deb had Mary | | | | | | | | | | |
| mop her kitchen floor. Mary cleaned out the | | | | | | | | | | |
| flower beds. Mary swept out the carport. | | | | | | | | | | |
| Finally Aunt Deb asked // *Mary to fold* | | | | | | | | | | |
| *her clean clothes.* | | | | | | | | | | |
| TOTALS | | | | | | | | | | |

**Summary of Reading Behaviors (Strengths and Needs)**

# PART II: ORAL READING AND ANALYSIS OF MISCUES

## Directions

Say, "Now I would like to hear you read this story out loud." Have the student read orally until the 100-word sample is completed. Follow along on the Miscue Grid, marking any oral reading errors as appropriate. *Remember to count miscues only up to the point in the story containing the oral reading stop-marker (//).* Then complete the Performance Summary to determine whether to continue the assessment. (*Note:* The Miscue Grid should be completed *after* the assessment session has been concluded in order to minimize stress for the student.)

# PART III: MISCUE ANALYSIS

## Directions

Circle all reading behaviors you observed.

## A. Fundamental Behaviors Observed

L → R Directionality          1-to-1 Matching          Searching for Clues          Cross-Checking

## B. Word Attack Behaviors

No Attempt          Mispronunciation (Invented Word Substitutions)          Substitutes

Skips/Reads On          Asks for Help          Repeats          Attempts to Self-Correct

"Sounds Out" (Segmenting)          Blends Sounds          Structural Analysis (Root Words, Affixes)

## C. Cueing Systems Used in Attempting Words

| CUEING TOOL | MISCUE EXAMPLES | ACTUAL TEXT |
|---|---|---|
| (M) Meaning | | |
| (S) Syntax | | |
| (V) Visual | | |

## D. Fluency (word by word → fluent reading)

Word by Word _____          Mixed Phrasing _____          Fluent Reading _____          Fluency Rate in Seconds _____

## E. Performance Summary

### Silent Reading Comprehension

_____ 0–1 questions missed = Easy

_____ 2 questions missed = Adequate

_____ 3+ questions missed = Too hard

### Oral Reading Accuracy

_____ 0–1 oral errors = Easy

_____ 2–5 oral errors = Adequate

_____ 6+ oral errors = Too hard

**Continue to the next reading passage?** _____ **Yes** _____ **No**

# PART IV: LISTENING COMPREHENSION

## Directions

If you have decided not to continue to have the student read any other passages, then use this passage to begin assessing the student's listening comprehension. Begin by reading the background statement for this passage and then say, "I am going to read this story to you. Please listen carefully because I will be asking you some questions after I finish reading it to you." After reading the passage, ask the student the questions associated with the passage. If the student correctly answers more than six questions, you will need to move to the next level and repeat the procedure.

## Listening Comprehension

_____ 0–2 questions missed = move to the next passage level

_____ more than 2 questions missed = stop assessment or move down a level

Examiner's Notes

# LEVEL 3 ASSESSMENT PROTOCOLS
Bedtime (247 words)

## PART I: SILENT READING COMPREHENSION

### Background Statement

"This is a story about a girl who has to go to bed. As you read the story, try to find out why she has to go to bed. Read it carefully because I'm going to ask you to tell me about it."

### Teacher Directions

Once the student completes the silent reading, say, "Tell me about the story you just read." Answers to the questions below that the student provides during the retelling should be marked "ua" in the appropriate blank to indicate that this response was unaided. Ask all remaining questions not addressed during the retelling and mark those that the student answers with an "a" to indicate that the correct response was given after prompting by the teacher.

| Questions/Answers | Story Grammar Element/ Level of Comprehension |
|---|---|
| _____ 1. Who were the people in the story? (*Wild Willie, Beth, and her mother*) | character-characterization/literal |
| _____ 2. Where was Wild Willie? (*the desert*) | setting/inferential |
| _____ 3. What was Wild Willie's problem? (*he was being followed*) | story problem(s)/literal |
| _____ 4. Why didn't Beth find out what was following Wild Willie? (*TV was turned off*) | story problem(s)/literal |
| _____ 5. How is Beth going to find out what was following Wild Willie? (*watch the reruns*) | problem resolution attempts/ inferential |
| _____ 6. If you were Beth, what other way can you think of to find out what was following Wild Willie? (*ask a friend, or any other plausible response*) | problem resolution/inferential |
| _____ 7. Describe Beth's feelings when she had to go to bed. (*disappointed, mad, upset, or other plausible responses*) | character-characterization/evaluative vocabulary/expressive language |
| _____ 8. What were the two reasons Beth's mother gave for turning off the TV? (*the next day was a school day and it was getting late*) | problem resolution attempts/literal |

## ERROR TYPES

## ERROR ANALYSIS

| Bedtime | Mis-pronun. | Sub-stitute | Inser-tions | Tchr. Assists | Omis-sions | Error Totals | Self-Correct. | Meaning (M) | Syntax (S) | Visual (V) |
|---|---|---|---|---|---|---|---|---|---|---|
| The sun was going down. The air was | | | | | | | | | | |
| hot and Wild Willie was afraid. Never | | | | | | | | | | |
| had he been in such a dry, hot place. His | | | | | | | | | | |
| horse, Wizard, was trying to find a few | | | | | | | | | | |
| blades of grass. Wild Willie was beginning | | | | | | | | | | |
| to fall asleep from staying awake so long. | | | | | | | | | | |
| Then he heard the sound again—the | | | | | | | | | | |
| same sound he had been hearing for | | | | | | | | | | |
| days. What could it be? Why was it | | | | | | | | | | |
| following him? How could he find out | | | | | | | | | | |
| what or who it was? Slowly Wizard | | | | | | | | | | |
| turned around. Willie stood up in the | | | | | | | | | | |
| stirrups to see over the sand dune. He | | | | | | | | | | |
| saw // *no one.* | | | | | | | | | | |
| TOTALS | | | | | | | | | | |

**Summary of Reading Behaviors (Strengths and Needs)**

# PART II: ORAL READING AND ANALYSIS OF MISCUES

## Directions

Say, "Now I would like to hear you read this story out loud." Have the student read orally until the 100-word sample is completed. Follow along on the Miscue Grid, marking any oral reading errors as appropriate. *Remember to count miscues only up to the point in the story containing the oral reading stop-marker (//).* Then complete the Performance Summary to determine whether to continue the assessment. (*Note:* The Miscue Grid should be completed *after* the assessment session has been concluded in order to minimize stress for the student.)

# PART III: MISCUE ANALYSIS

## Directions

Circle all reading behaviors you observed.

### A. Fundamental Behaviors Observed

L → R Directionality     1-to-1 Matching     Searching for Clues     Cross-Checking

### B. Word Attack Behaviors

No Attempt     Mispronunciation (Invented Word Substitutions)     Substitutes

Skips/Reads On     Asks for Help     Repeats     Attempts to Self-Correct

"Sounds Out" (Segmenting)     Blends Sounds     Structural Analysis (Root Words, Affixes)

### C. Cueing Systems Used in Attempting Words

| CUEING TOOL | MISCUE EXAMPLES | ACTUAL TEXT |
| --- | --- | --- |
| (M) Meaning | | |
| (S) Syntax | | |
| (V) Visual | | |

### D. Fluency (word by word → fluent reading)

Word by Word _____     Mixed Phrasing _____     Fluent Reading _____     Fluency Rate in Seconds _____

### E. Performance Summary

*Silent Reading Comprehension*

_____ 0–1 questions missed = Easy

_____ 2 questions missed = Adequate

_____ 3+ questions missed = Too hard

*Oral Reading Accuracy*

_____ 0–1 orals error = Easy

_____ 2–5 oral errors = Adequate

_____ 6+ oral errors = Too hard

**Continue to the next reading passage?** _____ Yes _____ No

# PART IV: LISTENING COMPREHENSION

## Directions

If you have decided not to continue to have the student read any other passages, then use this passage to begin assessing the student's listening comprehension. Begin by reading the background statement for this passage and then say, "I am going to read this story to you. Please listen carefully because I will be asking you some questions after I finish reading it to you." After reading the passage, ask the student the questions associated with the passage. If the student correctly answers more than six questions, you will need to move to the next level and repeat the procedure.

## Listening Comprehension

_____ 0–2 questions missed = move to the next passage level

_____ more than 2 questions missed = stop assessment or move down a level

Examiner's Notes

# LEVEL 4 ASSESSMENT PROTOCOLS

A Different Time (294 words)

## PART I: SILENT READING COMPREHENSION

### Background Statement

"This story is about a boy who lived a long time ago. Read the story to find out what Marlo wanted and why he couldn't have it. Read it carefully because I will ask you to tell me about it when you finish."

### Teacher Directions

Once the student completes the silent reading, say, "Tell me about the story you just read." Answers to the questions below that the student provides during the retelling should be marked "ua" in the appropriate blank to indicate that this response was unaided. Ask all remaining questions not addressed during the retelling and mark those that the student answers with an "a" to indicate that the correct response was given after prompting by the teacher.

| Questions/Answers | Story Grammar Element/ Level of Comprehension |
|---|---|
| _____ 1. Where did Marlo live? <br> (*in a hut*) | setting/literal |
| _____ 2. What was Marlo's problem? <br> (*he wanted to read*) | story problem(s)/literal |
| _____ 3. What did Marlo do that caused the old man to help him? <br> (*gave him some vegetables*) | problem resolution attempts/ inferential |
| _____ 4. Where did Marlo have to meet the old man? <br> (*old oak tree*) | setting/literal |
| _____ 5. How was Marlo's problem solved? <br> (*the old man gave him a book so he could learn to read*) | problem resolution attempts/ inferential |
| _____ 6. How would you describe Marlo? <br> (*kind, nice, thankful, other plausible responses*) | character-characterization/evaluative vocabulary/expressive language |
| _____ 7. How do you know that this story took place in olden times and not today? <br> (*castle, they lived in hut, used a cart, lots of people couldn't read, and other plausible responses*) | setting/inferential/vocabulary |
| _____ 8. Why is "be kind to others and they'll be kind to you" a good theme for this story? <br> (*responses will vary but should indicate that Marlo got his wish because of his kindness*) | theme/evaluative |

## ERROR ANALYSIS

## ERROR TYPES

| A Different Time | Mis-pronun. | Sub-stitute | Inser-tions | Tchr. Assists | Omis-sions | Error Totals | Self-Correct. | Meaning (M) | Syntax (S) | Visual (V) |
|---|---|---|---|---|---|---|---|---|---|---|
| Marlo lived in a different time and a | | | | | | | | | | |
| different place. He lived in a time of | | | | | | | | | | |
| darkness and gloom. Marlo lived in a | | | | | | | | | | |
| small hut with his poor parents. He didn't have | | | | | | | | | | |
| nice clothes and he didn't have much to eat. | | | | | | | | | | |
| But neither of these things bothered Marlo. | | | | | | | | | | |
| There was only one thing he wanted. But | | | | | | | | | | |
| he couldn't have it because the ruler | | | | | | | | | | |
| would not let any of his people have it. | | | | | | | | | | |
| This most important thing was to be able | | | | | | | | | | |
| to read. Today this may seem like a | | | | | | | | | | |
| dumb wish, but to Marlo it wasn't. One | | | | | | | | | | |
| day Marlo's father sent // *him* | | | | | | | | | | |
| *to the castle with a cart of vegetables.* | | | | | | | | | | |
| TOTALS | | | | | | | | | | |

**Summary of Reading Behaviors (Strengths and Needs)**

# PART II: ORAL READING AND ANALYSIS OF MISCUES

## Directions

Say, "Now I would like to hear you read this story out loud." Have the student read orally until the 100-word sample is completed. Follow along on the Miscue Grid, marking any oral reading errors as appropriate. *Remember to count miscues only up to the point in the story containing the oral reading stop-marker (//).* Then complete the Performance Summary to determine whether to continue the assessment. (*Note:* The Miscue Grid should be completed *after* the assessment session has been concluded in order to minimize stress for the student.)

# PART III: MISCUE ANALYSIS

## Directions

Circle all reading behaviors you observed.

## A. Fundamental Behaviors Observed

L → R Directionality        1-to-1 Matching        Searching for Clues        Cross-Checking

## B. Word Attack Behaviors

No Attempt        Mispronunciation (Invented Word Substitutions)        Substitutes

Skips/Reads On        Asks for Help        Repeats        Attempts to Self-Correct

"Sounds Out" (Segmenting)        Blends Sounds        Structural Analysis (Root Words, Affixes)

## C. Cueing Systems Used in Attempting Words

| CUEING TOOL | MISCUE EXAMPLES | ACTUAL TEXT |
|---|---|---|
| (M) Meaning | | |
| (S) Syntax | | |
| (V) Visual | | |

## D. Fluency (word by word → fluent reading)

Word by Word _____        Mixed Phrasing _____        Fluent Reading _____        Fluency Rate in Seconds _____

## E. Performance Summary

### Silent Reading Comprehension

_____ 0–1 questions missed = Easy

_____ 2 questions missed = Adequate

_____ 3+ questions missed = Too hard

### Oral Reading Accuracy

_____ 0–1 oral errors = Easy

_____ 2–5 oral errors = Adequate

_____ 6+ oral errors = Too hard

**Continue to the next reading passage?** _____ **Yes** _____ **No**

## PART IV: LISTENING COMPREHENSION

### Directions

If you have decided not to continue to have the student read any other passages, then use this passage to begin assessing the student's listening comprehension. Begin by reading the background statement for this passage and then say, "I am going to read this story to you. Please listen carefully because I will be asking you some questions after I finish reading it to you." After reading the passage, ask the student the questions associated with the passage. If the student correctly answers more than six questions, you will need to move to the next level and repeat the procedure.

## Listening Comprehension

_____ 0–2 questions missed = move to the next passage level

_____ more than 2 questions missed = stop assessment or move down a level

Examiner's Notes

# LEVEL 5 ASSESSMENT PROTOCOLS
## Afternoon Walk (388 words)

# PART I: SILENT READING COMPREHENSION

### Background Statement

"This story is about a young girl who goes walking in woods that are supposed to be haunted. Read the story to find out what happens to Allison when she ventures into the haunted woods. Read it carefully because I will ask you to tell me about it when you finish."

### Teacher Directions

Once the student completes the silent reading, say, "Tell me about the story you just read." Answers to the questions below that the student provides during the retelling should be marked "ua" in the appropriate blank to indicate that this response was unaided. Ask all remaining questions not addressed during the retelling and mark those that the student answers with an "a" to indicate that the correct response was given after prompting by the teacher.

| *Questions/Answers* | *Story Grammar Element/ Level of Comprehension* |
|---|---|
| _____ 1. Who is the main character in this story? *(Allison)* | character-characterization/literal |
| _____ 2. Where was Allison when she first met the old woman? *(in the woods or under an elm tree)* | setting/literal |
| _____ 3. The dwarf is described as "grim looking." What do you think that means? *(mean, stern, not kind, serious, any plausible response)* | vocabulary/expressive language |
| _____ 4. What was Allison's problem with the old woman? *(getting away before being sold to the dwarf or not acting tired)* | story problem(s)/inferential |
| _____ 5. How did Allison escape from the old woman? *(she ran out the door while the woman was looking for her dog)* | problem resolution/literal |
| _____ 6. What happened after Allison couldn't run any farther and fell asleep? *(her brother woke her up)* | problem resolution attempts/literal |
| _____ 7. What happened after Allison was safely back home? *(she found a small metal tag with "Spirit" printed on it)* | problem resolution attempts/literal |
| _____ 8. Why, in the story, did Allison always tell the old woman that she was not tired? *(because she didn't want to be sold)* | problem resolution attempts/ inferential |

ERROR TYPES / ERROR ANALYSIS

| | Mis-pronun. | Sub-stitute | Inser-tions | Tchr. Assists | Omis-sions | Error Totals | Self-Correct. | Meaning (M) | Syntax (S) | Visual (V) |
|---|---|---|---|---|---|---|---|---|---|---|
| **Afternoon Walk** | | | | | | | | | | |
| One day Allison was walking in the | | | | | | | | | | |
| woods behind her house. Some of the | | | | | | | | | | |
| other children in the neighborhood liked | | | | | | | | | | |
| to tease her by saying that the woods were | | | | | | | | | | |
| haunted. "There's an old, withered, | | | | | | | | | | |
| witch-like woman in those woods who | | | | | | | | | | |
| comes out at two o'clock every day to | | | | | | | | | | |
| catch children," they'd say. "She makes | | | | | | | | | | |
| them do housework and things like that. | | | | | | | | | | |
| Then she sells them to a grim-looking | | | | | | | | | | |
| dwarf from far away when they are | | | | | | | | | | |
| too tired to work. Once captured they | | | | | | | | | | |
| are never seen again." Allison knew her | | | | | | | | | | |
| friends were only telling stories, | | | | | | | | | | |
| but it still frightened // *her sometimes* | | | | | | | | | | |
| *when she went into the woods.* | | | | | | | | | | |
| TOTALS | | | | | | | | | | |

**Summary of Reading Behaviors (Strengths and Needs)**

# PART II: ORAL READING AND ANALYSIS OF MISCUES

*Directions*

Say, "Now I would like to hear you read this story out loud." Have the student read orally until the 100-word sample is completed. Follow along on the Miscue Grid, marking any oral reading errors as appropriate. *Remember to count miscues only up to the point in the story containing the oral reading stop-marker (//).* Then complete the Performance Summary to determine whether to continue the assessment. (*Note:* The Miscue Grid should be completed *after* the assessment session has been concluded in order to minimize stress for the student.)

# PART III: MISCUE ANALYSIS

*Directions*

Circle all reading behaviors you observed.

## A. Fundamental Behaviors Observed

L → R Directionality     1-to-1 Matching     Searching for Clues     Cross-Checking

## B. Word Attack Behaviors

No Attempt     Mispronunciation (Invented Word Substitutions)     Substitutes

Skips/Reads On     Asks for Help     Repeats     Attempts to Self-Correct

"Sounds Out" (Segmenting)     Blends Sounds     Structural Analysis (Root Words, Affixes)

## C. Cueing Systems Used in Attempting Words

| CUEING TOOL | MISCUE EXAMPLES | ACTUAL TEXT |
|-------------|-----------------|-------------|
| (M) Meaning |  |  |
| (S) Syntax |  |  |
| (V) Visual |  |  |

## D. Fluency (word by word → fluent reading)

Word by Word _____     Mixed Phrasing _____     Fluent Reading _____     Fluency Rate in Seconds _____

## E. Performance Summary

*Silent Reading Comprehension*

_____ 0–1 questions missed = Easy

_____ 2 questions missed = Adequate

_____ 3+ questions missed = Too hard

*Oral Reading Accuracy*

_____ 0–1 oral errors = Easy

_____ 2–5 oral errors = Adequate

_____ 6+ oral errors = Too hard

**Continue to the next reading passage?** _____ Yes _____ No

# PART IV: LISTENING COMPREHENSION

## Directions

If you have decided not to continue to have the student read any other passages, then use this passage to begin assessing the student's listening comprehension. Begin by reading the background statement for this passage and then say, "I am going to read this story to you. Please listen carefully because I will be asking you some questions after I finish reading it to you." After reading the passage, ask the student the questions associated with the passage. If the student correctly answers more than six questions, you will need to move to the next level and repeat the procedure.

## Listening Comprehension

_____ 0–2 questions missed = move to the next passage level

_____ more than 2 questions missed = stop assessment or move down a level

Examiner's Notes

# LEVEL 6 ASSESSMENT PROTOCOLS

Laser Boy (381 words)

## PART I: SILENT READING COMPREHENSION

*Background Statement*

"This story is about a boy who had problems in school. Read the story to find out how the boy's problems were solved. Read it carefully because I'm going to ask you to tell me about it when you finish."

*Teacher Directions*

Once the student completes the silent reading, say, "Tell me about the story you just read." Answers to the questions below that the student provides during the retelling should be marked "ua" in the appropriate blank to indicate that this response was unaided. Ask all remaining questions not addressed during the retelling and mark those that the student answers with an "a" to indicate that the correct response was given after prompting by the teacher.

*Questions/Answers*

*Story Grammar Element/ Level of Comprehension*

_____ 1. Who was the story mainly about?
(*Matthew*)

character-characterization/literal

_____ 2. What was Matthew's problem?
(*he wasn't doing well in school, or other plausible responses*)

story problem(s)/inferential

_____ 3. What did Matthew's teacher decide to do about Matthew's problem?
(*have Matthew tested for a learning problem*)

problem resolution attempts/literal

_____ 4. Summarize what the school found out about Matthew's problem.
(*he was gifted in math and science*)

problem resolution/inferential

_____ 5. How did the school try to solve the problem?
(*it allowed Matthew to study what interested him the most*)

problem resolution attempts/ inferential

_____ 6. How was Matthew affected by being allowed to study what most interested him?
(*he improved as a student and made friends*)

character-characterization/inferential

_____ 7. How did Matthew's story affect the writer of this story?
(*the writer believes everyone has special talents if you look for them*)

theme/evaluative/ expressive language

_____ 8. Why were the phone calls with the professor set up for Matthew?
(*so he could ask the professor about lasers when he needed to*)

problem resolution attempts/literal

## ERROR TYPES / ERROR ANALYSIS

| Laser Boy | Mis-pronun. | Sub-stitute | Inser-tions | Tchr. Assists | Omis-sions | Error Totals | Self-Correct. | Meaning (M) | Syntax (S) | Visual (V) |
|---|---|---|---|---|---|---|---|---|---|---|
| My name is Bob and I'm a teacher. | | | | | | | | | | |
| Several years ago I knew a student | | | | | | | | | | |
| that I'd like to tell you about. | | | | | | | | | | |
| Matthew was a 13-year-old who never | | | | | | | | | | |
| seemed to do well in school. Some | | | | | | | | | | |
| say that he was a misfit, someone | | | | | | | | | | |
| who doesn't quite fit in with the | | | | | | | | | | |
| other kids his age. Not only that, | | | | | | | | | | |
| Matthew had trouble in school nearly | | | | | | | | | | |
| his whole life. He failed to complete his | | | | | | | | | | |
| homework even when it was an easy assignment. | | | | | | | | | | |
| By not participating in class, not turning in | | | | | | | | | | |
| homework, and only doing a fair job on tests, | | | | | | | | | | |
| Matthew always seemed //to be just barely passing. | | | | | | | | | | |
| TOTALS | | | | | | | | | | |

Summary of Reading Behaviors (Strengths and Needs)

# PART II: ORAL READING AND ANALYSIS OF MISCUES

## Directions

Say, "Now I would like to hear you read this story out loud." Have the student read orally until the 100-word sample is completed. Follow along on the Miscue Grid, marking any oral reading errors as appropriate. *Remember to count miscues only up to the point in the story containing the oral reading stop-marker (//).* Then complete the Performance Summary to determine whether to continue the assessment. (*Note:* The Miscue Grid should be completed *after* the assessment session has been concluded in order to minimize stress for the student.)

# PART III: MISCUE ANALYSIS

## Directions

Circle all reading behaviors you observed.

## A. Fundamental Behaviors Observed

L → R Directionality        1-to-1 Matching        Searching for Clues        Cross-Checking

## B. Word Attack Behaviors

No Attempt        Mispronunciation (Invented Word Substitutions)        Substitutes

Skips/Reads On        Asks for Help        Repeats        Attempts to Self-Correct

"Sounds Out" (Segmenting)        Blends Sounds        Structural Analysis (Root Words, Affixes)

## C. Cueing Systems Used in Attempting Words

| CUEING TOOL | MISCUE EXAMPLES | ACTUAL TEXT |
|---|---|---|
| (M) Meaning | | |
| (S) Syntax | | |
| (V) Visual | | |

## D. Fluency (word by word → fluent reading)

Word by Word _____        Mixed Phrasing _____        Fluent Reading _____        Fluency Rate in Seconds _____

## E. Performance Summary

### Silent Reading Comprehension

_____ 0–1 questions missed = Easy

_____ 2 questions missed = Adequate

_____ 3+ questions missed = Too hard

### Oral Reading Accuracy

_____ 0–1 oral errors = Easy

_____ 2–5 oral errors = Adequate

_____ 6+ oral errors = Too hard

**Continue to the next reading passage?** _____ Yes _____ No

# PART IV: LISTENING COMPREHENSION

### *Directions*

If you have decided not to continue to have the student read any other passages, then use this passage to begin assessing the student's listening comprehension. Begin by reading the background statement for this passage and then say, "I am going to read this story to you. Please listen carefully because I will be asking you some questions after I finish reading it to you." After reading the passage, ask the student the questions associated with the passage. If the student correctly answers more than six questions, you will need to move to the next level and repeat the procedure.

## Listening Comprehension

_____ 0–2 questions missed = move to the next passage level

_____ more than 2 questions missed = stop assessment or move down a level

Examiner's Notes

# LEVEL 7 ASSESSMENT PROTOCOLS

The Paper Route (436 words)

## PART I: SILENT READING COMPREHENSION

### Background Statement

"This story is about a boy who begins his first job as a paper boy. Read it to find out what his first year was like. Read it carefully because I will ask you to tell me about it when you finish."

### Teacher Directions

Once the student completes the silent reading, say, "Tell me about the story you just read." Answers to the questions below that the student provides during the retelling should be marked "ua" in the appropriate blank to indicate that this response was unaided. Ask all remaining questions not addressed during the retelling and mark those that the student answers with an "a" to indicate that the correct response was given after prompting by the teacher.

### Questions/Answers

_____ 1. Who were the main characters in the story?
*(Scott and Mr. Miley)*

_____ 2. How did Scott get a chance to earn money?
*(by answering an ad for newspaper carriers)*

_____ 3. What did Scott have to do each morning after picking up his newspapers?
*(roll them and put them in plastic bags)*

_____ 4. Why were Thursdays and Sundays problems for Scott?
*(papers were extra large and it took many trips to get them delivered)*

_____ 5. What were the two main problems Scott faced with his job?
*(bad weather and cranky customers)*

_____ 6. How did Scott handle the problem of cranky customers?
*(by going out of his way to please them)*

_____ 7. What words would you use to describe Scott?
*(responses will vary but should reflect the idea of hardworking, conscientious)*

_____ 8. What lessons would a job like Scott's teach?
*(responses will vary but should indicate a theme related to benefits of hard work)*

### Story Grammar Element/ Level of Comprehension

character-characterization/literal

problem resolution attempts/literal

problem resolution attempts/literal

story problem(s)/inferential

story problem(s)/literal

problem resolution/literal

character-characterization/evaluative

theme/evaluative/
expressive vocabulary

## ERROR TYPES | ERROR ANALYSIS

| The Paper Route | Mis-pronun. | Sub-stitute | Inser-tions | Tchr. Assists | Omis-sions | Error Totals | Self-Correct. | Meaning (M) | Syntax (S) | Visual (V) |
|---|---|---|---|---|---|---|---|---|---|---|
| Scott had a chance to earn his own money | | | | | | | | | | |
| for the first time. Answering an advertisement | | | | | | | | | | |
| for newspaper carriers, he set up an appointment | | | | | | | | | | |
| with Mr. Miley, the distribution manager. | | | | | | | | | | |
| Mr. Miley was a rather short and stocky | | | | | | | | | | |
| man who spoke with a loud voice. After | | | | | | | | | | |
| reviewing Scott's application, Mr. Miley | | | | | | | | | | |
| said, "You look like a dependable young | | | | | | | | | | |
| man to me. Do your parents approve of | | | | | | | | | | |
| your becoming a paper carrier?" "Yes, sir," | | | | | | | | | | |
| replied Scott, "and I have a letter from my | | | | | | | | | | |
| dad saying it's OK with him." "You | | | | | | | | | | |
| can have the job, Scott," said Mr. Miley. | | | | | | | | | | |
| "However, I want // you to realize that this is | | | | | | | | | | |
| *a long route and you will have to get up very early.* | | | | | | | | | | |
| TOTALS | | | | | | | | | | |

**Summary of Reading Behaviors (Strengths and Needs)**

# PART II: ORAL READING AND ANALYSIS OF MISCUES

## Directions

Say, "Now I would like to hear you read this story out loud." Have the student read orally until the 100-word sample is completed. Follow along on the Miscue Grid, marking any oral reading errors as appropriate. *Remember to count miscues only up to the point in the story containing the oral reading stop-marker ( / / ).* Then complete the Performance Summary to determine whether to continue the assessment. (*Note:* The Miscue Grid should be completed *after* the assessment session has been concluded in order to minimize stress for the student.)

# PART III: MISCUE ANALYSIS

## Directions

Circle all reading behaviors you observed.

## A. Fundamental Behaviors Observed

L → R Directionality          1-to-1 Matching          Searching for Clues          Cross-Checking

## B. Word Attack Behaviors

No Attempt          Mispronunciation (Invented Word Substitutions)          Substitutes

Skips/Reads On          Asks for Help          Repeats          Attempts to Self-Correct

"Sounds Out" (Segmenting)          Blends Sounds          Structural Analysis (Root Words, Affixes)

## C. Cueing Systems Used in Attempting Words

| CUEING TOOL | MISCUE EXAMPLES | ACTUAL TEXT |
|---|---|---|
| (M) Meaning | | |
| (S) Syntax | | |
| (V) Visual | | |

## D. Fluency (word by word → fluent reading)

Word by Word _____          Mixed Phrasing _____          Fluent Reading _____          Fluency Rate in Seconds _____

## E. Performance Summary

| *Silent Reading Comprehension* | *Oral Reading Accuracy* |
|---|---|
| _____ 0–1 questions missed = Easy | _____ 0–1 oral errors = Easy |
| _____ 2 questions missed = Adequate | _____ 2–5 oral errors = Adequate |
| _____ 3+ questions missed = Too hard | _____ 6+ oral errors = Too hard |

**Continue to the next reading passage?** _____ Yes _____ No

# PART IV: LISTENING COMPREHENSION

## Directions

If you have decided not to continue to have the student read any other passages, then use this passage to begin assessing the student's listening comprehension. Begin by reading the background statement for this passage and then say, "I am going to read this story to you. Please listen carefully because I will be asking you some questions after I finish reading it to you." After reading the passage, ask the student the questions associated with the passage. If the student correctly answers more than six questions, you will need to move to the next level and repeat the procedure.

## Listening Comprehension

_____ 0–2 questions missed = move to the next passage level

_____ more than 2 questions missed = stop assessment or move down a level

Examiner's Notes

# LEVEL 8 ASSESSMENT PROTOCOLS

Riley and Leonard (431 words)

## PART I: SILENT READING COMPREHENSION

*Background Statement*

"This is a story about a boy named Leonard who was very unpopular in school. Read this story to find out how Leonard deals with his problem. Read it carefully because I'm going to ask you to tell me about it when you finish."

*Teacher Directions*

Once the student completes the silent reading, say, "Tell me about the story you just read." Answers to the questions below that the student provides during the retelling should be marked "ua" in the appropriate blank to indicate that this response was unaided. Ask all remaining questions not addressed during the retelling and mark those that the student answers with an "a" to indicate that the correct response was given after prompting by the teacher.

| *Questions/Answers* | *Story Grammar Element/ Level of Comprehension* |
|---|---|
| _____ 1. Who were the main characters in the story? *(Leonard, Riley, Lorrie)* | character-characterization/literal |
| _____ 2. What was Leonard's problem when he was in school? *(he was unpopular)* | story problem(s)/literal |
| _____ 3. What problem resolution attempts did Leonard make when his fellow students made negative comments about his family? *(he started a fight)* | problem resolution attempts/literal |
| _____ 4. What does the phrase "familiar mockery" mean? *(repeated teasing, words he had heard before, etc.)* | inferential/vocabulary |
| _____ 5. How did Leonard solve his problem of being unpopular? *(by becoming successful and involved in civic projects)* | problem resolution/inferential |
| _____ 6. Where did the accident take place? *(outside the fancy restaurant)* | setting/literal |
| _____ 7. What caused the beggar to step into the path of the truck? *(surprise at both the amount of money and the fact that it was Leonard)* | problem resolution attempts/ inferential |
| _____ 8. What is the theme/moral of this passage? *(responses will vary but should indicate a theme/ moral related to "what goes around comes around")* | theme/evaluative/ expressive vocabulary |

## ERROR TYPES

## ERROR ANALYSIS

| | Mis-pronun. | Sub-stitute | Inser-tions | Tchr. Assists | Omis-sions | Error Totals | Self-Correct. | Meaning (M) | Syntax (S) | Visual (V) |
|---|---|---|---|---|---|---|---|---|---|---|
| **Riley and Leonard** | | | | | | | | | | |
| At times Leonard felt like the most | | | | | | | | | | |
| unpopular boy in school. No matter what | | | | | | | | | | |
| he did, he was constantly ridiculed by his classmates. | | | | | | | | | | |
| Maybe it was because he was small in stature | | | | | | | | | | |
| and wore thick bifocals. Or maybe it was | | | | | | | | | | |
| because he didn't like sports. Possibly | | | | | | | | | | |
| it was because he couldn't afford the designer | | | | | | | | | | |
| clothes the other kids seemed to live for. | | | | | | | | | | |
| Regardless, Leonard felt like a loser and | | | | | | | | | | |
| was unhappy with his situation. One | | | | | | | | | | |
| day, while putting his books in his locker, | | | | | | | | | | |
| the familiar mockery began. A small covey | | | | | | | | | | |
| of classmates formed a semicircle around | | | | | | | | | | |
| Leonard. Each began to // *taunt him* | | | | | | | | | | |
| *and call him names.* | | | | | | | | | | |
| TOTALS | | | | | | | | | | |

Summary of Reading Behaviors (Strengths and Needs)

# PART II: ORAL READING AND ANALYSIS OF MISCUES

*Directions*

Say, "Now I would like to hear you read this story out loud." Have the student read orally until the 100-word sample is completed. Follow along on the Miscue Grid, marking any oral reading errors as appropriate. *Remember to count miscues only up to the point in the story containing the oral reading stop-marker ( // ).* Then complete the Performance Summary to determine whether to continue the assessment. (*Note:* The Miscue Grid should be completed *after* the assessment session has been concluded in order to minimize stress for the student.)

# PART III: MISCUE ANALYSIS

*Directions*

Circle all reading behaviors you observed.

## A. Fundamental Behaviors Observed

L → R Directionality          1-to-1 Matching          Searching for Clues          Cross-Checking

## B. Word Attack Behaviors

No Attempt          Mispronunciation (Invented Word Substitutions)          Substitutes

Skips/Reads On          Asks for Help          Repeats          Attempts to Self-Correct

"Sounds Out" (Segmenting)          Blends Sounds          Structural Analysis (Root Words, Affixes)

## C. Cueing Systems Used in Attempting Words

| CUEING TOOL | MISCUE EXAMPLES | ACTUAL TEXT |
|---|---|---|
| (M) Meaning | | |
| (S) Syntax | | |
| (V) Visual | | |

## D. Fluency (word by word → fluent reading)

Word by Word _____          Mixed Phrasing _____          Fluent Reading _____          Fluency Rate in Seconds _____

## E. Performance Summary

*Silent Reading Comprehension*

_____ 0–1 questions missed = Easy

_____ 2 questions missed = Adequate

_____ 3+ questions missed = Too hard

*Oral Reading Accuracy*

_____ 0–1 oral errors = Easy

_____ 2–5 oral errors = Adequate

_____ 6+ oral errors = Too hard

**Continue to the next reading passage?** _____ Yes _____ No

# PART IV: LISTENING COMPREHENSION

## Directions

If you have decided not to continue to have the student read any other passages, then use this passage to begin assessing the student's listening comprehension. Begin by reading the background statement for this passage and then say, "I am going to read this story to you. Please listen carefully because I will be asking you some questions after I finish reading it to you." After reading the passage, ask the student the questions associated with the passage. If the student correctly answers more than six questions, you will need to move to the next level and repeat the procedure.

## Listening Comprehension

_____ 0–2 questions missed = move to the next passage level

_____ more than 2 questions missed = stop assessment or move down a level

Examiner's Notes

# LEVEL 9 ASSESSMENT PROTOCOLS

## The Long Night (476 words)

## PART I: SILENT READING COMPREHENSION

### Background Statement

"This story is about mistaken identity. Read it carefully because I will ask you to tell me about the story when you finish reading."

### Teacher Directions

Once the student completes the silent reading, say, "Tell me about the story you just read." Answers to the questions below that the student provides during the retelling should be marked "ua" in the appropriate blank to indicate that this response was unaided. Ask all remaining questions not addressed during the retelling and mark those that the student answers with an "a" to indicate that the correct response was given after prompting by the teacher.

| Questions/Answers | Story Grammar Element/ Level of Comprehension |
|---|---|
| _____ 1. Where and at what time of day did this story take place? <br> *(nighttime in New Orleans)* | setting/literal |
| _____ 2. What was the problem facing the writer of this story while he walked up Rampart? <br> *(he was being followed and someone gave him a note that said he was going to die)* | story problem(s)/inferential |
| _____ 3. How did the police officer react to his story? <br> *(didn't really believe him)* | problem resolution attempts/literal |
| _____ 4. What happened after he left the police officer? <br> *(he was taken into a building by two men)* | problem resolution attempts/literal |
| _____ 5. How did the writer of this story solve the problem(s)? <br> *(it turned out to be a case of mistaken identity)* | problem resolution/inferential |
| _____ 6. Who was Nero, and how would you describe him? <br> *(he was the boss, a criminal, and a nasty kind of character)* | story problem(s)/inferential/ vocabulary |
| _____ 7. What series of events got the person in this story into such trouble? <br> *(flight delay, walking alone at night, and he looked like someone else)* | story problem(s)/inferential |
| _____ 8. What did the author do after he was released? <br> *(stayed two more days and never returned)* | problem resolution attempts/literal |

ERROR ANALYSIS

| | Meaning (M) | Syntax (S) | Visual (V) |
|---|---|---|---|

ERROR TYPES

| | Mis-pronun. | Sub-stitute | Inser-tions | Tchr. Assists | Omis-sions | Error Totals | Self-Correct. |
|---|---|---|---|---|---|---|---|

**The Long Night**

I arrived late at the New Orleans International

Airport because of delays in St. Louis. The

night was descending on the Crescent City as

I entered the cab for the short ride to city

center. As the cab headed toward the city,

the cabbie engaged me in an informative

conversation about the Crescent City.

She had an island accent and her multicolored

dress was very nontraditional. After I told

her I wanted to go to Rampart in the

French Quarter, she abruptly turned

left and headed southwest. Fifteen minutes

later, without a word, I got out of the

cab and // *proceeded up Rampart.*

TOTALS

**Summary of Reading Behaviors (Strengths and Needs)**

# PART II: ORAL READING AND ANALYSIS OF MISCUES

*Directions*

Say, "Now I would like to hear you read this story out loud." Have the student read orally until the 100-word sample is completed. Follow along on the Miscue Grid, marking any oral reading errors as appropriate. *Remember to count miscues only up to the point in the story containing the oral reading stop-marker ( / / ).* Then complete the Performance Summary to determine whether to continue the assessment. (*Note:* The Miscue Grid should be completed *after* the assessment session has been concluded in order to minimize stress for the student.)

# PART III: MISCUE ANALYSIS

*Directions*

Circle all reading behaviors you observed.

## A. Fundamental Behaviors Observed

L → R Directionality       1-to-1 Matching       Searching for Clues       Cross-Checking

## B. Word Attack Behaviors

No Attempt       Mispronunciation (Invented Word Substitutions)       Substitutes

Skips/Reads On       Asks for Help       Repeats       Attempts to Self-Correct

"Sounds Out" (Segmenting)       Blends Sounds       Structural Analysis (Root Words, Affixes)

## C. Cueing Systems Used in Attempting Words

| CUEING TOOL | MISCUE EXAMPLES | ACTUAL TEXT |
| --- | --- | --- |
| (M) Meaning | | |
| (S) Syntax | | |
| (V) Visual | | |

## D. Fluency (word by word → fluent reading)

Word by Word _____       Mixed Phrasing _____       Fluent Reading _____       Fluency Rate in Seconds _____

## E. Performance Summary

### Silent Reading Comprehension

_____ 0–1 questions missed = Easy

_____ 2 questions missed = Adequate

_____ 3+ questions missed = Too hard

### Oral Reading Accuracy

_____ 0–1 oral errors = Easy

_____ 2–5 oral errors = Adequate

_____ 6+ oral errors = Too hard

# PART IV: LISTENING COMPREHENSION

## Directions

If you have decided not to continue to have the student read any other passages, then use this passage to begin assessing the student's listening comprehension. Begin by reading the background statement for this passage and then say, "I am going to read this story to you. Please listen carefully because I will be asking you some questions after I finish reading it to you." After reading the passage, ask the student the questions associated with the passage. If the student correctly answers more than six questions, you will need to move to the next level and repeat the procedure.

## Listening Comprehension

_____ 0–2 questions missed = move to the next passage level

_____ more than 2 questions missed = stop assessment or move down a level

Examiner's Notes

# SENTENCES FOR INITIAL PASSAGE SELECTION

## FORM C: LEVEL 1

1. Some animals are fun.

2. I eat lots of food.

3. He can smell good.

## FORM C: LEVEL 2

1. It was a very clear night.

2. I get hot when the sun shines bright.

3. We can't see air moving.

## FORM C: LEVEL 3

1. Many insects are very helpful.

2. Some adults are slender; some are fat.

3. I agree that it is the most beautiful flower.

## FORM C: LEVEL 4

1. A famous man would know what to do.

2. The invention was very important.

3. Instead of jam I like syrup on my food.

## FORM C: LEVEL 5

1. The estimate for my car was not acceptable.

2. Various people came immediately to the fire.

3. The amount of water you drink is important.

## FORM C: LEVEL 6

1. He considered it carefully, but it was too expensive.

2. The new method of raising the temperature got good results.

3. What is common today is the result of many years of experimenting.

## FORM C: LEVEL 7

1. Scientists hope to transform the industrial site before the end of the year.

2. Foreign minerals are used to develop usable compounds.

3. The presence of impurities lowers the value of all gems.

## FORM C: LEVEL 8

1. Scientists are always looking for advancements to improve the world.

2. The prearranged site was eliminated.

3. To compress hundreds of wires into one is called "fiber optics."

## FORM C: LEVEL 9

1. He moved in a circular motion, then ran off laterally.

2. The vertical object couldn't be viewed easily.

3. At the intersection, a series of accidents occurred.

# EXPOSITORY READING PASSAGES

## Bears

There are many kinds of bears.
Some bears are brown. Others are black.
Still others are white and are called polar bears.
The biggest bears are called grizzly bears.

Bears can smell and hear very well.
Bears have small eyes and cannot see very well.
They eat all kinds of food.
They eat small animals, plants, and berries.
Most bears sleep during the winter.
When they wake up they are hungry.

Bears can run very fast.
They can climb trees.
They are not safe animals to be around.
The best place to be around bears is at the zoo.

## The Night Sky

Look up at the sky at night. If it is a clear night, you will see stars. How many stars are there? No one knows for sure. But there is one star that you know by name. You can see it in the daytime. It is our sun. The sun is a star. All stars are suns. Our sun is so close that we cannot see other stars in the day. We only see the other suns at night.

Stars are made up of very hot gas, and they seem to twinkle because of the air moving across them. Even though we can't always see them, they are always in the sky, even in the daytime.

## Flying Flowers

There are many kinds of insects. There are big ones, little ones, ugly ones, biting ones, and helpful ones. But there is one kind of insect that most people agree is the most beautiful one. This insect is often called the flying flower. It is the butterfly.

Butterflies are insects that have two pairs of wings. The wings are covered with tiny scales. The scales are different colors. These scales give the butterfly its beautiful colors. Butterflies smell and hear by using their long, thin antennae. Butterflies can't bite or chew. They use long, tube-like tongues to get at the food they eat from flowers.

Butterflies begin as eggs. Then they hatch into caterpillars. A caterpillar forms a hard skin. When they finally break out of the hard skin, they are butterflies with colorful wings. Adult butterflies must lay eggs soon. They do not live very long.

Butterflies and moths are different. Butterflies like the day. Moths like the night. Moths are not as colorful as butterflies. Butterfly bodies are slender, while moths tend to have large, fat bodies. Moths form cocoons before turning into winged insects. Most butterflies do not form cocoons.

### The Story of Coca-Cola

Lots of people all over the world have heard of the soft drink called Coca-Cola. But not many people know the real story about how this drink was invented.

Coca-Cola was the invention of a Mr. John Pemberton. Although he wasn't a doctor, most people called him Dr. Pemberton. He was a druggist in a town in the South. Dr. Pemberton liked to invent new things. He lived during the time just after the Civil War.

One day Dr. Pemberton decided to make a headache medicine. He made it from nuts, fruits, and leaves. He also added the drugs necessary to cure a headache. Dr. Pemberton now thought he had something to sell that tasted good.

In the summer of 1886, Dr. Pemberton took a jug of this headache syrup to one of the best drugstores in Atlanta, Georgia. He told the manager of the drugstore to mix some of the syrup with water and have just people with headaches drink it. At first it did not sell very well. Then one day a clerk sold some of the new medicine to a customer with a bad headache. But instead of using regular water, he used carbonated water by accident. Carbonated water has bubbles in it. Everyone loved this new change, and carbonated water is still used in Coca-Cola today.

Most of the medicine that cures headaches was taken out of Coca-Cola as time went on. But Dr. Pemberton's drink is still one of the world's favorite soft drinks.

### Popcorn

There are three major types of corn grown in this country. First, there is the type of corn people eat most of the time. It is called sweet corn because of its flavor. Second, there is field corn, which is used mainly for feeding livestock. Sometimes people eat field corn too. However, its taste is not as good as sweet corn and its kernels are not as full. The third type of corn, often called Indian corn, is popcorn. Popcorn is grown commercially in the United States because the average American eats almost two pounds of popcorn a year, according to various estimates.

When America was discovered by Columbus, Native Americans had been eating popcorn for thousands of years. They prepared it several different ways. One way was to stick the ear of corn on a stick and place it over a campfire. Any kernels that popped out of the fire were gathered up and eaten. Another method was to scrape the cob and throw the kernels into the fire. Any kernels that popped out of the fire were immediately eaten. Since these methods limited how many kernels could actually be eaten, the Native Americans began to use small clay bowls that they would heat sand in. When the sand got really hot, they placed the popcorn in the bowls and waited for the kernels to pop.

Popcorn is popcorn because of the amount of water content of the kernel. Most experts agree that, ideally, a kernel should have at least fourteen percent water content to be good corn for popping. If the corn kernels have less than twelve percent water content, then the kernels will be duds. They won't pop right.

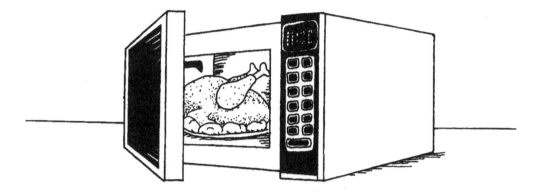

## Cooking Without Fire: The Microwave Oven

Microwave cooking is very common today. It is, however, a recent invention. The microwave oven one uses today was developed from the invention of the magnetron tube in 1940. The invention of the magnetron tube, by Sir John Randall and Dr. H. A. Boot, was a very important part of the radar defense of England during World War II. Neither man considered it as a means of preparing food after they invented it.

It wasn't until the late 1940s that Dr. Percy Spencer discovered the magnetron's ability to heat and cook food from the inside out. Spencer experimented with many different foods, all with the same results: The inside got hot first.

It took several years for the company Spencer worked for to develop what we know today as the microwave oven. Not until around 1952 could a person purchase a microwave oven, then called a Radar Range, for home use. These early models were expensive and bulky.

Today's microwave ovens are inexpensive and come with a variety of features. The features include: defrost, constant temperature cooking, and automatic reheat. Microwave cooking, many claim, was the first completely new method of cooking food since early humans discovered fire. Why? Because microwave cooking requires no fire or element of fire to cook food. The food is cooked by electromagnetic energy.

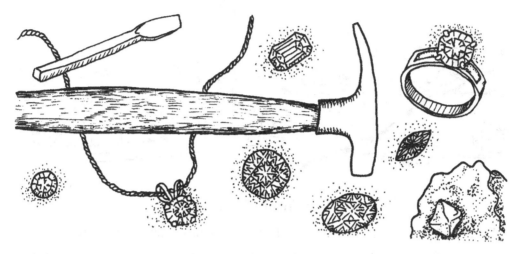

### Diamonds

A diamond is one of the most beautiful treasures that nature ever created, and one of the rarest. It takes thousands of years for nature to transform a chunk of carbon into a rough diamond. Only three important diamond fields have been found in the world—in India, South America, and Africa.

The first diamonds were found in the sand and gravel of stream beds. These types of diamonds are called alluvial diamonds. Later, diamonds were found deep in the earth in rock formations called pipes. These formations resemble extinct volcanoes. The rock in which diamonds are found is called blue ground. Yet even where diamonds are plentiful, it takes digging and sorting through tons of rock and gravel to find enough diamonds for a one-carat ring.

Gem diamonds' quality is based on weight, purity, color, and cut. The weight of a diamond is measured by the carat. Its purity is determined by the presence or absence of impurities, such as foreign minerals and uncrystallized carbon. The color of diamonds varies, but most diamonds are tinged yellow or brown. The cut of a diamond also figures into its value. A fully cut diamond, often called flawless, would have fifty-eight facets. Facets, or sides, cause the brilliance that is produced when a diamond is struck by light.

Humans have learned how to make artificial diamonds. Manufactured diamonds are placed in a machine that creates the same pressure that exists about two hundred and fifty miles beneath the surface of the earth. Besides intense pressure, the carbon compounds are heated to temperatures over five thousand degrees Fahrenheit. Unfortunately, the created diamonds are small and are used mainly in industrial settings. They have no value as gems.

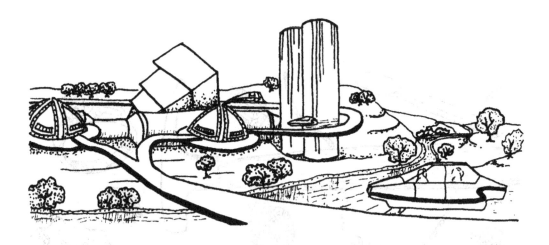

### The Future Is Here

What will the twenty-first century bring in terms of new inventions and space-age technologies? No one knows for sure. But scientists, inventors, and futurists are predicting a variety of new inventions. These new advancements will affect the way we live and play. Some of them are already on the drawing board.

One example is the levitation vehicle. The idea of a vertical take-off and landing aircraft that can also be driven on the road is the invention of Paul Moeller. He named his first version of this type of craft the Moeller 400. People involved in this type of technology see increases in population and crowded highways as reasons that a levitation vehicle will be needed. Imagine flying into the city, hovering over a prearranged landing site, landing, and then driving the rest of the way to work.

Another innovation developed in the 1990s is the dental laser. Researchers created a laser that they hope will replace the much feared dental drill. The laser basically vaporizes the cavity without affecting the surrounding enamel. As a bonus, the laser will eliminate the need for a shot to deaden surrounding tissue.

Probably one of the most significant new technologies that will continue to affect people in the future is fiber optics. Fiber optics has the effect of compressing hundreds of wires into one, thus allowing for the communication of huge amounts of information over very thin wires. One example of the application of fiber optics will be the development of full-motion, color video telephones. These will be particularly important to the deaf.

Another advancement that is becoming commonplace in the early twenty-first century is high-definition television. The average consumer will be able to upgrade his or her current televiewing dramatically when high-definition television becomes widely available at affordable prices. The color of these televisions has the vividness of 35-millimeter movies and the sound quality of compact discs (CDs). This refinement will lead to improvements in at-home movies and video games, both of which will be available in three-dimensional formats.

Regardless of new advancements in technology, people must be prepared to face the challenges of the future: namely, to assist each other as we travel through time, and to help preserve our home, the earth.

## Visual Illusions

A visual illusion is an unreal or misleading appearance or image, according to *Webster's* dictionary. In other words, visual illusions are sometimes caused by ideas one holds about what one expects to see. In other instances, the illusion is caused by the brain's difficulty in choosing from two or more visual patterns.

If you look at a bull's-eye and move it slowly in circular motions, you should see spokes moving. The spokes, if you see them, aren't really there. This type of visual illusion is called lateral inhibition.

Another type of visual illusion occurs when a person tries to estimate the height of a vertical object. It is referred to as length distortion. The famous Gateway Arch in St. Louis is an example of length distortion, because the arch seems much higher than it is wide. In reality the height and width of the arch are identical. Length distortion occurs because our eyes move more easily from side to side than up and down. This greater effort to look up causes the brain to over-interpret the height of vertical objects.

If you look at a series of squares, you should see small gray spots at each intersection. If you look directly at one intersection, the spots should disappear. This illusion is known as Hermann's Grid. It is often seen in modern high-rise office buildings. Many of these buildings have windows separated by crossing strips of metal or concrete.

The above are only three examples of the many ways that our eyes can deceive us. But they do reinforce the old axiom, "Don't believe everything you see."

# EXAMINER'S ASSESSMENT PROTOCOLS

# LEVEL 1 ASSESSMENT PROTOCOLS

Bears (99 words)

## PART I: SILENT READING COMPREHENSION

### Background Statement

"This story is about bears. Read this story to find out information about the different kinds of bears. Read it carefully because I'm going to ask you to tell me about what you read."

### Teacher Directions

Once the student completes the silent reading, say, "Tell me about the story you just read." Answers to the questions below that the student provides during the retelling should be marked "ua" in the appropriate blank to indicate that this response was unaided. Ask all remaining questions not addressed during the retelling and mark those that the student answers with an "a" to indicate that the correct response was given after prompting by the teacher.

| Questions/Answers | Expository Grammar Element/ Level of Comprehension |
|---|---|
| _____ 1. What kinds of bears did you read about? *(brown, black, polar, and grizzly)* | literal/collection |
| _____ 2. What kind of bear is the biggest of all? *(grizzly bear)* | literal/description |
| _____ 3. Explain why bears are not safe to be around. *(accept plausible responses related to bears being wild and having been known to attack humans)* | inferential/problem-solution/ expressive vocabulary |
| _____ 4. What are some things bears can do very well? *(smell, hear, run, climb—any three)* | literal/collection |
| _____ 5. How do bears find their food? *(smelling and hearing)* | inferential/problem-solution |
| _____ 6. Why are bears often hungry after winter? *(because they sleep most of the winter)* | inferential/causation |
| _____ 7. Can you name two things that bears eat? *(plants, berries, and small animals)* | literal/collection |
| _____ 8. Where did the story say was the best place to be around bears? *(at the zoo)* | literal/description |

## ERROR TYPES

## ERROR ANALYSIS

| | Mis-pronun. | Sub-stitute | Inser-tions | Tchr. Assists | Omis-sions | Error Totals | Self-Correct. | Meaning (M) | Syntax (S) | Visual (V) |
|---|---|---|---|---|---|---|---|---|---|---|
| **Bears** | | | | | | | | | | |
| There are many kinds of bears. | | | | | | | | | | |
| Some bears are brown. Others are | | | | | | | | | | |
| black. Still others are white and | | | | | | | | | | |
| are called polar bears. The biggest | | | | | | | | | | |
| bears are called grizzly bears. | | | | | | | | | | |
| Bears can smell and hear very | | | | | | | | | | |
| well. Bears have small eyes and | | | | | | | | | | |
| cannot see very well. They eat all | | | | | | | | | | |
| kinds of food. They eat small animals, | | | | | | | | | | |
| plants, and berries. Most bears sleep during | | | | | | | | | | |
| the winter. When they wake up they | | | | | | | | | | |
| are hungry. Bears can run very fast. | | | | | | | | | | |
| They can climb trees. They are not safe | | | | | | | | | | |
| animals to be around. The best place | | | | | | | | | | |
| to be around bears is at the zoo. // | | | | | | | | | | |
| **TOTALS** | | | | | | | | | | |

**Summary of Reading Behaviors (Strengths and Needs)**

# PART II: ORAL READING AND ANALYSIS OF MISCUES

## Directions

Say, "Now I would like to hear you read this story out loud." Have the student read orally until the sample is completed. Follow along on the Miscue Grid, marking any oral reading errors as appropriate. *Remember to count miscues only up to the point in the story containing the oral reading stop-marker (//).* Then complete the Performance Summary to determine whether to continue the assessment. (*Note:* The Miscue Grid should be completed *after* the assessment session has been concluded in order to minimize stress for the student.)

# PART III: MISCUE ANALYSIS

## Directions

Circle all reading behaviors you observed.

## A. Fundamental Behaviors Observed

L → R Directionality      1-to-1 Matching      Searching for Clues      Cross-Checking

## B. Word Attack Behaviors

No Attempt      Mispronunciation (Invented Word Substitutions)      Substitutes

Skips/Reads On      Asks for Help      Repeats      Attempts to Self-Correct

"Sounds Out" (Segmenting)      Blends Sounds      Structural Analysis (Root Words, Affixes)

## C. Cueing Systems Used in Attempting Words

| CUEING TOOL | MISCUE EXAMPLES | ACTUAL TEXT |
|---|---|---|
| (M) Meaning | | |
| (S) Syntax | | |
| (V) Visual | | |

## D. Fluency (word by word → fluent reading)

Word by Word _____      Mixed Phrasing _____      Fluent Reading _____      Fluency Rate in Seconds _____

## E. Performance Summary

### Silent Reading Comprehension

_____ 0–1 questions missed = Easy

_____ 2 questions missed = Adequate

_____ 3+ questions missed = Too hard

### Oral Reading Accuracy

_____ 0–1 oral errors = Easy

_____ 2–5 oral errors = Adequate

_____ 6+ oral errors = Too hard

Continue to the next reading passage? _____ Yes _____ No

# PART IV: LISTENING COMPREHENSION

## Directions

If you have decided not to continue to have the student read any other passages, then use this passage to begin assessing the student's listening comprehension. Begin by reading the background statement for this passage and then say, "I am going to read this story to you. Please listen carefully because I will be asking you some questions after I finish reading it to you." After reading the passage, ask the student the questions associated with the passage. If the student correctly answers more than six questions, you will need to move to the next level and repeat the procedure.

## Listening Comprehension

_____ 0–2 questions missed = move to the next passage level

_____ more than 2 questions missed = stop assessment or move down a level

Examiner's Notes

# LEVEL 2 ASSESSMENT PROTOCOLS

The Night Sky (116 words)

## PART I: SILENT READING COMPREHENSION

### Background Statement

"This story is about stars. Read it and try to remember some of the important facts about stars because I'm going to ask you to tell me about what you have read."

### Teacher Directions

Once the student completes the silent reading, say, "Tell me about the story you just read." Answers to the questions below that the student provides during the retelling should be marked "ua" in the appropriate blank to indicate that this response was unaided. Ask all remaining questions not addressed during the retelling and mark those that the student answers with an "a" to indicate that the correct response was given after prompting by the teacher.

| Questions/Answers | Expository Grammar Element/ Level of Comprehension |
|---|---|
| _____ 1. What kind of night is best for seeing stars? *(clear night)* | literal/description |
| _____ 2. Stars are made up of what? *(hot gases)* | literal/description |
| _____ 3. What star can you see only in the daytime? *(the sun)* | literal/causation |
| _____ 4. What causes stars to twinkle? *(the air moving across them)* | literal/causation |
| _____ 5. Why can't people on earth see other stars during the day? *(the sun is so close and bright that it blocks our view)* | literal/causation |
| _____ 6. If one night you looked up at the sky and could see no stars, what could be the reason? *(cloudy night)* | evaluative/causation |
| _____ 7. Explain why saying "look at all the suns in the night sky" would be an accurate statement. *(because all stars are "suns")* | inferential/comparison/ expressive vocabulary |
| _____ 8. Can you name one reason why the earth cannot be called a star? *(it is not made up of hot gases, it is a planet not a star, it has water, and any other plausible responses)* | evaluative/comparison/ expressive vocabulary |

## ERROR ANALYSIS

## ERROR TYPES

| The Night Sky | Mis-pronun. | Sub-stitute | Inser-tions | Tchr. Assists | Omis-sions | Error Totals | Self-Correct. | Meaning (M) | Syntax (S) | Visual (V) |
|---|---|---|---|---|---|---|---|---|---|---|
| Look up at the sky at night. If it is a clear | | | | | | | | | | |
| night, you will see stars. How many stars are | | | | | | | | | | |
| there? No one knows for sure. But there | | | | | | | | | | |
| is one star that you know by name. You | | | | | | | | | | |
| can see it in the daytime. It is our sun. | | | | | | | | | | |
| The sun is a star. All stars are suns. | | | | | | | | | | |
| Our sun is so close that we cannot see | | | | | | | | | | |
| other stars in the day. We only see | | | | | | | | | | |
| the other suns at night. Stars are made | | | | | | | | | | |
| up of very hot gas, and they seem to | | | | | | | | | | |
| twinkle because of the air moving across | | | | | | | | | | |
| them. Even // *though we can't always see* | | | | | | | | | | |
| *them, they are always in the sky,* | | | | | | | | | | |
| *even in the daytime.* | | | | | | | | | | |
| TOTALS | | | | | | | | | | |

Summary of Reading Behaviors (Strengths and Needs)

# PART II: ORAL READING AND ANALYSIS OF MISCUES

*Directions*

Say, "Now I would like to hear you read this story out loud." Have the student read orally until the 100-word sample is completed. Follow along on the Miscue Grid, marking any oral reading errors as appropriate. *Remember to count miscues only up to the point in the story containing the oral reading stop-marker (//).* Then complete the Performance Summary to determine whether to continue the assessment. (*Note:* The Miscue Grid should be completed *after* the assessment session has been concluded in order to minimize stress for the student.)

# PART III: MISCUE ANALYSIS

*Directions*

Circle all reading behaviors you observed.

## A. Fundamental Behaviors Observed

L → R Directionality       1-to-1 Matching       Searching for Clues       Cross-Checking

## B. Word Attack Behaviors

No Attempt       Mispronunciation (Invented Word Substitutions)       Substitutes

Skips/Reads On       Asks for Help       Repeats       Attempts to Self-Correct

"Sounds Out" (Segmenting)       Blends Sounds       Structural Analysis (Root Words, Affixes)

## C. Cueing Systems Used in Attempting Words

| CUEING TOOL | MISCUE EXAMPLES | ACTUAL TEXT |
|---|---|---|
| (M) Meaning | | |
| (S) Syntax | | |
| (V) Visual | | |

## D. Fluency (word by word → fluent reading)

Word by Word \_\_\_\_\_       Mixed Phrasing \_\_\_\_\_       Fluent Reading \_\_\_\_\_       Fluency Rate in Seconds \_\_\_\_\_

## E. Performance Summary

*Silent Reading Comprehension*

\_\_\_\_\_ 0–1 questions missed = Easy

\_\_\_\_\_ 2 questions missed = Adequate

\_\_\_\_\_ 3+ questions missed = Too hard

*Oral Reading Accuracy*

\_\_\_\_\_ 0–1 oral errors = Easy

\_\_\_\_\_ 2–5 oral errors = Adequate

\_\_\_\_\_ 6+ oral errors = Too hard

**Continue to the next reading passage?** \_\_\_\_\_ Yes \_\_\_\_\_ No

# PART IV: LISTENING COMPREHENSION

## Directions

If you have decided not to continue to have the student read any other passages, then use this passage to begin assessing the student's listening comprehension. Begin by reading the background statement for this passage and then say, "I am going to read this story to you. Please listen carefully because I will be asking you some questions after I finish reading it to you." After reading the passage, ask the student the questions associated with the passage. If the student correctly answers more than six questions, you will need to move to the next level and repeat the procedure.

## Listening Comprehension

_____ 0–2 questions missed = move to the next passage level

_____ more than 2 questions missed = stop assessment or move down a level

Examiner's Notes

# LEVEL 3 ASSESSMENT PROTOCOLS

Flying Flowers (194 words)

## PART I: SILENT READING COMPREHENSION

### Background Statement

"This selection is about a special kind of insect. It is about butterflies. Read this selection to find out some interesting facts about butterflies. I will ask you to tell me about what you read, so read carefully."

### Teacher Directions

Once the student completes the silent reading, say, "Tell me about the story you just read." Answers to the questions below that the student provides during the retelling should be marked "ua" in the appropriate blank to indicate that this response was unaided. Ask all remaining questions not addressed during the retelling and mark those that the student answers with an "a" to indicate that the correct response was given after prompting by the teacher.

| *Questions/Answers* | *Expository Grammar Element/ Level of Comprehension* |
|---|---|
| _____ 1. What kind of insect was the passage mainly about? <br> *(butterfly)* | literal/descriptive |
| _____ 2. Why is the butterfly referred to as the flying flower? <br> *(because of its many different colors)* | literal/collection |
| _____ 3. What gives the butterfly its colors? <br> *(scales)* | literal/causation |
| _____ 4. Can you name two ways in which a butterfly and moth are different? <br> *(butterflies like the day, are more colorful, are thinner, and most don't form cocoons—moths are the opposite)* | literal/comparison |
| _____ 5. Can you name two ways in which a butterfly and a moth are alike? <br> *(they fly, lay eggs, have scales, have wings, etc.)* | inferential/comparison |
| _____ 6. What is the purpose of the butterfly's antennae? <br> *(to smell and hear)* | literal/collection |
| _____ 7. Why do grown-up butterflies have to lay eggs as soon as possible? <br> *(they don't live very long)* | inferential/problem-solution |
| _____ 8. What happens after a butterfly egg becomes a caterpillar? <br> *(it forms a hard skin that it has to break out of)* | literal/causation/expressive vocabulary |

## ERROR TYPES / ERROR ANALYSIS

| | Mis-pronun. | Sub-stitute | Inser-tions | Tchr. Assists | Omis-sions | Error Totals | Self-Correct. | Meaning (M) | Syntax (S) | Visual (V) |
|---|---|---|---|---|---|---|---|---|---|---|
| **Flying Flowers** | | | | | | | | | | |
| There are many kinds of insects. There are | | | | | | | | | | |
| big ones, little ones, ugly ones, biting ones, | | | | | | | | | | |
| and helpful ones. But there is one kind of insect | | | | | | | | | | |
| that most people agree is the most beautiful one. | | | | | | | | | | |
| This insect is often called the flying flower. | | | | | | | | | | |
| It is the butterfly. Butterflies are insects | | | | | | | | | | |
| that have two pairs of wings. The wings | | | | | | | | | | |
| are covered with tiny scales. These scales | | | | | | | | | | |
| are different colors. These scales | | | | | | | | | | |
| give the butterfly its beautiful colors. | | | | | | | | | | |
| Butterflies smell and hear by using | | | | | | | | | | |
| their long, thin antennae. Butterflies | | | | | | | | | | |
| can't bite or chew. They use long, | | | | | | | | | | |
| tube-like tongues to get at // the food | | | | | | | | | | |
| they eat from flowers. | | | | | | | | | | |
| **TOTALS** | | | | | | | | | | |

**Summary of Reading Behaviors (Strengths and Needs)**

# PART II: ORAL READING AND ANALYSIS OF MISCUES

*Directions*

Say, "Now I would like to hear you read this story out loud." Have the student read orally until the 100-word sample is completed. Follow along on the Miscue Grid, marking any oral reading errors as appropriate. *Remember to count miscues only up to the point in the story containing the oral reading stop-marker (//).* Then complete the Performance Summary to determine whether to continue the assessment. (*Note:* The Miscue Grid should be completed *after* the assessment session has been concluded in order to minimize stress for the student.)

# PART III: MISCUE ANALYSIS

*Directions*

Circle all reading behaviors you observed.

## A. Fundamental Behaviors Observed

L → R Directionality       1-to-1 Matching       Searching for Clues       Cross-Checking

## B. Word Attack Behaviors

No Attempt       Mispronunciation (Invented Word Substitutions)       Substitutes

Skips/Reads On       Asks for Help       Repeats       Attempts to Self-Correct

"Sounds Out" (Segmenting)       Blends Sounds       Structural Analysis (Root Words, Affixes)

## C. Cueing Systems Used in Attempting Words

| CUEING TOOL | MISCUE EXAMPLES | ACTUAL TEXT |
|---|---|---|
| (M) Meaning | | |
| (S) Syntax | | |
| (V) Visual | | |

## D. Fluency (word by word → fluent reading)

Word by Word _____       Mixed Phrasing _____       Fluent Reading _____       Fluency Rate in Seconds _____

## E. Performance Summary

*Silent Reading Comprehension*

_____ 0–1 questions missed = Easy

_____ 2 questions missed = Adequate

_____ 3+ questions missed = Too hard

*Oral Reading Accuracy*

_____ 0–1 oral errors = Easy

_____ 2–5 oral errors = Adequate

_____ 6+ oral errors = Too hard

Continue to the next reading passage? _____ Yes _____ No

# PART IV: LISTENING COMPREHENSION

*Directions*

If you have decided not to continue to have the student read any other passages, then use this passage to begin assessing the student's listening comprehension. Begin by reading the background statement for this passage and then say, "I am going to read this story to you. Please listen carefully because I will be asking you some questions after I finish reading it to you." After reading the passage, ask the student the questions associated with the passage. If the student correctly answers more than six questions, you will need to move to the next level and repeat the procedure.

## Listening Comprehension

_____ 0–2 questions missed = move to the next passage level

_____ more than 2 questions missed = stop assessment or move down a level

Examiner's Notes

# LEVEL 4 ASSESSMENT PROTOCOLS

The Story of Coca-Cola (253 words)

## PART I: SILENT READING COMPREHENSION

### Background Statement

"This selection is about the history of Coca-Cola. Read it carefully and try to find out some facts about Coca-Cola, because I'm going to ask you to tell me about what you find."

### Teacher Directions

Once the student completes the silent reading, say, "Tell me about the story you just read." Answers to the questions below that the student provides during the retelling should be marked "ua" in the appropriate blank to indicate that this response was unaided. Ask all remaining questions not addressed during the retelling and mark those that the student answers with an "a" to indicate that the correct response was given after prompting by the teacher.

| *Questions/Answers* | *Expository Grammar Element/ Level of Comprehension* |
|---|---|
| _____ 1. Who invented Coca-Cola? *(Mr./Dr. Pemberton)* | literal/causation |
| _____ 2. What was Dr. Pemberton trying to invent when he invented Coca-Cola? *(a headache medicine)* | literal/description |
| _____ 3. Besides drugs for headaches, what other things were put into Dr. Pemberton's new medicine? *(leaves, fruits, and nuts)* | literal/description |
| _____ 4. Why didn't the medicine sell very well at first? *(because the syrup was mixed with regular water)* | inferential/causation |
| _____ 5. Why could one say that Coca-Cola became popular because of a mistake? *(because a clerk accidentally mixed the syrup with carbonated water)* | inferential/problem-solution |
| _____ 6. Based on your reading, has Coca-Cola been around for a long time? How do you know? *(some reference to the Civil War)* | inferential |
| _____ 7. Explain what is different between today's Coca-Cola and the original version. *(no headache medicine, or other plausible responses)* | inferential/comparison/expressive vocabulary |
| _____ 8. What's the difference between regular water and carbonated water? *(regular water doesn't have bubbles)* | inferential/comparison |

## ERROR TYPES | ERROR ANALYSIS

| The Story of Coca-Cola | Mis-pronun. | Sub-stitute | Inser-tions | Tchr. Assists | Omis-sions | Error Totals | Self-Correct. | Meaning (M) | Syntax (S) | Visual (V) |
|---|---|---|---|---|---|---|---|---|---|---|
| Lots of people all over the world have heard | | | | | | | | | | |
| of the soft drink called Coca-Cola. But not | | | | | | | | | | |
| many people know the real story about | | | | | | | | | | |
| how this drink was invented. Coca-Cola | | | | | | | | | | |
| was the invention of a Mr. John Pemberton. | | | | | | | | | | |
| Although he wasn't a doctor, most people | | | | | | | | | | |
| called him Dr. Pemberton. He was a | | | | | | | | | | |
| druggist in a town in the South. Dr. | | | | | | | | | | |
| Pemberton liked to invent new things. He | | | | | | | | | | |
| lived during the time just after the Civil | | | | | | | | | | |
| War. One day Dr. Pemberton decided to | | | | | | | | | | |
| make a headache medicine. He made it from | | | | | | | | | | |
| nuts, fruits, and leaves. He also added | | | | | | | | | | |
| the // *drugs necessary to cure a headache.* | | | | | | | | | | |
| **TOTALS** | | | | | | | | | | |

**Summary of Reading Behaviors (Strengths and Needs)**

# PART II: ORAL READING AND ANALYSIS OF MISCUES

*Directions*

Say, "Now I would like to hear you read this story out loud." Have the student read orally until the 100-word sample is completed. Follow along on the Miscue Grid, marking any oral reading errors as appropriate. *Remember to count miscues only up to the point in the story containing the oral reading stop-marker (//).* Then complete the Performance Summary to determine whether to continue the assessment. (*Note:* The Miscue Grid should be completed *after* the assessment session has been concluded in order to minimize stress for the student.)

# PART III: MISCUE ANALYSIS

*Directions*

Circle all reading behaviors you observed.

## A. Fundamental Behaviors Observed

L → R Directionality        1-to-1 Matching        Searching for Clues        Cross-Checking

## B. Word Attack Behaviors

No Attempt        Mispronunciation (Invented Word Substitutions)        Substitutes

Skips/Reads On        Asks for Help        Repeats        Attempts to Self-Correct

"Sounds Out" (Segmenting)        Blends Sounds        Structural Analysis (Root Words, Affixes)

## C. Cueing Systems Used in Attempting Words

| CUEING TOOL | MISCUE EXAMPLES | ACTUAL TEXT |
|---|---|---|
| (M) Meaning | | |
| (S) Syntax | | |
| (V) Visual | | |

## D. Fluency (word by word → fluent reading)

Word by Word _____        Mixed Phrasing _____        Fluent Reading _____        Fluency Rate in Seconds _____

## E. Performance Summary

### Silent Reading Comprehension

_____ 0–1 questions missed = Easy

_____ 2 questions missed = Adequate

_____ 3+ questions missed = Too hard

### Oral Reading Accuracy

_____ 0–1 oral errors = Easy

_____ 2–5 oral errors = Adequate

_____ 6+ oral errors = Too hard

Continue to the next reading passage? _____ Yes _____ No

# PART IV: LISTENING COMPREHENSION

*Directions*

If you have decided not to continue to have the student read any other passages, then use this passage to begin assessing the student's listening comprehension. Begin by reading the background statement for this passage and then say, "I am going to read this story to you. Please listen carefully because I will be asking you some questions after I finish reading it to you." After reading the passage, ask the student the questions associated with the passage. If the student correctly answers more than six questions, you will need to move to the next level and repeat the procedure.

## Listening Comprehension

_____ 0–2 questions missed = move to the next passage level

_____ more than 2 questions missed = stop assessment or move down a level

Examiner's Notes

# LEVEL 5 ASSESSMENT PROTOCOLS

Popcorn (282 words)

## PART I: SILENT READING COMPREHENSION

### Background Statement

"This selection is about corn, and *popcorn* in particular. Read the passage to discover some interesting facts about corn. Read it carefully because I'm going to ask you to tell me about what you read."

### Teacher Directions

Once the student completes the silent reading, say, "Tell me about the story you just read." Answers to the questions below that the student provides during the retelling should be marked "ua" in the appropriate blank to indicate that this response was unaided. Ask all remaining questions not addressed during the retelling and mark those that the student answers with an "a" to indicate that the correct response was given after prompting by the teacher.

| *Questions/Answers* | *Expository Grammar Element/ Level of Comprehension* |
|---|---|
| _____ 1. Which type of corn is this passage mainly about? <br> *(Indian corn or popcorn)* | inferential/descriptive |
| _____ 2. Explain how sweet corn differs from field corn. <br> *(sweet corn is not used to feed livestock, tastes better, and has fuller kernels)* | inferential/comparison |
| _____ 3. What makes popcorn pop? <br> *(water in the kernel)* | inferential/causation |
| _____ 4. What does the term *duds* mean when talking about popcorn? <br> *(unpopped kernels)* | literal/description vocabulary |
| _____ 5. Which of the methods to pop corn used by the Native Americans was the most effective, and why? <br> *(the hot sand/clay bowl method because more kernels could be saved)* | inferential/problem-solution |
| _____ 6. How many pounds of popcorn did the passage say that the typical person in this country eats per year? <br> *(two pounds)* | literal/description |
| _____ 7. How long did the passage say popcorn has been eaten by humans? <br> *(thousands of years)* | literal/description |
| _____ 8. What is one limitation or problem associated with all three methods used by the Native Americans to pop corn? <br> *(all lost kernels)* | inferential/problem-solution |

## ERROR TYPES / ERROR ANALYSIS

| | Mis-pronun. | Sub-stitute | Inser-tions | Tchr. Assists | Omis-sions | Error Totals | Self-Correct. | Meaning (M) | Syntax (S) | Visual (V) |
|---|---|---|---|---|---|---|---|---|---|---|
| **Popcorn** | | | | | | | | | | |
| There are three major types of corn grown | | | | | | | | | | |
| in this country. First, there is the type of | | | | | | | | | | |
| corn people eat most of the time. It is | | | | | | | | | | |
| called sweet corn because of its flavor. | | | | | | | | | | |
| Second, there is field corn, which is | | | | | | | | | | |
| used mainly for feeding livestock. | | | | | | | | | | |
| Sometimes people eat field corn too. | | | | | | | | | | |
| However, its taste is not as good as sweet | | | | | | | | | | |
| corn and its kernels are not as full. The | | | | | | | | | | |
| third type of corn, often called Indian | | | | | | | | | | |
| corn, is popcorn. Popcorn is grown | | | | | | | | | | |
| commercially in the United States because | | | | | | | | | | |
| the average American eats almost two | | | | | | | | | | |
| pounds of popcorn a year, according // | | | | | | | | | | |
| to various estimates. | | | | | | | | | | |
| **TOTALS** | | | | | | | | | | |

Summary of Reading Behaviors (Strengths and Needs)

# PART II: ORAL READING AND ANALYSIS OF MISCUES

## Directions

Say, "Now I would like to hear you read this story out loud." Have the student read orally until the 100-word sample is completed. Follow along on the Miscue Grid, marking any oral reading errors as appropriate. *Remember to count miscues only up to the point in the story containing the oral reading stop-marker (//).* Then complete the Performance Summary to determine whether to continue the assessment. (*Note:* The Miscue Grid should be completed *after* the assessment session has been concluded in order to minimize stress for the student.)

# PART III: MISCUE ANALYSIS

## Directions

Circle all reading behaviors you observed.

## A. Fundamental Behaviors Observed

L → R Directionality    1-to-1 Matching    Searching for Clues    Cross-Checking

## B. Word Attack Behaviors

No Attempt    Mispronunciation (Invented Word Substitutions)    Substitutes

Skips/Reads On    Asks for Help    Repeats    Attempts to Self-Correct

"Sounds Out" (Segmenting)    Blends Sounds    Structural Analysis (Root Words, Affixes)

## C. Cueing Systems Used in Attempting Words

| CUEING TOOL | MISCUE EXAMPLES | ACTUAL TEXT |
|---|---|---|
| (M) Meaning | | |
| (S) Syntax | | |
| (V) Visual | | |

## D. Fluency (word by word → fluent reading)

Word by Word _____    Mixed Phrasing _____    Fluent Reading _____    Fluency Rate in Seconds _____

## E. Performance Summary

### Silent Reading Comprehension

_____ 0–1 questions missed = Easy

_____ 2 questions missed = Adequate

_____ 3+ questions missed = Too hard

### Oral Reading Accuracy

_____ 0–1 oral errors = Easy

_____ 2–5 oral errors = Adequate

_____ 6+ oral errors = Too hard

**Continue to the next reading passage?** _____ Yes _____ No

# PART IV: LISTENING COMPREHENSION

## *Directions*

If you have decided not to continue to have the student read any other passages, then use this passage to begin assessing the student's listening comprehension. Begin by reading the background statement for this passage and then say, "I am going to read this story to you. Please listen carefully because I will be asking you some questions after I finish reading it to you." After reading the passage, ask the student the questions associated with the passage. If the student correctly answers more than six questions, you will need to move to the next level and repeat the procedure.

## Listening Comprehension

_____ 0–2 questions missed = move to the next passage level

_____ more than 2 questions missed = stop assessment or move down a level

## Examiner's Notes

# LEVEL 6 ASSESSMENT PROTOCOLS

Cooking Without Fire: The Microwave Oven (219 words)

## PART I: SILENT READING COMPREHENSION

### Background Statement

"This passage is about microwave ovens. Read the selection to find out how microwave ovens were developed. Read it carefully because I'm going to ask you to tell me about what you read."

### Teacher Directions

Once the student completes the silent reading, say, "Tell me about the story you just read." Answers to the questions below that the student provides during the retelling should be marked "ua" in the appropriate blank to indicate that this response was unaided. Ask all remaining questions not addressed during the retelling and mark those that the student answers with an "a" to indicate that the correct response was given after prompting by the teacher.

| Questions/Answers | Expository Grammar Element/ Level of Comprehension |
|---|---|
| _____ 1. What invention led to the development of the microwave oven? *(magnetron tube)* | literal/causation |
| _____ 2. For what job was the magnetron tube first used? *(radar)* | literal/description |
| _____ 3. What did Dr. Percy Spencer discover about the magnetron tube? *(it could heat food from the inside out)* | literal/description |
| _____ 4. What was the name given to the first microwave oven? *(Radar Range)* | literal/description |
| _____ 5. Name two ways that today's microwave ovens differ from the first ones. *(not as bulky, more features, less expensive)* | literal/comparison/vocabulary |
| _____ 6. Explain why some people consider microwave cooking the first new method of cooking since the discovery of fire. *(it requires no fire or element of fire to cook food)* | literal/causation/expressive language |
| _____ 7. What type of energy is used by the microwave to cook food? *(electromagnetic)* | literal/description |
| _____ 8. What are two features found on most microwave ovens, according to the passage? *(defrost, reheat, constant temperature cooking)* | literal/description |

## ERROR TYPES

| | Mis-pronun. | Sub-stitute | Inser-tions | Tchr. Assists | Omis-sions | Error Totals | Self-Correct. |
|---|---|---|---|---|---|---|---|

## ERROR ANALYSIS

| | Meaning (M) | Syntax (S) | Visual (V) |
|---|---|---|---|

**Cooking Without Fire: The Microwave Oven**

Microwave cooking is very common today. It

is, however, a recent invention. The microwave

oven one uses today was developed from the

invention of the magnetron tube in 1940. The

invention of the magnetron tube, by Sir John

Randall and Dr. H. A. Boot, was a very important

part of the radar defense of England during

World War II. Neither man considered it as a

means of preparing food after they invented it. It

wasn't until the late 1940s that Dr. Percy

Spencer discovered the magnetron's ability to

heat and cook food from the inside out. Spencer

experimented with many // *different foods, all*

*with the same results: The inside got hot first.*

**TOTALS**

**Summary of Reading Behaviors (Strengths and Needs)**

# PART II: ORAL READING AND ANALYSIS OF MISCUES

## Directions

Say, "Now I would like to hear you read this story out loud." Have the student read orally until the 100-word sample is completed. Follow along on the Miscue Grid, marking any oral reading errors as appropriate. *Remember to count miscues only up to the point in the story containing the oral reading stop-marker (//).* Then complete the Performance Summary to determine whether to continue the assessment. (*Note:* The Miscue Grid should be completed *after* the assessment session has been concluded in order to minimize stress for the student.)

# PART III: MISCUE ANALYSIS

## Directions

Circle all reading behaviors you observed.

## A. Fundamental Behaviors Observed

L → R Directionality     1-to-1 Matching     Searching for Clues     Cross-Checking

## B. Word Attack Behaviors

No Attempt     Mispronunciation (Invented Word Substitutions)     Substitutes

Skips/Reads On     Asks for Help     Repeats     Attempts to Self-Correct

"Sounds Out" (Segmenting)     Blends Sounds     Structural Analysis (Root Words, Affixes)

## C. Cueing Systems Used in Attempting Words

| CUEING TOOL | MISCUE EXAMPLES | ACTUAL TEXT |
|---|---|---|
| (M) Meaning | | |
| (S) Syntax | | |
| (V) Visual | | |

## D. Fluency (word by word → fluent reading)

Word by Word _____     Mixed Phrasing _____     Fluent Reading _____     Fluency Rate in Seconds _____

## E. Performance Summary

### Silent Reading Comprehension

_____ 0–1 questions missed = Easy

_____ 2 questions missed = Adequate

_____ 3+ questions missed = Too hard

### Oral Reading Accuracy

_____ 0–1 oral errors = Easy

_____ 2–5 oral errors = Adequate

_____ 6+ oral errors = Too hard

**Continue to the next reading passage?** _____ Yes _____ No

# PART IV: LISTENING COMPREHENSION

## Directions

If you have decided not to continue to have the student read any other passages, then use this passage to begin assessing the student's listening comprehension. Begin by reading the background statement for this passage and then say, "I am going to read this story to you. Please listen carefully because I will be asking you some questions after I finish reading it to you." After reading the passage, ask the student the questions associated with the passage. If the student correctly answers more than six questions, you will need to move to the next level and repeat the procedure.

## Listening Comprehension

_____ 0–2 questions missed = move to the next passage level

_____ more than 2 questions missed = stop assessment or move down a level

Examiner's Notes

# LEVEL 7 ASSESSMENT PROTOCOLS

Diamonds (286 words)

## PART I: SILENT READING COMPREHENSION

### Background Statement

"The following selection is about diamonds. Read it carefully to find out about how diamonds are made, because I'm going to ask you to tell me all about what you read."

### Teacher Directions

Once the student completes the silent reading, say, "Tell me about the story you just read." Answers to the questions below that the student provides during the retelling should be marked "ua" in the appropriate blank to indicate that this response was unaided. Ask all remaining questions not addressed during the retelling and mark those that the student answers with an "a" to indicate that the correct response was given after prompting by the teacher.

| *Questions/Answers* | *Expository Grammar Element/ Level of Comprehension* |
|---|---|
| _____ 1. Where are the most important diamond fields located? *(India, South America, and Africa)* | literal/description |
| _____ 2. What information in the passage supports the idea that diamonds are rare? *(only located in certain areas, and even when present tons of rock must be sorted through)* | inferential/problem-solution |
| _____ 3. Where were the first diamonds found? *(sand and gravel in stream beds)* | literal/description |
| _____ 4. What four things determine the quality of a diamond? *(purity, color, weight, and cut)* | literal/description |
| _____ 5. What causes the brilliance of a diamond? *(the way it is cut, or number of facets)* | literal/causation |
| _____ 6. What two factors lower the purity of a diamond? *(uncrystallized carbon and foreign substances)* | inferential/causation |
| _____ 7. Explain how artificial diamonds are made. *(they result from carbon being placed under high pressure and temperature)* | inferential/collection/expressive language |
| _____ 8. Describe where natural diamonds are found. *(in rock formations that look like volcanoes)* | literal/description/expressive vocabulary |

## ERROR TYPES

## ERROR ANALYSIS

| Diamonds | Mis-pronun. | Sub-stitute | Inser-tions | Tchr. Assists | Omis-sions | Error Totals | Self-Correct. | Meaning (M) | Syntax (S) | Visual (V) |
|---|---|---|---|---|---|---|---|---|---|---|
| A diamond is one of the most beautiful | | | | | | | | | | |
| treasures that nature ever created, and one | | | | | | | | | | |
| of the rarest. It takes thousands of years | | | | | | | | | | |
| for nature to transform a chunk of carbon | | | | | | | | | | |
| into a rough diamond. Only three important | | | | | | | | | | |
| diamond fields have been found in the | | | | | | | | | | |
| world—in India, South America, and Africa. | | | | | | | | | | |
| The first diamonds were found in the sand | | | | | | | | | | |
| and gravel of stream beds. These types of | | | | | | | | | | |
| diamonds are called alluvial diamonds. | | | | | | | | | | |
| Later, diamonds were found deep in | | | | | | | | | | |
| the earth in rock formations called pipes. | | | | | | | | | | |
| These formations resemble extinct volcanoes. | | | | | | | | | | |
| The rock in which diamonds are found is | | | | | | | | | | |
| called // *blue ground*. | | | | | | | | | | |
| **TOTALS** | | | | | | | | | | |

**Summary of Reading Behaviors (Strengths and Needs)**

# PART II: ORAL READING AND ANALYSIS OF MISCUES

## Directions

Say, "Now I would like to hear you read this story out loud." Have the student read orally until the 100-word sample is completed. Follow along on the Miscue Grid, marking any oral reading errors as appropriate. *Remember to count miscues only up to the point in the story containing the oral reading stop-marker (//).* Then complete the Performance Summary to determine whether to continue the assessment. (*Note:* The Miscue Grid should be completed *after* the assessment session has been concluded in order to minimize stress for the student.)

# PART III: MISCUE ANALYSIS

## Directions

Circle all reading behaviors you observed.

## A. Fundamental Behaviors Observed

L → R Directionality        1-to-1 Matching        Searching for Clues        Cross-Checking

## B. Word Attack Behaviors

No Attempt        Mispronunciation (Invented Word Substitutions)        Substitutes

Skips/Reads On        Asks for Help        Repeats        Attempts to Self-Correct

"Sounds Out" (Segmenting)        Blends Sounds        Structural Analysis (Root Words, Affixes)

## C. Cueing Systems Used in Attempting Words

| CUEING TOOL | MISCUE EXAMPLES | ACTUAL TEXT |
|---|---|---|
| (M) Meaning | | |
| (S) Syntax | | |
| (V) Visual | | |

## D. Fluency (word by word → fluent reading)

Word by Word _____        Mixed Phrasing _____        Fluent Reading _____        Fluency Rate in Seconds _____

## E. Performance Summary

### Silent Reading Comprehension

_____ 0–1 questions missed = Easy

_____ 2 questions missed = Adequate

_____ 3+ questions missed = Too hard

### Oral Reading Accuracy

_____ 0–1 oral errors = Easy

_____ 2–5 oral errors = Adequate

_____ 6+ oral errors = Too hard

Continue to the next reading passage? _____ Yes _____ No

# PART IV: LISTENING COMPREHENSION

## Directions

If you have decided not to continue to have the student read any other passages, then use this passage to begin assessing the student's listening comprehension. Begin by reading the background statement for this passage and then say, "I am going to read this story to you. Please listen carefully because I will be asking you some questions after I finish reading it to you." After reading the passage, ask the student the questions associated with the passage. If the student correctly answers more than six questions, you will need to move to the next level and repeat the procedure.

## Listening Comprehension

_____ 0–2 questions missed = move to the next passage level

_____ more than 2 questions missed = stop assessment or move down a level

Examiner's Notes

# LEVEL 8 ASSESSMENT PROTOCOLS

## The Future Is Here (382 words)

## PART I: SILENT READING COMPREHENSION

### Background Statement

"This selection is about some inventions that will affect people in the near future. Read it carefully to find out what some of the inventions are and the ways they will affect people because I'm going to ask you to tell me about what you read."

### Teacher Directions

Once the student completes the silent reading, say, "Tell me about the story you just read." Answers to the questions below that the student provides during the retelling should be marked "ua" in the appropriate blank to indicate that this response was unaided. Ask all remaining questions not addressed during the retelling and mark those that the student answers with an "a" to indicate that the correct response was given after prompting by the teacher.

### Questions/Answers

**Expository Grammar Element/ Level of Comprehension**

_____ 1. What is a levitation vehicle?
(*a machine that is part aircraft and part car*)
inferential/collection

_____ 2. Why are people working on this type of vehicle?
(*crowded highways and increase in population*)
literal/causation

_____ 3. Explain how a dental laser works.
(*a laser destroys the cavity without pain*)
inferential/causation

_____ 4. Explain why a full-motion, color video telephone will benefit people who are deaf.
(*they will be able to call people who know sign language and communicate with them*)
inferential/causation/expressive language

_____ 5. What can fiber optics do that traditional technology is unable to do?
(*allow communication of lots of information over very thin wires*)
inferential/comparison/expressive vocabulary

_____ 6. What two aspects of your current television will be upgraded when high-definition TV becomes common?
(*sound and picture*)
literal/description

_____ 7. What does the sound and picture quality of high-definition TV compare to?
(*compact discs and 35-millimeter movies*)
literal/comparison

_____ 8. What did the passage say about how new advancements will affect people?
(*responses will vary but should relate to helping people meet the challenges of the future*)
inferential/causation/ expressive vocabulary

## The Future Is Here

| | ERROR TYPES | | | | | | | ERROR ANALYSIS | | |
|---|---|---|---|---|---|---|---|---|---|---|
| | Mis-pronun. | Sub-stitute | Inser-tions | Tchr. Assists | Omis-sions | Error Totals | Self-Correct. | Meaning (M) | Syntax (S) | Visual (V) |
| What will the twenty-first century bring | | | | | | | | | | |
| in terms of new inventions and space-age | | | | | | | | | | |
| technologies? No one knows for sure. But | | | | | | | | | | |
| scientists, inventors, and futurists are predicting | | | | | | | | | | |
| a variety of new inventions. These new | | | | | | | | | | |
| advancements will affect the way we live | | | | | | | | | | |
| and play. Some of them are already on the | | | | | | | | | | |
| drawing board. One example is the levitation | | | | | | | | | | |
| vehicle. The idea of a vertical take-off and | | | | | | | | | | |
| landing aircraft that can also be driven on | | | | | | | | | | |
| the road is the invention of Paul Moeller. | | | | | | | | | | |
| He named his first version of this type of | | | | | | | | | | |
| craft the Moeller 400. People involved in | | | | | | | | | | |
| this // type of technology see increases in | | | | | | | | | | |
| population and crowded highways as reasons | | | | | | | | | | |
| that a levitation vehicle will be needed. | | | | | | | | | | |
| **TOTALS** | | | | | | | | | | |

**Summary of Reading Behaviors (Strengths and Needs)**

# PART II: ORAL READING AND ANALYSIS OF MISCUES

## Directions

Say, "Now I would like to hear you read this story out loud." Have the student read orally until the 100-word sample is completed. Follow along on the Miscue Grid, marking any oral reading errors as appropriate. *Remember to count miscues only up to the point in the story containing the oral reading stop-marker (//).* Then complete the Performance Summary to determine whether to continue the assessment. (*Note:* The Miscue Grid should be completed *after* the assessment session has been concluded in order to minimize stress for the student.)

# PART III: MISCUE ANALYSIS

## Directions

Circle all reading behaviors you observed.

## A. Fundamental Behaviors Observed

L → R Directionality        1-to-1 Matching        Searching for Clues        Cross-Checking

## B. Word Attack Behaviors

No Attempt        Mispronunciation (Invented Word Substitutions)        Substitutes

Skips/Reads On        Asks for Help        Repeats        Attempts to Self-Correct

"Sounds Out" (Segmenting)        Blends Sounds        Structural Analysis (Root Words, Affixes)

## C. Cueing Systems Used in Attempting Words

| CUEING TOOL | MISCUE EXAMPLES | ACTUAL TEXT |
|---|---|---|
| (M) Meaning | | |
| (S) Syntax | | |
| (V) Visual | | |

## D. Fluency (word by word → fluent reading)

Word by Word _____        Mixed Phrasing _____        Fluent Reading _____        Fluency Rate in Seconds _____

## E. Performance Summary

### Silent Reading Comprehension

_____ 0–1 questions missed = Easy

_____ 2 questions missed = Adequate

_____ 3+ questions missed = Too hard

### Oral Reading Accuracy

_____ 0–1 oral errors = Easy

_____ 2–5 oral errors = Adequate

_____ 6+ oral errors = Too hard

**Continue to the next reading passage?** _____ Yes _____ No

# PART IV: LISTENING COMPREHENSION

*Directions*

If you have decided not to continue to have the student read any other passages, then use this passage to begin assessing the student's listening comprehension. Begin by reading the background statement for this passage and then say, "I am going to read this story to you. Please listen carefully because I will be asking you some questions after I finish reading it to you." After reading the passage, ask the student the questions associated with the passage. If the student correctly answers more than six questions, you will need to move to the next level and repeat the procedure.

## Listening Comprehension

_____ 0–2 questions missed = move to the next passage level

_____ more than 2 questions missed = stop assessment or move down a level

Examiner's Notes

# LEVEL 9 ASSESSMENT PROTOCOLS

Visual Illusions (269 words)

## PART I: SILENT READING COMPREHENSION

### Background Statement

"This selection is about visual illusions. Read it to find out about three specific types of visual illusions. Read it carefully because when you finish I will ask you to tell me about what you have read."

### Teacher Directions

Once the student completes the silent reading, say, "Tell me about the story you just read." Answers to the questions below that the student provides during the retelling should be marked "ua" in the appropriate blank to indicate that this response was unaided. Ask all remaining questions not addressed during the retelling and mark those that the student answers with an "a" to indicate that the correct response was given after prompting by the teacher.

| Questions/Answers | Expository Grammar Element/ Level of Comprehension |
|---|---|
| _____ 1. What two reasons were given for visual illusions? *(preconceptions and the brain's difficulty in choosing from two or more patterns)* | literal/description |
| _____ 2. What is an example of a lateral inhibition illusion? *(a bull's-eye)* | literal/description |
| _____ 3. The Gateway Arch in St. Louis is an example of what distortion? *(length distortion)* | literal/description |
| _____ 4. Explain why length distortion occurs. *(because the eyes work better side to side than up and down)* | literal/collection |
| _____ 5. What's an example of the visual illusion called "Hermann's Grid"? *(modern buildings)* | literal/description/expressive vocabulary |
| _____ 6. How does Hermann's Grid affect what you see visually? *(it causes the eyes to see gray spots at the corners of squares)* | inferential/causation |
| _____ 7. Explain why the old axiom "Don't believe everything you see" is valid in everyday life. *(examples of visual illusions are all around us, or other plausible responses)* | inferential/collection/figurative language |
| _____ 8. How does the tendency of eyes to move more easily from side to side rather than up and down affect the way we perceive tall objects? *(they seem taller than they actually are)* | literal/causation |

## ERROR ANALYSIS

## ERROR TYPES

| | Mis-pronun. | Sub-stitute | Inser-tions | Tchr. Assists | Omis-sions | Error Totals | Self-Correct. | Meaning (M) | Syntax (S) | Visual (V) |
|---|---|---|---|---|---|---|---|---|---|---|
| **Visual Illusions** | | | | | | | | | | |
| A visual illusion is an unreal or misleading | | | | | | | | | | |
| appearance or image, according to *Webster's* | | | | | | | | | | |
| dictionary. In other words, visual illusions are | | | | | | | | | | |
| sometimes caused by ideas one holds about | | | | | | | | | | |
| what one expects to see. In other instances, | | | | | | | | | | |
| the illusion is caused by the brain's difficulty | | | | | | | | | | |
| in choosing from two or more visual patterns. | | | | | | | | | | |
| If you look at a bull's-eye and move it | | | | | | | | | | |
| slowly in circular motions, you should see | | | | | | | | | | |
| spokes moving. The spokes, if you see them, | | | | | | | | | | |
| aren't really there. This type of visual illusion is | | | | | | | | | | |
| called lateral inhibition. Another type of | | | | | | | | | | |
| visual illusion occurs when a person tries | | | | | | | | | | |
| to // *estimate the height of a vertical object.* | | | | | | | | | | |
| **TOTALS** | | | | | | | | | | |

Summary of Reading Behaviors (Strengths and Needs)

# PART II: ORAL READING AND ANALYSIS OF MISCUES

*Directions*

Say, "Now I would like to hear you read this story out loud." Have the student read orally until the 100-word sample is completed. Follow along on the Miscue Grid, marking any oral reading errors as appropriate. *Remember to count miscues only up to the point in the story containing the oral reading stop-marker (///).* Then complete the Performance Summary to determine whether to continue the assessment. (*Note:* The Miscue Grid should be completed *after* the assessment session has been concluded in order to minimize stress for the student.)

# PART III: MISCUE ANALYSIS

*Directions*

Circle all reading behaviors you observed.

## A. Fundamental Behaviors Observed

L → R Directionality       1-to-1 Matching       Searching for Clues       Cross-Checking

## B. Word Attack Behaviors

No Attempt       Mispronunciation (Invented Word Substitutions)       Substitutes

Skips/Reads On       Asks for Help       Repeats       Attempts to Self-Correct

"Sounds Out" (Segmenting)       Blends Sounds       Structural Analysis (Root Words, Affixes)

## C. Cueing Systems Used in Attempting Words

| CUEING TOOL | MISCUE EXAMPLES | ACTUAL TEXT |
|---|---|---|
| (M) Meaning | | |
| (S) Syntax | | |
| (V) Visual | | |

## D. Fluency (word by word → fluent reading)

Word by Word _____       Mixed Phrasing _____       Fluent Reading _____       Fluency Rate in Seconds _____

## E. Performance Summary

*Silent Reading Comprehension*

_____ 0–1 questions missed = Easy

_____ 2 questions missed = Adequate

_____ 3+ questions missed = Too hard

*Oral Reading Accuracy*

_____ 0–1 oral errors = Easy

_____ 2–5 oral errors = Adequate

_____ 6+ oral errors = Too hard

# PART IV: LISTENING COMPREHENSION

### Directions

If you have decided not to continue to have the student read any other passages, then use this passage to begin assessing the student's listening comprehension. Begin by reading the background statement for this passage and then say, "I am going to read this story to you. Please listen carefully because I will be asking you some questions after I finish reading it to you." After reading the passage, ask the student the questions associated with the passage. If the student correctly answers more than six questions, you will need to move to the next level and repeat the procedure.

## Listening Comprehension

_____ 0–2 questions missed = move to the next passage level

_____ more than 2 questions missed = stop assessment or move down a level

Examiner's Notes

# SENTENCES FOR INITIAL PASSAGE SELECTION

# FORM D: LEVEL 1

1. Dogs can bark.

2. Cats can be friends.

3. There are many kinds of animals.


# FORM D: LEVEL 2

1. Look at things in your bedroom.

2. These shapes have color.

3. Purple is made by mixing other colors.


# FORM D: LEVEL 3

1. Some books are interesting.

2. It had not been invented.

3. He allowed the book to be read over.


# FORM D: LEVEL 4

1. They trapped animals in the mountains.

2. He lived in unknown parts of the country.

3. He discovered a pass out West.


# FORM D: LEVEL 5

1. Mexico lies south of the United States.

2. Some music is played with violins.

3. Guitar music is unique when played in a group.

# FORM D: LEVEL 6

1. Some laws still discriminate against people.

2. Celebrations were held for the national hero.

3. A stormy argument took place.

# FORM D: LEVEL 7

1. There are literally hundreds of measurements.

2. They frequently are pointed or barbed to make for better fastening.

3. The profession usually uses a gauge to determine a product's value.

# FORM D: LEVEL 8

1. The continent is home to a large population.

2. There was not suitable soil in the central part of the region.

3. The grassland was a fascinating place to visit.

# FORM D: LEVEL 9

1. The amount of cholesterol in your diet can affect your health.

2. There are myriad ways to monitor your caloric intake.

3. The continuum provides a wide range of nutritional options.

# EXPOSITORY READING PASSAGES

## Animal Friends

There are many kinds of animals.
Some animals are our friends. Others are not.
Dogs and cats can be good friends.

Dogs and cats make sounds to talk to us.
Some dogs bark when they hear something.
Some dogs bark when they are hungry.
Cats purr when they are happy.
Cats meow when they are hungry.

Not all cats and dogs are your friends.
If you do not know a dog, do not pet it.
It might bite you.
Cats can hurt you too.
Cats have claws and they can bite.

## Making Pictures Is Art

Look around and you can see art everywhere. Look at things in your bedroom. They all have lines, shape, and color. People who do art, or *artists,* use lines, shape, and color to make pictures.

Lines can be thick or thin. Lines can be short or long. You would need to use lines to draw your face. Lines are used to make shapes. In your room at home, your bed, night light, and wall have shape. These things also have color.
Red, yellow, and blue are the main colors.
All other colors can be made by mixing these colors.
Orange is made by mixing red and yellow.
Green is made by mixing yellow and blue.
Purple is made by mixing red and blue.
Black and white are not colors.
They do not have blue, yellow, or red in them.

## The History of Books

The history of books is interesting. A long time ago most people could not read. The people who could read didn't have many books to read. They didn't have many books because the printing press had not been invented. All books had to be hand written on either an animal skin or a kind of paper.

Most books were written on stretched sheepskin or stretched calfskin. The cost of writing a book on skin limited how many could be made. Only the rich could own books. Most books were written on skins because they were stronger and prettier than those written on paper. Hundreds of years ago it could have taken a whole flock of sheep to make one book because it took one sheepskin for each page.

The invention of the printing press changed the world. The printing press allowed many more books to be made. As books became more common, many people began to learn how to read. For the first time, books began to be used to teach people about art, science, and faraway places. No longer were people required to remember everything. They could read about the world in books over and over again if they chose to do so.

## Mountain Man

During the early history of our country, the West was full of stories about cowboys and American Indians. Another group that helped settle the West were the mountain men. These were men who wanted to trap animals for their furs. These men went into unknown parts of the West beyond the Rocky Mountains. They carried a gun, a knife, coffee, flour, and little else. They planned to eat the animals they shot and the berries they found. They went to trap beaver for their furs. Some of these men made friends with the American Indians who lived in the far West. Others did not. One famous mountain man who made friends with the American Indians was Jim Beckwourth.

Jim Beckwourth was a black man. He had been a slave. At the age of 20 he decided he didn't want to be a slave. He ran away. He made it to the Rocky Mountains and became a mountain man. Jim began trapping and made friends with an American Indian tribe called the Crow. Jim married an American Indian woman. He even became a chief of the Crows. Later on, Jim moved farther west. He headed off for California and discovered a pass through the mountains to California. The pass through the mountains still bears his name today. Jim Beckwourth couldn't read or write but he got his story written down. His story is in a book called *The Life and Adventures of James P. Beckwourth.*

### Music of Mexico

Much of the music you hear in the United States comes from other countries. Most people who come to the United States from other countries adapt to the lifestyle here. However, they do not give up the music of their homelands.

Many people have come to the United States from Mexico. Mexico is a large country that lies south of the United States. The music of Mexico is unique and has contributed much to the music heard in the United States. Music from Mexico often uses instruments such as the folk harp, violin, and various types of guitars.

Music in Mexico is used to celebrate birthdays, weddings, anniversaries, and other holidays. The people like music and they show it. They sing along with the musicians and often burst out with yells, laughter, clapping, and dancing.

Two types of music that are popular throughout Mexico are from states in the east and west. In the east, music is performed on four instruments. A band in the east generally has a 35-string harp that plays the melody and bass, a thin guitar, a six-string guitar, and a four-string guitar. The music is lively and fast paced. A famous song from this part of Mexico is "La Bamba." Music from the western part of Mexico is usually played by a musical group. These musical groups called "mariachi" (mah-ree-AH-chee) play many types of music. The group usually consists of several violins, two trumpets, a large bass guitar, a short five-string guitar, and a six-string guitar. Mariachi often play for special events. Other times mariachi can be seen strolling along the street playing and singing to people eating or shopping.

### Jesse Owens

In 1936, the Olympic games were to be held in Germany. For months before the games took place, a stormy argument took place in the United States. Germany was ruled by Adolf Hitler and the Nazi Party. Hitler had been mistreating German Jews for some time, and many people in the United States wondered whether we should send a team or stay home and protest German racism. It was finally decided that we should send a team.

At the same time, many black athletes wondered if they should go because of racism in the United States. Finally, led by Jesse Owens, the black American athletes decided they should go to Germany to show the Germans how great they were. Jesse Owens led the American team to victory by capturing four Gold Medals. Jesse returned home a national hero. Many cities held parades and celebrations in his honor. Yet in much of the United States, laws still discriminated against black citizens.

In his later life, Jesse Owens, without bitterness, wrote the following. "In the early 1830s my ancestors were brought on a boat across the Atlantic Ocean from Africa to America as slaves for men who felt they had the right to own other men. In August of 1936, I boarded a boat to go back across the Atlantic Ocean to do battle with Adolf Hitler, a man who thought all other men should be slave to him and his armies."

Jesse Owens's Gold Medals did little to stop the direction of Germany in 1936. However, they did help move the United States a step closer toward providing equal treatment for all Americans regardless of their race.

## Nails: A Carpenter's "Fastener"

Carpenters use a variety of tools in their profession such as hammers, saws, and power tools. They also use what are called *fasteners* to hold pieces of wood and other materials together. The most widely used fasteners are nails, screws, and bolts. Nails are perhaps the most commonly used fasteners in the carpenter's toolbox.

There are literally hundreds of kinds of nails that can be used for just about any kind of fastening job. The size of nails is usually designated using the *penny system*. While we are not exactly sure how the penny system came about, many people believe that it is an ancient measurement based on the price of nails according to weight per one hundred nails. Larger and heavier nails would cost more pennies than smaller nails, thus a six-penny nail (written as "6d") would cost more than a two-penny (2d) nail. In the penny system, the smallest nail is a two-penny (2d) nail and the largest is a sixty-penny (60d) nail. The thickness or *gauge* of nails usually increases as nails get longer, so a 50d nail will typically be much thicker in gauge than a 10d nail.

There are many ways of making nails, and each type is better suited to different purposes. One type of nail that is not used very often is called the *cut* nail. Cut nails are given that name because they are literally cut or *stamped* from thin metal sheets and are wedge-shaped.

*Wire nails* are cut from long rolls of metal wire and most often come in three types: common, box, and finish nails. *Common nails* have a smooth shaft, are of fairly heavy gauge, and have a medium-sized head. They frequently have a pointed or barbed section under the head to improve holding power and make for better fastening. *Box nails* are very much like common nails except they are much thinner (smaller gauge). This makes them better suited to fastening edges of wood with less danger of splitting the wood. *Finish nails* are light gauge (very thin) and are ideal for what is called "finishing work" on the inside of homes. They have a small head and can be driven into the wood so as to become almost invisible.

An old saying among carpenters is "always use the right tool for the right job." Knowing just which nail is the correct fastening tool is one way master carpenters live up to this important motto.

## The Environments of Africa

Africa is the Earth's second largest continent. It is home to about one-tenth of the world's population. While it is about three times larger than the United States in terms of landmass, many people still do not know very much about it. Some think of Africa as a single country and it is not. In this selection we take a brief tour of this continent.

Africa is almost completely surrounded by water. Two oceans and two seas are on its borders. The Atlantic Ocean borders Africa on the west, while the Indian Ocean borders to the east. The Mediterranean Sea and the Red Sea are to the north. The famous Sahara Desert stretches across Africa. It separates North African countries from the southern countries, which are often called sub-Saharan Africa. As of the 1990s, there were some 49 countries in sub-Saharan Africa alone. Because the equator runs through sub-Saharan Africa, most of this region has a climate that is quite warm and moist or *tropical.*

Central and West African countries are thinly populated because of a lack of suitable soil for farming. They do, however, have many tropical rain forests, which are of great benefit to people around the Earth. A major concern to many is that these splendid rain forests are being cut down to make way for farming and houses. Among other things, the loss of the rain forests leads to a great deal of soil erosion and the loss of plant and animal habitats.

As we move further away from the equator, we find that the African rain forests disappear and are replaced by grasslands known as *savannas.* In East Africa, there are thick grasslands where large herds of big game animals such as the giraffe, antelope, and zebra roam. Farming is also an important way of life in these East Africa countries.

The *African Horn* is also part of East Africa and bulges out into the Indian Ocean. It is a mass of hills, mountains, canyons, and valleys that slope down toward the dry lowlands near the Red Sea. Because of overpopulation and other problems, there is a great deal of poverty in this region. The African Horn is home to four countries: Ethiopia, Somalia, Eritrea, and Djibouti.

Southern Africa is a fascinating place that features wooded areas to the north and, because of less rainfall, grasslands to the south. Some of the countries located in Southern Africa include Angola, Zambia, Namibia, and South Africa. There has been a great deal of political change in South Africa over the last twenty years as this country moved from government ruled by white citizens only to a democracy that allows everyone to vote for her leaders.

Finally, as we travel to North Africa above the Sahara Desert, we see that it is home to such ancient countries as Egypt, Sudan, Libya, Algeria, and Morocco. These nations have their own special character and traditions that can vary greatly from their African neighbors to the south. Without doubt, Africa is a continent rich in traditions, culture, and varied geography.

### The Mathematics of Health

Americans spend billions of dollars every year on medical care. Doctor bills, medicine, dental work, optical products (glasses, contacts, etc.), health insurance, nursing homes, and other health-related costs are all part of the health care picture. As the associated costs of medical care continue to escalate, more and more Americans are making efforts to stay healthy in a myriad of ways. These efforts range on a continuum from daily exercise to careful control of one's diet. This passage will focus on the mathematics involved in monitoring one's diet.

People sometimes try to remain healthy by limiting the amount of fat, sodium (salt), cholesterol, and sugar in their diet. Too much fat in your diet, for instance, can lead to heart disease and other deadly health problems. Years ago many food producers began marketing products carrying labels like "LITE" (low in fat or sugar) or "Lo-Cal" (low in calories) to suggest that their foods were more healthy than some of their competitors' products. Sometimes, however, these food products were not any more healthy than their competitors that did not carry the "LITE" or "Lo-Cal" markings.

In 1994, the federal Food and Drug Administration (FDA) in Washington, D.C., created new rules for food producers marking their products "LITE," "Lo-Cal," or "Light." Now all companies, except for the very smallest, must provide nutritional information on their labels for consumers so that we can judge for ourselves whether the food is as low in fat, sodium, cholesterol, or sugar as we expect.

Sometimes when we are shopping for groceries, it can be interesting to compare products just to see how much fat is contained in them. This can help us to choose foods that are as healthy as they are pleasing to the taste. For example, a frankfurter typically has about thirteen grams of fat. (*Note:* This is written as "13 g" on the label next to where it says "Fat.") Roast turkey, on the other hand, has 12.5 g *less* fat than a frankfurter! Here is another example. A can of orange soda has about 110 calories, mostly due to the amount of sugar it contains. However, a LITE or diet soda only has about one calorie. If a grown person should usually consume about 1,500 calories per day from all foods, think of how many calories can be saved for other more pleasing foods just by switching to a diet soda without sugar.

Becoming a "label reader" can be a great way to add years to your life while also helping you enjoy the foods you eat. Maybe, as the old saying goes, "You *can* have your cake and eat it, too!" as long as you pay close attention to *what* you put into the cake.

# EXAMINER'S ASSESSMENT PROTOCOLS

## FORM
## D

# LEVEL 1 ASSESSMENT PROTOCOLS

Animal Friends (91 words)

## PART I: SILENT READING COMPREHENSION

*Background Statement*

"This story is about dogs and cats. Read it and try to remember some of the important facts about these animals because I'm going to ask you to tell me about what you have read."

*Teacher Directions*

Once the student completes the silent reading, say, "Tell me about the story you just read." Answers to the questions below that the student provides during the retelling should be marked "ua" in the appropriate blank to indicate that this response was unaided. Ask all remaining questions not addressed during the retelling and mark those student answers with an "a" to indicate that the correct response was given after prompting by the teacher.

| *Questions/Answers* | *Expository Grammar Element/ Level of Comprehension* |
|---|---|
| _____ 1. What two kinds of animals were in this story? <br> *(dogs and cats)* | literal/description |
| _____ 2. Why do cats purr? <br> *(they are happy)* | literal/description |
| _____ 3. What were the two reasons given for dogs barking? <br> *(hungry and when they hear something)* | literal/collection |
| _____ 4. Why is it best not to pet a dog you do not know? <br> *(it might bite you)* | literal/problem-solution |
| _____ 5. What two ways can a cat hurt someone? <br> *(scratch or bite)* | literal/collection |
| _____ 6. What do cats do when they are hungry? <br> *(meow)* | literal/description |
| _____ 7. What does "dogs and cats like to talk to us" mean? <br> *(it means that when they bark or meow or make other noises, they are trying to let people know they hear something, are hungry, or are happy)* | inferential/causation |
| _____ 8. Can you think of any animals that aren't our friends? <br> *(accept plausible responses)* | evaluative/comparison |

**ERROR TYPES**

**ERROR ANALYSIS**

| | Mis-pronun. | Sub-stitute | Inser-tions | Tchr. Assists | Omis-sions | Error Totals | Self-Correct. | Meaning (M) | Syntax (S) | Visual (V) |
|---|---|---|---|---|---|---|---|---|---|---|
| **Animal Friends** | | | | | | | | | | |
| There are many kinds of animals. | | | | | | | | | | |
| Some animals are our friends. Others are not. | | | | | | | | | | |
| Dogs and cats can be good friends. | | | | | | | | | | |
| Dogs and cats make sounds to talk to us. | | | | | | | | | | |
| Some dogs bark when they hear something. | | | | | | | | | | |
| Some dogs bark when they are hungry. | | | | | | | | | | |
| Cats purr when they are happy. | | | | | | | | | | |
| Cats meow when they are hungry. | | | | | | | | | | |
| Not all cats and dogs are your friends. | | | | | | | | | | |
| If you do not know a dog, do not pet it. | | | | | | | | | | |
| It might bite you. | | | | | | | | | | |
| Cats can hurt you too. | | | | | | | | | | |
| Cats have claws and they can bite.// | | | | | | | | | | |
| **TOTALS** | | | | | | | | | | |

**Summary of Reading Behaviors (Strengths and Needs)**

# PART II: ORAL READING AND ANALYSIS OF MISCUES

## Directions

Say, "Now I would like to hear you read this story out loud." Have the student read orally until the sample is completed. Follow along on the Miscue Grid, marking any oral reading errors as appropriate. *Remember to count miscues only up to the point in the story containing the oral reading stop-marker (//).* Then complete the Performance Summary to determine whether to continue the assessment. (*Note:* The Miscue Grid should be completed *after* the assessment session has been concluded in order to minimize stress for the student.)

# PART III: MISCUE ANALYSIS

## Directions

Circle all reading behaviors you observed.

## A. Fundamental Behaviors Observed

L → R Directionality       1-to-1 Matching       Searching for Clues       Cross-Checking

## B. Word Attack Behaviors

No Attempt       Mispronunciation (Invented Word Substitutions)       Substitutes

Skips/Reads On       Asks for Help       Repeats       Attempts to Self-Correct

"Sounds Out" (Segmenting)       Blends Sounds       Structural Analysis (Root Words, Affixes)

## C. Cueing Systems Used in Attempting Words

| CUEING TOOL | MISCUE EXAMPLES | ACTUAL TEXT |
|---|---|---|
| (M) Meaning | | |
| (S) Syntax | | |
| (V) Visual | | |

## D. Fluency (word by word → fluent reading)

Word by Word _____       Mixed Phrasing _____       Fluent Reading _____       Fluency Rate in Seconds _____

## E. Performance Summary

### Silent Reading Comprehension

_____ 0–1 questions missed = Easy

_____ 2 questions missed = Adequate

_____ 3+ questions missed = Too hard

### Oral Reading Accuracy

_____ 0–1 oral errors = Easy

_____ 2–5 oral errors = Adequate

_____ 6+ oral errors = Too hard

**Continue to the next reading passage?** _____ Yes _____ No

## PART IV: LISTENING COMPREHENSION

### Directions

If you have decided not to continue to have the student read any other passages, then use this passage to begin assessing the student's listening comprehension. Begin by reading the background statement for this passage and then say, "I am going to read this story to you. Please listen carefully because I will be asking you some questions after I finish reading it to you." After reading the passage, ask the student the questions associated with the passage. If the student correctly answers more than six questions, you will need to move to the next level and repeat the procedure.

## Listening Comprehension

_____ 0–2 questions missed = move to the next passage level

_____ more than 2 questions missed = stop assessment or move down a level

## Examiner's Notes

# LEVEL 2 ASSESSMENT PROTOCOLS

Making Pictures Is Art (139 words)

## PART I: SILENT READING COMPREHENSION

### Background Statement

"This story is about how we create art. Read it and try to remember some of the important facts about making pictures because I'm going to ask you to tell me about what you have read."

### Teacher Directions

Once the student completes the silent reading, say, "Tell me about the story you just read." Answers to the questions below that the student provides during the retelling should be marked "ua" in the appropriate blank to indicate that this response was unaided. Ask all remaining questions not addressed during the retelling and mark those the student answers with an "a" to indicate that the correct response was given after prompting by the teacher.

| Questions/Answers | Expository Grammar Element/ Level of Comprehension |
|---|---|
| _____ 1. Where around us do we find art? *(everywhere; or the student may name several places)* | literal/description |
| _____ 2. All art has several things in common (alike). Can you name two? *(line, shape, and/or color)* | literal/collection |
| _____ 3. What is an *artist*? *(someone who creates art, or a similar response)* | literal/description |
| _____ 4. Lines can be different. What are two ways lines can be different? *(thick, thin, short, long)* | literal/comparison |
| _____ 5. What are the three main colors? *(red, yellow, blue)* | literal/collection |
| _____ 6. What can you do to make a brand new color? *(mix two or more of the main colors)* | inferential/problem-solution |
| _____ 7. Why does the story say that white and black are not colors? *(they do not contain red, yellow, or blue)* | inferential/literal |
| _____ 8. A person may look at a drawing and say that he thinks it is beautiful art. Another person can look at the very same drawing and say that she thinks it is bad art. Why do people sometimes disagree about what is good or bad art? *(accept any reasonable response, but something implicit of "art is in the eye of the beholder" is best)* | evaluative/comparison |

## Making Pictures Is Art

| | ERROR TYPES | | | | | | | ERROR ANALYSIS | | |
|---|---|---|---|---|---|---|---|---|---|---|
| | Mis-pronun. | Sub-stitute | Inser-tions | Tchr. Assists | Omis-sions | Error Totals | Self-Correct. | Meaning (M) | Syntax (S) | Visual (V) |
| Look around and you can see art everywhere. | | | | | | | | | | |
| Look at things in your bedroom. They all | | | | | | | | | | |
| have lines, shape, and color. People who do | | | | | | | | | | |
| art, or *artists*, use lines, shape, and color to | | | | | | | | | | |
| make pictures. Lines can be thick or thin. | | | | | | | | | | |
| Lines can be short or long. You would need to | | | | | | | | | | |
| use lines to draw your face. Lines are used to | | | | | | | | | | |
| make shapes. In your room at home, your | | | | | | | | | | |
| bed, night light, and wall have shape. These | | | | | | | | | | |
| things also have color. Red, yellow, and blue | | | | | | | | | | |
| are the main colors. All other colors can be | | | | | | | | | | |
| made by mixing these colors. Orange// *is* | | | | | | | | | | |
| *made by mixing red and yellow.* | | | | | | | | | | |
| TOTALS | | | | | | | | | | |

Summary of Reading Behaviors (Strengths and Needs)

# PART II: ORAL READING AND ANALYSIS OF MISCUES

*Directions*

Say, "Now I would like to hear you read this story out loud." Have the student read orally until the 100-word sample is completed. Follow along on the Miscue Grid, marking any oral reading errors as appropriate. *Remember to count miscues only up to the point in the story containing the oral reading stop-marker (//).* Then complete the Performance Summary to determine whether to continue the assessment. (*Note:* The Miscue Grid should be completed *after* the assessment session has been concluded in order to minimize stress for the student.)

# PART III: MISCUE ANALYSIS

*Directions*

Circle all reading behaviors you observed.

## A. Fundamental Behaviors Observed

L → R Directionality      1-to-1 Matching      Searching for Clues      Cross-Checking

## B. Word Attack Behaviors

No Attempt      Mispronunciation (Invented Word Substitution)      Substitutes

Skips/Reads On      Asks for Help      Repeats      Attempts to Self-Correct

"Sounds Out" (Segmenting)      Blends Sounds      Structural Analysis (Root Words, Affixes)

## C. Cueing Systems Used in Attempting Words

| CUEING TOOL | MISCUE EXAMPLES | ACTUAL TEXT |
|---|---|---|
| (M) Meaning | | |
| (S) Syntax | | |
| (V) Visual | | |

## D. Fluency (word by word → fluent reading)

Word by Word _____      Mixed Phrasing _____      Fluent Reading _____      Fluency Rate in Seconds _____

## E. Performance Summary

**Silent Reading Comprehension**

_____ 0–1 questions missed = Easy

_____ 2 questions missed = Adequate

_____ 3+ questions missed = Too hard

**Oral Reading Accuracy**

_____ 0–1 oral errors = Easy

_____ 2–5 oral errors = Adequate

_____ 6+ oral errors = Too hard

**Continue to the next reading passage?** _____ Yes _____ No

## PART IV: LISTENING COMPREHENSION

### Directions

If you have decided not to continue to have the student read any other passages, then use this passage to begin assessing the student's listening comprehension. Begin by reading the background statement for this passage and then say, "I am going to read this story to you. Please listen carefully because I will be asking you some questions after I finish reading it to you." After reading the passage, ask the student the questions associated with the passage. If the student correctly answers more than six questions, you will need to move to the next level and repeat the procedure.

## Listening Comprehension

_____ 0–2 questions missed = move to the next passage level

_____ more than 2 questions missed = stop assessment or move down a level

Examiner's Notes

# LEVEL 3 ASSESSMENT PROTOCOLS

The History of Books (204 words)

## PART I: SILENT READING COMPREHENSION

### Background Statement

"This story is about how books were first made. Read it and try to remember some of the important facts about books because I'm going to ask you to tell me about what you have read."

### Teacher Directions

Once the student completes the silent reading, say, "Tell me about the story you just read." Answers to the questions below that the student provides during the retelling should be marked "ua" in the appropriate blank to indicate that this response was unaided. Ask all remaining questions not addressed during the retelling and mark those the student answers with an "a" to indicate that the correct response was given after prompting by the teacher.

| Questions/Answers | Expository Grammar Element/ Level of Comprehension |
|---|---|
| _____ 1. Why were there so few books a long time ago? *(the printing press hadn't been invented)* | literal/causation |
| _____ 2. How were early books produced? *(they were hand written on skin or paper)* | inferential/problem-solution |
| _____ 3. Early books were written on what kinds of skin? *(sheep and calf)* | literal/description |
| _____ 4. Why were animal skins preferred to paper when making a book a long time ago? *(animal skins were stronger than paper)* | literal/comparison |
| _____ 5. Early in the history of books only the rich had books. Why? *(because the cost of making the books made them expensive)* | inferential/causation |
| _____ 6. What invention allowed people who were not rich to begin reading books? *(printing press)* | literal/problem-solution |
| _____ 7. Why could it have taken a whole flock of sheep to make a book? *(because it took one sheepskin for each page)* | literal/causation |
| _____ 8. How has the invention of the printing press helped people throughout the world? *(response should be related to the ideas of more people learned to read, people can learn about lots of different topics, or other plausible responses)* | evaluative/language |

|  | ERROR TYPES | | | | | | SELF | ERROR ANALYSIS | | |
|---|---|---|---|---|---|---|---|---|---|---|
|  | Mis-pronun. | Sub-stitute | Inser-tions | Tchr. Assists | Omis-sions | Error Totals | Self-Correct. | Meaning (M) | Syntax (S) | Visual (V) |
| **The History of Books** | | | | | | | | | | |
| The history of books is interesting. A long | | | | | | | | | | |
| time ago most people could not read. The | | | | | | | | | | |
| people who could read didn't have many | | | | | | | | | | |
| books to read. They didn't have many books | | | | | | | | | | |
| because the printing press had not been | | | | | | | | | | |
| invented. All books had to be hand written | | | | | | | | | | |
| on either an animal skin or a kind of paper. | | | | | | | | | | |
| Most books were written on stretched | | | | | | | | | | |
| sheepskin or stretched calfskin. The cost | | | | | | | | | | |
| of writing a book on skin limited how | | | | | | | | | | |
| many could be made. Only the rich | | | | | | | | | | |
| could own books. Most books were written | | | | | | | | | | |
| on skins because they were stronger and | | | | | | | | | | |
| prettier than those//*written on paper.* | | | | | | | | | | |
| **TOTALS** | | | | | | | | | | |

Summary of Reading Behaviors (Strengths and Needs)

# PART II: ORAL READING AND ANALYSIS OF MISCUES

*Directions*

Say, "Now I would like to hear you read this story out loud." Have the student read orally until the 100-word sample is completed. Follow along on the Miscue Grid, marking any oral reading errors as appropriate. *Remember to count miscues only up to the point in the story containing the oral reading stop-marker (///).* Then complete the Performance Summary to determine whether to continue the assessment. (*Note:* The Miscue Grid should be completed *after* the assessment session has been concluded in order to minimize stress for the student.)

# PART III: MISCUE ANALYSIS

*Directions*

Circle all reading behaviors you observed.

## A. Fundamental Behaviors Observed

L → R Directionality        1-to-1 Matching        Searching for Clues        Cross-Checking

## B. Word Attack Behaviors

No Attempt        Mispronunciation (Invented Word Substitutions)        Substitutes

Skips/Reads On        Asks for Help        Repeats        Attempts to Self-Correct

"Sounds Out" (Segmenting)        Blends Sounds        Structural Analysis (Root Words, Affixes)

## C. Cueing Systems Used in Attempting Words

| CUEING TOOL | MISCUE EXAMPLES | ACTUAL TEXT |
|---|---|---|
| (M) Meaning | | |
| (S) Syntax | | |
| (V) Visual | | |

## D. Fluency (word by word → fluent reading)

Word by Word _____        Mixed Phrasing _____        Fluent Reading _____        Fluency Rate in Seconds _____

## E. Performance Summary

*Silent Reading Comprehension*

_____ 0–1 questions missed = Easy

_____ 2 questions missed = Adequate

_____ 3+ questions missed = Too hard

*Oral Reading Accuracy*

_____ 0–1 oral errors = Easy

_____ 2–5 oral errors = Adequate

_____ 6+ oral errors = Too hard

**Continue to the next reading passage?** _____ Yes _____ No

## PART IV: LISTENING COMPREHENSION

### *Directions*

If you have decided not to continue to have the student read any other passages, then use this passage to begin assessing the student's listening comprehension. Begin by reading the background statement for this passage and then say, "I am going to read this story to you. Please listen carefully because I will be asking you some questions after I finish reading it to you." After reading the passage, ask the student the questions associated with the passage. If the student correctly answers more than six questions, you will need to move to the next level and repeat the procedure.

## Listening Comprehension

\_\_\_\_\_ 0–2 questions missed = move to the next passage level

\_\_\_\_\_ more than 2 questions missed = stop assessment or move down a level

## Examiner's Notes

FORM D Assessment Protocols

# LEVEL 4 ASSESSMENT PROTOCOLS

## Mountain Man (244 words)

## PART I: SILENT READING COMPREHENSION

### Background Statement

"This story is about a man who went to live in the mountains. Read it and try to remember some of the important facts about this mountain man because I'm going to ask you to tell me about what you have read."

### Teacher Directions

Once the student completes the silent reading, say, "Tell me about the story you just read." Answers to the questions below that the student provides during the retelling should be marked "ua" in the appropriate blank to indicate that this response was unaided. Ask all remaining questions not addressed during the retelling and mark those the student answers with an "a" to indicate that the correct response was given after prompting by the teacher.

| *Questions/Answers* | *Expository Grammar Element/ Level of Comprehension* |
|---|---|
| _____ 1. Who was the famous mountain man the story was about? <br> *(Jim Beckwourth)* | literal/description |
| _____ 2. What four things did most mountain men take with them into the mountains? <br> *(gun, knife, coffee, flour)* | literal/collection |
| _____ 3. What made Jim Beckwourth go to the mountains? <br> *(he wanted to escape slavery)* | literal/causation |
| _____ 4. What animal did Jim trap? <br> *(beaver)* | inferential/causation |
| _____ 5. Why would mountain men want to be on good terms with the American Indians? <br> *(accept plausible responses)* | evaluative/problem-solution |
| _____ 6. What did the author mean by "he discovered a pass through the mountains"? <br> *(he meant he found a way to get through the mountains that was easier than other ways)* | inferential/problem-solution |
| _____ 7. Why is it unusual that Jim became a chief of the Crow Indians? <br> *(he was not born a Crow Indian; he was a black man; he was a runaway slave)* | inferential/language |
| _____ 8. Who did Jim marry? <br> *(an American Indian woman)* | literal/causation |

## ERROR TYPES | ERROR ANALYSIS

| | Mis-pronun. | Sub-stitute | Inser-tions | Tchr. Assists | Omis-sions | Error Totals | Self-Correct. | Meaning (M) | Syntax (S) | Visual (V) |
|---|---|---|---|---|---|---|---|---|---|---|
| **Mountain Man** | | | | | | | | | | |
| During the early history of our country, | | | | | | | | | | |
| the West was full of stories about cowboys | | | | | | | | | | |
| and American Indians. Another group that helped settle | | | | | | | | | | |
| the West were the mountain men. These were | | | | | | | | | | |
| men who wanted to trap animals for their furs. | | | | | | | | | | |
| These men went into unknown parts of the | | | | | | | | | | |
| West beyond the Rocky Mountains. They | | | | | | | | | | |
| carried a gun, a knife, coffee, flour, and little | | | | | | | | | | |
| else. They planned to eat the animals they | | | | | | | | | | |
| shot and the berries they found. They went to | | | | | | | | | | |
| trap beaver for their furs. Some of these men | | | | | | | | | | |
| made friends with the American Indians who | | | | | | | | | | |
| lived in the far // West. | | | | | | | | | | |
| **TOTALS** | | | | | | | | | | |

**Summary of Reading Behaviors (Strengths and Needs)**

# PART II: ORAL READING AND ANALYSIS OF MISCUES

## Directions

Say, "Now I would like to hear you read this story out loud." Have the student read orally until the 100-word sample is completed. Follow along on the Miscue Grid, marking any oral reading errors as appropriate. *Remember to count miscues only up to the point in the story containing the oral reading stop-marker (//).* Then complete the Performance Summary to determine whether to continue the assessment. (*Note:* The Miscue Grid should be completed *after* the assessment session has been concluded in order to minimize stress for the student.)

# PART III: MISCUE ANALYSIS

## Directions

Circle all reading behaviors you observed.

## A. Fundamental Behaviors Observed

L → R Directionality        1-to-1 Matching        Searching for Clues        Cross-Checking

## B. Word Attack Behaviors

No Attempt        Mispronunciation (Invented Word Substitutions)        Substitutes

Skips/Reads On        Asks for Help        Repeats        Attempts to Self-Correct

"Sounds Out" (Segmenting)        Blends Sounds        Structural Analysis (Root Words, Affixes)

## C. Cueing Systems Used in Attempting Words

| CUEING TOOL | MISCUE EXAMPLES | ACTUAL TEXT |
|-------------|-----------------|-------------|
| (M) Meaning |  |  |
| (S) Syntax  |  |  |
| (V) Visual  |  |  |

## D. Fluency (word by word → fluent reading)

Word by Word _____        Mixed Phrasing _____        Fluent Reading _____        Fluency Rate in Seconds _____

## E. Performance Summary

### Silent Reading Comprehension

_____ 0–1 questions missed = Easy

_____ 2 questions missed = Adequate

_____ 3+ questions missed = Too hard

### Oral Reading Accuracy

_____ 0–1 oral errors = Easy

_____ 2–5 oral errors = Adequate

_____ 6+ oral errors = Too hard

**Continue to the next reading passage?** _____ Yes _____ No

# PART IV: LISTENING COMPREHENSION

## Directions

If you have decided not to continue to have the student read any other passages, then use this passage to begin assessing the student's listening comprehension. Begin by reading the background statement for this passage and then say, "I am going to read this story to you. Please listen carefully because I will be asking you some questions after I finish reading it to you." After reading the passage, ask the student the questions associated with the passage. If the student correctly answers more than six questions, you will need to move to the next level and repeat the procedure.

## Listening Comprehension

\_\_\_\_\_ 0–2 questions missed = move to the next passage level

\_\_\_\_\_ more than 2 questions missed = stop assessment or move down a level

Examiner's Notes

# LEVEL 5 ASSESSMENT PROTOCOLS

Music of Mexico (283 words)

## PART I: SILENT READING COMPREHENSION

### Background Statement

"This story is about music that people in Mexico enjoy. Read it and try to remember some of the important facts about their music because I'm going to ask you to tell me about what you have read."

### Teacher Directions

Once the student completes the silent reading, say, "Tell me about the story you just read." Answers to the questions below that the student provides during the retelling should be marked "ua" in the appropriate blank to indicate that this response was unaided. Ask all remaining questions not addressed during the retelling and mark those the student answers with an "a" to indicate that the correct response was given after prompting by the teacher.

| Questions/Answers | Expository Grammar Element/ Level of Comprehension |
|---|---|
| _____ 1. Where is Mexico located? *(south of the United States)* | literal/description |
| _____ 2. What types of events are celebrated with music in Mexico? *(weddings, birthdays, anniversaries)* | literal/collection |
| _____ 3. Musical groups from the eastern part of Mexico differ from those in the west. Can you name two instruments used in western Mexico that musicians in eastern Mexico don't use? *(violins and trumpets)* | inferential/comparison |
| _____ 4. What is the name of a famous song from the eastern part of Mexico? *(La Bamba)* | literal/collection |
| _____ 5. What does the word *mariachi* refer to in the passage you just read? *(a musical group from the western part of Mexico)* | literal/vocabulary |
| _____ 6. Let me read the second sentence to you again. "Most people who come to the United States from other countries ADAPT to the lifestyle here." What does the word ADAPT mean? *(adapt means to become familiar with; become a part of; become adjusted; become comfortable; accept plausible responses)* | inferential/language/vocabulary |
| _____ 7. How many instruments are used by bands from the eastern part of Mexico? *(four)* | literal/collection |
| _____ 8. Many of the people who move to the United States do not give up the music of their homeland. Why do you think that is? *(accept plausible responses associated with keeping in touch with their cultures)* | evaluative/comparison/language |

## ERROR TYPES / ERROR ANALYSIS

| | Mis-pronun. | Sub-stitute | Inser-tions | Tchr. Assists | Omis-sions | Error Totals | Self-Correct. | Meaning (M) | Syntax (S) | Visual (V) |
|---|---|---|---|---|---|---|---|---|---|---|
| **Music of Mexico** | | | | | | | | | | |
| Much of the music you hear in the United | | | | | | | | | | |
| States comes from other countries. Most | | | | | | | | | | |
| people who come to the United States from | | | | | | | | | | |
| other countries adapt to the lifestyle here. | | | | | | | | | | |
| However, they do not give up the music | | | | | | | | | | |
| of their homelands. Many people have | | | | | | | | | | |
| come to the United States from Mexico. | | | | | | | | | | |
| Mexico is a large country that lies | | | | | | | | | | |
| south of the United States. The music of | | | | | | | | | | |
| Mexico is unique and has contributed | | | | | | | | | | |
| much to the music heard in the United | | | | | | | | | | |
| States. Music from Mexico often uses | | | | | | | | | | |
| instruments such as the folk harp, violin, | | | | | | | | | | |
| and various types of guitars. Music in // | | | | | | | | | | |
| *Mexico is used to celebrate birthdays,* | | | | | | | | | | |
| *weddings, anniversaries, and other holidays.* | | | | | | | | | | |
| **TOTALS** | | | | | | | | | | |

Summary of Reading Behaviors (Strengths and Needs)

# PART II: ORAL READING AND ANALYSIS OF MISCUES

## Directions

Say, "Now I would like to hear you read this story out loud." Have the student read orally until the 100-word sample is completed. Follow along on the Miscue Grid, marking any oral reading errors as appropriate. *Remember to count miscues only up to the point in the story containing the oral reading stop-marker (//).* Then complete the Performance Summary to determine whether to continue the assessment. (*Note:* The Miscue Grid should be completed *after* the assessment session has been concluded in order to minimize stress for the student.)

# PART III: MISCUE ANALYSIS

## Directions

Circle all reading behaviors you observed.

## A. Fundamental Behaviors Observed

L → R Directionality        1-to-1 Matching        Searching for Clues        Cross-Checking

## B. Word Attack Behaviors

No Attempt        Mispronunciation (Invented Word Substitutions)        Substitutes

Skips/Reads On        Asks for Help        Repeats        Attempts to Self-Correct

"Sounds Out" (Segmenting)        Blends Sounds        Structural Analysis (Root Words, Affixes)

## C. Cueing Systems Used in Attempting Words

| CUEING TOOL | MISCUE EXAMPLES | ACTUAL TEXT |
|---|---|---|
| (M) Meaning | | |
| (S) Syntax | | |
| (V) Visual | | |

## D. Fluency (word by word → fluent reading)

Word by Word _____        Mixed Phrasing _____        Fluent Reading _____        Fluency Rate in Seconds _____

## E. Performance Summary

### Silent Reading Comprehension

_____ 0–1 questions missed = Easy

_____ 2 questions missed = Adequate

_____ 3+ questions missed = Too hard

### Oral Reading Accuracy

_____ 0–1 oral errors = Easy

_____ 2–5 oral errors = Adequate

_____ 6+ oral errors = Too hard

**Continue to the next reading passage?** _____ Yes _____ No

# PART IV: LISTENING COMPREHENSION

## Directions

If you have decided not to continue to have the student read any other passages, then use this passage to begin assessing the student's listening comprehension. Begin by reading the background statement for this passage and then say, "I am going to read this story to you. Please listen carefully because I will be asking you some questions after I finish reading it to you." After reading the passage, ask the student the questions associated with the passage. If the student correctly answers more than six questions, you will need to move to the next level and repeat the procedure.

## Listening Comprehension

_____ 0–2 questions missed = move to the next passage level

_____ more than 2 questions missed = stop assessment or move down a level

## Examiner's Notes

# LEVEL 6 ASSESSMENT PROTOCOLS

Jesse Owens (276 words)

## PART I: SILENT READING COMPREHENSION

*Background Statement*

"This story is about a famous athlete in the 1936 Olympics. Read it and try to remember some of the important facts about this man because I'm going to ask you to tell me about what you have read."

*Teacher Directions*

Once the student completes the silent reading, say, "Tell me about the story you just read." Answers to the questions below that the student provides during the retelling should be marked "ua" in the appropriate blank to indicate that this response was unaided. Ask all remaining questions not addressed during the retelling and mark those the student answers with an "a" to indicate that the correct response was given after prompting by the teacher.

| *Questions/Answers* | *Expository Grammar Element/ Level of Comprehension* |
|---|---|
| _____ 1. Where were the 1936 Olympic Games held? *(Germany)* | literal/collection |
| _____ 2. Who ruled Germany during this time? *(Adolf Hitler)* | literal/collection |
| _____ 3. Why did some Americans think we should not send a team and stay home? *(Hitler had been mistreating German Jews, or German racism)* | literal/problem-solution |
| _____ 4. Why did black athletes at the time question whether they should go to the Olympics? *(American racism)* | literal/comparison |
| _____ 5. What did Jesse Owens do during the 1936 Olympics? *(led the U.S. team to victory and/or won four Gold Medals)* | literal/collection |
| _____ 6. How did Jesse Owens's accomplishments help the United States? *(they helped move the United States toward equal treatment for all Americans)* | literal/causation |
| _____ 7. How was Adolf Hitler like slave owners during the early part of the United States's history? *(he thought he had the right to own people)* | inferential/comparison |
| _____ 8. In our story we read about how Jesse Owens fought racism. What does it mean to say someone is a *racist*? *(accept plausible responses but they should relate to the idea of mistreating another person or thinking your own race is superior to others)* | evaluative/language |

## ERROR TYPES | ERROR ANALYSIS

| | Mis-pronun. | Sub-stitute | Inser-tions | Tchr. Assists | Omis-sions | Error Totals | Self-Correct. | Meaning (M) | Syntax (S) | Visual (V) |
|---|---|---|---|---|---|---|---|---|---|---|
| **Jesse Owens** | | | | | | | | | | |
| In 1936, the Olympic games were to | | | | | | | | | | |
| be held in Germany. For months before | | | | | | | | | | |
| the games took place, a stormy argument | | | | | | | | | | |
| took place in the United States. Germany | | | | | | | | | | |
| was ruled by Adolf Hitler and the Nazi Party. | | | | | | | | | | |
| Hitler had been mistreating German Jews for | | | | | | | | | | |
| some time, and many people in the United | | | | | | | | | | |
| States wondered whether we should send | | | | | | | | | | |
| a team or stay home and protest German | | | | | | | | | | |
| racism. It was finally decided that we should | | | | | | | | | | |
| send a team. At the same time, many black | | | | | | | | | | |
| athletes wondered if they should go because | | | | | | | | | | |
| of racism in the United States. Finally, led | | | | | | | | | | |
| by Jesse// Owens, the black American athletes | | | | | | | | | | |
| decided they should go to Germany to | | | | | | | | | | |
| show the Germans how great they were. | | | | | | | | | | |
| **TOTALS** | | | | | | | | | | |

**Summary of Reading Behaviors (Strengths and Needs)**

# PART II: ORAL READING AND ANALYSIS OF MISCUES

## Directions

Say, "Now I would like to hear you read this story out loud." Have the student read orally until the 100-word sample is completed. Follow along on the Miscue Grid, marking any oral reading errors as appropriate. *Remember to count miscues only up to the point in the story containing the oral reading stop-marker (//).* Then complete the Performance Summary to determine whether to continue the assessment. (*Note:* The Miscue Grid should be completed *after* the assessment session has been concluded in order to minimize stress for the student.)

# PART III: MISCUE ANALYSIS

## Directions

Circle all reading behaviors you observed.

## A. Fundamental Behaviors Observed

L → R Directionality        1-to-1 Matching        Searching for Clues        Cross-Checking

## B. Word Attack Behaviors

No Attempt        Mispronunciation (Invented Word Substitutions)        Substitutes

Skips/Reads On        Asks for Help        Repeats        Attempts to Self-Correct

"Sounds Out" (Segmenting)        Blends Sounds        Structural Analysis (Root Words, Affixes)

## C. Cueing Systems Used in Attempting Words

| CUEING TOOL | MISCUE EXAMPLES | ACTUAL TEXT |
|-------------|-----------------|-------------|
| (M) Meaning |  |  |
| (S) Syntax |  |  |
| (V) Visual |  |  |

## D. Fluency (word by word → fluent reading)

Word by Word _____        Mixed Phrasing _____        Fluent Reading _____        Fluency Rate in Seconds _____

## E. Performance Summary

*Silent Reading Comprehension*                 *Oral Reading Accuracy*

_____ 0–1 questions missed = Easy                 _____ 0–1 oral errors = Easy

_____ 2 questions missed = Adequate                 _____ 2–5 oral errors = Adequate

_____ 3+ questions missed = Too hard                 _____ 6+ oral errors = Too hard

**Continue to the next reading passage?** _____ Yes _____ No

# PART IV: LISTENING COMPREHENSION

## Directions

If you have decided not to continue to have the student read any other passages, then use this passage to begin assessing the student's listening comprehension. Begin by reading the background statement for this passage and then say, "I am going to read this story to you. Please listen carefully because I will be asking you some questions after I finish reading it to you." After reading the passage, ask the student the questions associated with the passage. If the student correctly answers more than six questions, you will need to move to the next level and repeat the procedure.

## Listening Comprehension

_____ 0–2 questions missed = move to the next passage level

_____ more than 2 questions missed = stop assessment or move down a level

Examiner's Notes

# LEVEL 7 ASSESSMENT PROTOCOLS

Nails: A Carpenter's "Fastener" (413 words)

## PART I: SILENT READING COMPREHENSION

### Background Statement

"This story is about the different kinds of nails used by carpenters. Read it and try to remember some of the important facts about nails because I'm going to ask you to tell me about what you have read."

### Teacher Directions

Once the student completes the silent reading, say, "Tell me about the story you just read." Answers to the questions below that the student provides during the retelling should be marked "ua" in the appropriate blank to indicate that this response was unaided. Ask all remaining questions not addressed during the retelling and mark those the student answers with an "a" to indicate that the correct response was given after prompting by the teacher.

| Questions/Answers | Expository Grammar Element/ Level of Comprehension |
|---|---|
| _____ 1. Other than nails, what are two widely used hardware fasteners? <br> *(screws and bolts)* | literal/collection |
| _____ 2. What is the most common explanation of how the penny system originated? <br> *(most people think the penny system originated by the weight of one hundred nails determining the price)* | inferential/causation |
| _____ 3. What are the three common types of wire nails? <br> *(common, box, finish)* | literal/collection |
| _____ 4. What is the difference between wire nails and cut nails? <br> *(cut nails are stamped from metal sheets, whereas wire nails are cut from rolls of wire)* | inferential/comparison |
| _____ 5. What does the term "gauge" mean in reference to nails? <br> *(thickness)* | literal/vocabulary |
| _____ 6. What is a difference between common nails and finish nails? <br> *(common nails are thicker and have a larger head than finish nails)* | inferential/comparison |
| _____ 7. Why are box nails preferred for fastening edges of wood? <br> *(they are thin and are less likely to cause the wood to split)* | inferential/comparison |
| _____ 8. What is the motto of many carpenters? <br> *(always use the right tool for the right job)* | literal/collection |

**ERROR TYPES**

**ERROR ANALYSIS**

| | Mis-pronun. | Sub-stitute | Inser-tions | Tchr. Assists | Omis-sions | Error Totals | Self-Correct. | Meaning (M) | Syntax (S) | Visual (V) |
|---|---|---|---|---|---|---|---|---|---|---|
| **Nails: A Carpenter's "Fastener"** | | | | | | | | | | |
| Carpenters use a variety of tools in their | | | | | | | | | | |
| profession such as hammers, saws, and power | | | | | | | | | | |
| tools. They also use what are called *fasteners* | | | | | | | | | | |
| to hold pieces of wood and other materials | | | | | | | | | | |
| together. The most widely used fasteners are | | | | | | | | | | |
| nails, screws, and bolts. Nails are perhaps the | | | | | | | | | | |
| most commonly used fasteners in the | | | | | | | | | | |
| carpenter's toolbox. There are literally | | | | | | | | | | |
| hundreds of kinds of nails that can be used | | | | | | | | | | |
| for just about any kind of fastening job. The | | | | | | | | | | |
| size of nails is usually designated using the | | | | | | | | | | |
| *penny system.* While we are not exactly sure | | | | | | | | | | |
| how the penny system came about, many | | | | | | | | | | |
| people believe// *that it is an ancient* | | | | | | | | | | |
| *measurement based on the price of nails* | | | | | | | | | | |
| *according to weight per one hundred nails.* | | | | | | | | | | |
| **TOTALS** | | | | | | | | | | |

Summary of Reading Behaviors (Strengths and Needs)

# PART II: ORAL READING AND ANALYSIS OF MISCUES

## Directions

Say, "Now I would like to hear you read this story out loud." Have the student read orally until the 100-word sample is completed. Follow along on the Miscue Grid, marking any oral reading errors as appropriate. *Remember to count miscues only up to the point in the story containing the oral reading stop-marker (//).* Then complete the Performance Summary to determine whether to continue the assessment. (*Note:* The Miscue Grid should be completed *after* the assessment session has been concluded in order to minimize stress for the student.)

# PART III: MISCUE ANALYSIS

## Directions

Circle all reading behaviors you observed.

## A. Fundamental Behaviors Observed

L → R Directionality        1-to-1 Matching        Searching for Clues        Cross-Checking

## B. Word Attack Behaviors

No Attempt        Mispronunciation (Invented Word Substitutions)        Substitutes

Skips/Reads On        Asks for Help        Repeats        Attempts to Self-Correct

"Sounds Out" (Segmenting)        Blends Sounds        Structural Analysis (Root Words, Affixes)

## C. Cueing Systems Used in Attempting Words

| CUEING TOOL | MISCUE EXAMPLES | ACTUAL TEXT |
|---|---|---|
| (M) Meaning | | |
| (S) Syntax | | |
| (V) Visual | | |

## D. Fluency (word by word → fluent reading)

Word by Word _____        Mixed Phrasing _____        Fluent Reading _____        Fluency Rate in Seconds _____

## E. Performance Summary

### Silent Reading Comprehension

_____ 0–1 questions missed = Easy

_____ 2 questions missed = Adequate

_____ 3+ questions missed = Too hard

### Oral Reading Accuracy

_____ 0–1 oral errors = Easy

_____ 2–5 oral errors = Adequate

_____ 6+ oral errors = Too hard

**Continue to the next reading passage?** _____ Yes _____ No

## PART IV: LISTENING COMPREHENSION

### Directions

If you have decided not to continue to have the student read any other passages, then use this passage to begin assessing the student's listening comprehension. Begin by reading the background statement for this passage and then say, "I am going to read this story to you. Please listen carefully because I will be asking you some questions after I finish reading it to you." After reading the passage, ask the student the questions associated with the passage. If the student correctly answers more than six questions, you will need to move to the next level and repeat the procedure.

### Listening Comprehension

\_\_\_\_\_ 0–2 questions missed = move to the next passage level

\_\_\_\_\_ more than 2 questions missed = stop assessment or move down a level

Examiner's Notes

# LEVEL 8 ASSESSMENT PROTOCOLS

## The Environments of Africa (513 words)

## PART I: SILENT READING COMPREHENSION

### Background Statement

"This story is about parts of Africa. Read it and try to remember some of the important facts about this continent because I'm going to ask you to tell me about what you have read."

### Teacher Directions

Once the student completes the silent reading, say, "Tell me about the story you just read." Answers to the questions below that the student provides during the retelling should be marked "ua" in the appropriate blank to indicate that this response was unaided. Ask all remaining questions not addressed during the retelling and mark those the student answers with an "a" to indicate that the correct response was given after prompting by the teacher.

| Questions/Answers | Expository Grammar Element/ Level of Comprehension |
|---|---|
| _____ 1. What four bodies of water nearly surround Africa? (*Atlantic and Indian Oceans, Mediterranean and Red Seas*) | literal/collection |
| _____ 2. Why are the countries in Central and West Africa thinly populated? (*lack of suitable soil for farming*) | literal/causation |
| _____ 3. Which section of Africa is often called the sub-Sahara? (*southern*) | literal/collection |
| _____ 4. What are *savannas*? (*grasslands*) | literal/vocabulary |
| _____ 5. In which part of Africa is the Sahara Desert located? (*northern*) | literal/description |
| _____ 6. What type of political change occurred in South Africa during the latter portion of the 20th century? (*South Africa became a democracy because everyone was given the right to vote.*) | literal/causation |
| _____ 7. What is the name of the region of Africa where the countries of Ethiopia and Somalia are located? (*African Horn*) | literal/collection |
| _____ 8. What causes the climate of the sub-Sahara to be warm and moist? (*the equator runs through the sub-Sahara*) | literal/causation |

**ERROR TYPES**

**ERROR ANALYSIS**

| | Mis-pronun. | Sub-stitute | Inser-tions | Tchr. Assists | Omis-sions | Error Totals | Self-Correct. | Meaning (M) | Syntax (S) | Visual (V) |
|---|---|---|---|---|---|---|---|---|---|---|
| **The Environments of Africa** | | | | | | | | | | |
| Africa is the Earth's second largest continent. | | | | | | | | | | |
| It is home to about one-tenth of the world's | | | | | | | | | | |
| population. While it is about three times | | | | | | | | | | |
| larger than the United States in terms of | | | | | | | | | | |
| landmass, many people still do not know | | | | | | | | | | |
| very much about it. Some think of Africa | | | | | | | | | | |
| as a single country and it is not. In this | | | | | | | | | | |
| selection we take a brief tour of this continent. | | | | | | | | | | |
| Africa is almost completely surrounded by | | | | | | | | | | |
| water. Two oceans and two seas are on its | | | | | | | | | | |
| borders. The Atlantic Ocean borders Africa | | | | | | | | | | |
| on the west, while the Indian Ocean borders | | | | | | | | | | |
| to the east. The Mediterranean // Sea | | | | | | | | | | |
| and the Red Sea are to the north. | | | | | | | | | | |
| **TOTALS** | | | | | | | | | | |

Summary of Reading Behaviors (Strengths and Needs)

# PART II: ORAL READING AND ANALYSIS OF MISCUES

*Directions*

Say, "Now I would like to hear you read this story out loud." Have the student read orally until the 100-word sample is completed. Follow along on the Miscue Grid, marking any oral reading errors as appropriate. *Remember to count miscues only up to the point in the story containing the oral reading stop-marker (//).* Then complete the Performance Summary to determine whether to continue the assessment. (*Note:* The Miscue Grid should be completed *after* the assessment session has been concluded in order to minimize stress for the student.)

# PART III: MISCUE ANALYSIS

*Directions*

Circle all reading behaviors you observed.

## A. Fundamental Behaviors Observed

L → R Directionality        1-to-1 Matching        Searching for Clues        Cross-Checking

## B. Word Attack Behaviors

No Attempt        Mispronunciation (Invented Word Substitutions)        Substitutes

Skips/Reads On        Asks for Help        Repeats        Attempts to Self-Correct

"Sounds Out" (Segmenting)        Blends Sounds        Structural Analysis (Root Words, Affixes)

## C. Cueing Systems Used in Attempting Words

| CUEING TOOL | MISCUE EXAMPLES | ACTUAL TEXT |
|---|---|---|
| (M) Meaning | | |
| (S) Syntax | | |
| (V) Visual | | |

## D. Fluency (word by word → fluent reading)

Word by Word _____        Mixed Phrasing _____        Fluent Reading _____        Fluency Rate in Seconds _____

## E. Performance Summary

*Silent Reading Comprehension*

_____ 0–1 questions missed = Easy

_____ 2 questions missed = Adequate

_____ 3+ questions missed = Too hard

*Oral Reading Accuracy*

_____ 0–1 oral errors = Easy

_____ 2–5 oral errors = Adequate

_____ 6+ oral errors = Too hard

**Continue to the next reading passage?** _____ Yes _____ No

# PART IV: LISTENING COMPREHENSION

## *Directions*

If you have decided not to continue to have the student read any other passages, then use this passage to begin assessing the student's listening comprehension. Begin by reading the background statement for this passage and then say, "I am going to read this story to you. Please listen carefully because I will be asking you some questions after I finish reading it to you." After reading the passage, ask the student the questions associated with the passage. If the student correctly answers more than six questions, you will need to move to the next level and repeat the procedure.

## Listening Comprehension

\_\_\_\_\_ 0–2 questions missed = move to the next passage level

\_\_\_\_\_ more than 2 questions missed = stop assessment or move down a level

Examiner's Notes

# LEVEL 9 ASSESSMENT PROTOCOLS

The Mathematics of Health (456 words)

## PART I: SILENT READING COMPREHENSION

### Background Statement

"This story is about the foods we eat. Read it and try to remember some of the important facts because I'm going to ask you to tell me about what you have read."

### Teacher Directions

Once the student completes the silent reading, say, "Tell me about the story you just read." Answers to the questions below that the student provides during the retelling should be marked "ua" in the appropriate blank to indicate that this response was unaided. Ask all remaining questions not addressed during the retelling and mark those the student answers with an "a" to indicate that the correct response was given after prompting by the teacher.

### Questions/Answers

**Expository Grammar Element/ Level of Comprehension**

_____ 1. What has caused more and more people to try to stay healthy?
*(rising cost of health care)*
    inferential/causation

_____ 2. What are four things people try to limit the amount of in their diets?
*(sugar, fat, salt/sodium, cholesterol)*
    literal/collection

_____ 3. What was an initial problem with products labeled Lo-Cal or LITE?
*(they weren't really any healthier than foods that didn't have the labels)*
    literal/problem-solution

_____ 4. According to the passage, how can comparing food labels benefit the health-conscious buyer?
*(a person can select foods that have less fat content or less caloric content)*
    inferential/problem-solution

_____ 5. What caused companies to begin providing nutritional information on their products?
*(Food and Drug Administration rules)*
    literal/causation

_____ 6. The title of this selection is "The Mathematics of Health." Why is this an appropriate title?
*(accept plausible responses related to the idea of determining the amounts of fat, salt, etc., in food)*
    inferential/problem-solution

_____ 7. What did the selection indicate as the optimum amount of calories per day for a grown person?
*(1,500)*
    literal/collection

_____ 8. What does the lowercase "g" mean on a food label that says a food has 20 g of fat?
*(grams)*
    literal/description

## ERROR ANALYSIS

## ERROR TYPES

| | Mis-pronun. | Sub-stitute | Inser-tions | Tchr. Assists | Omis-sions | Error Totals | Self-Correct. | Meaning (M) | Syntax (S) | Visual (V) |
|---|---|---|---|---|---|---|---|---|---|---|
| **The Mathematics of Health** | | | | | | | | | | |
| Americans spend billions of dollars every | | | | | | | | | | |
| year on medical care. Doctor bills, medicine, | | | | | | | | | | |
| dental work, optical products (glasses, | | | | | | | | | | |
| contacts, etc.), health insurance, nursing | | | | | | | | | | |
| homes, and other health-related costs are all | | | | | | | | | | |
| part of the health care picture. As the | | | | | | | | | | |
| associated costs of medical care continue | | | | | | | | | | |
| to escalate, more and more Americans are | | | | | | | | | | |
| making efforts to stay healthy in a myriad of | | | | | | | | | | |
| ways. These efforts range on a continuum | | | | | | | | | | |
| from daily exercise to careful control of one's | | | | | | | | | | |
| diet. This passage will focus on the | | | | | | | | | | |
| mathematics involved in monitoring one's diet. | | | | | | | | | | |
| People sometimes try to remain healthy by | | | | | | | | | | |
| limiting the amount of // *fat, sodium (salt),* | | | | | | | | | | |
| *cholesterol, and sugar in their diet.* | | | | | | | | | | |
| **TOTALS** | | | | | | | | | | |

Summary of Reading Behaviors (Strengths and Needs)

# PART II: ORAL READING AND ANALYSIS OF MISCUES

## Directions

Say, "Now I would like to hear you read this story out loud." Have the student read orally until the 100-word sample is completed. Follow along on the Miscue Grid, marking any oral reading errors as appropriate. *Remember to count miscues only up to the point in the story containing the oral reading stop-marker (///).* Then complete the Performance Summary to determine whether to continue the assessment. (*Note:* The Miscue Grid should be completed *after* the assessment session has been concluded in order to minimize stress for the student.)

# PART III: MISCUE ANALYSIS

## Directions

Circle all reading behaviors you observed.

## A. Fundamental Behaviors Observed

L → R Directionality     1-to-1 Matching     Searching for Clues     Cross-Checking

## B. Word Attack Behaviors

No Attempt     Mispronunciation (Invented Word Substitutions)     Substitutes

Skips/Reads On     Asks for Help     Repeats     Attempts to Self-Correct

"Sounds Out" (Segmenting)     Blends Sounds     Structural Analysis (Root Words, Affixes)

## C. Cueing Systems Used in Attempting Words

| CUEING TOOL | MISCUE EXAMPLES | ACTUAL TEXT |
|---|---|---|
| (M) Meaning | | |
| (S) Syntax | | |
| (V) Visual | | |

## D. Fluency (word by word → fluent reading)

Word by Word _____     Mixed Phrasing _____     Fluent Reading _____     Fluency Rate in Seconds _____

## E. Performance Summary

*Silent Reading Comprehension*

_____ 0–1 questions missed = Easy

_____ 2 questions missed = Adequate

_____ 3+ questions missed = Too hard

*Oral Reading Accuracy*

_____ 0–1 oral errors = Easy

_____ 2–5 oral errors = Adequate

_____ 6+ oral errors = Too hard

# PART IV: LISTENING COMPREHENSION

## Directions

If you have decided not to continue to have the student read any other passages, then use this passage to begin assessing the student's listening comprehension. Begin by reading the background statement for this passage and then say, "I am going to read this story to you. Please listen carefully because I will be asking you some questions after I finish reading it to you." After reading the passage, ask the student the questions associated with the passage. If the student correctly answers more than six questions, then you may assume listening comprehension to be higher than Level 9.

## Listening Comprehension

_____ 0–2 questions missed = move to the next passage level

_____ more than 2 questions missed = stop assessment or move down a level

Examiner's Notes

# APPENDIX: STUDENT SUMMARY FORM

# Student Summary Form

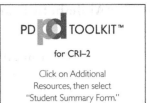
**Student's name** _____ **Age** _____

**School** _____ **Grade** _____

**Examiner** _____ **Date** _____

**Directions:** Record all significant summary information collected from the subtest administered.

## Part I. Student Interview

> **Background Knowledge, Reading Interests, Speaking Vocabulary**

*Student's interests and background knowledge* (These may be useful in making text selections):

*Informal evaluation of verbal skills* (If the student was interviewed one-on-one):

# Part II. "Alphabetics" and Vocabulary Knowledge

> **Phonemic Awareness Tests (PATs), Letter Naming, Phonics, Vocabulary**

**Phonemic Awareness Tests** (Rate as one of these—Emergent, Developing, or Proficient—according to the criteria found in the instructions for each subtest.)

*Initial Consonant Sounds Test* (ICST)  ☐ Emergent  ☐ Developing  ☐ Proficient
Student needs:

*Phonemic Segmentation Test* (PST)  ☐ Emergent  ☐ Developing  ☐ Proficient
Student needs:

*Blending Sounds Test* (BST)  ☐ Emergent  ☐ Developing  ☐ Proficient
Student needs:

*Composite phonemic awareness skills*  ☐ **Emergent**  ☐ **Developing**  ☐ **Proficient**

---

**Letter Naming**

*Letter Naming Test* (LNT)  ☐ Emergent  ☐ Developing  ☐ Proficient
Student needs:

---

**Phonics**

*Phonics Test* (PT)  ☐ Emergent  ☐ Developing  ☐ Proficient
Student needs:

---

**Vocabulary Knowledge**

*High-Frequency Word Knowledge Survey* (HFWKS)—
Unknown words:

# Part III. Reading Comprehension, Fluency, and Oral Reading Assessments

**Reading Fluency and Reading Comprehension: Passages (Forms PP–9)**

## Overall Performance Levels on Reading Passages

|  | *Narrative passages* (A, B) | *Expository* (nonfiction) *passages* (C, D) |
|---|---|---|
| Easy (independent) | _____ | _____ |
| Adequate (instructional) | _____ | _____ |
| Too hard (frustration) | _____ | _____ |

## Miscue Summary Chart

**Directions:** *Enter total number of miscues from all passages into each block indicated.*

(Purpose: To identify patterns of miscues based on highest frequency of errors to inform instructional decisions.)

|  | Nonsense words | Substitutions | Insertions | Teacher Assists | Omissions |
|---|---|---|---|---|---|
| Total miscues from all passages | | | | | |

## Error Analyses (Cueing Systems)

**Directions:** *Enter total number of times (all passages) the student used each of the cueing systems when a miscue was made.*

(Purpose: To determine the extent to which cueing systems are used to identify unknown words in print.)

Meaning cues (M) _____    Syntax cues (S) _____    Visual cues (V) _____

**Listening Comprehension** (highest level reached): _____

**Fluency** (Reading rate/wpm at "adequate" or instructional level)

_____ wpm for Narrative texts (Forms A or B); grade level (approximate) _____

_____ wpm for Expository texts (Forms C or D); grade level (approximate) _____

## Oral Language and Vocabulary Observations

Maria was able to answer questions about vocabulary in the context of the stories with relative ease. She did have some trouble interpreting figurative language; example - Maria was not sure what "to cut back" or "secret weapon" meant in the stories.

## Part IV. Student's Intervention History for Tiers 1 and 2

Describe below the history of interventions attempted with this student and his or her responses to these interventions.

| | Date(s) | Description | Response to Intervention (RTI) |
|---|---|---|---|
| **Example** | 11/2013–5/2014 | Tutoring 1:1 after school | Grades in reading, spelling, and writing improved |
| | | | |
| | | | |

## Part V. Instructional Implications (IF–THEN Analyses)

The CRI–2 uses findings from the National Reading Panel and other recent scientific research that identify the critical components of reading as *phonemic awareness, phonics, vocabulary, comprehension,* and *fluency,* as well as rapid letter naming. Performance for this student on the CRI–2 indicates the following:

*Strengths:*

\_\_\_\_ Phonemic awareness

\_\_\_\_ Rapid letter naming

\_\_\_\_ Phonics

\_\_\_\_ Vocabulary

\_\_\_\_ Comprehension—narrative

\_\_\_\_ Comprehension—expository

\_\_\_\_ Comprehension—listening

\_\_\_\_ Fluency—narrative

\_\_\_\_ Fluency—expository

\_\_\_\_ Vocabulary in context

\_\_\_\_ Figurative language

*Weaknesses:*

\_\_\_\_ Phonemic awareness

\_\_\_\_ Rapid letter naming

\_\_\_\_ Phonics

\_\_\_\_ Vocabulary

\_\_\_\_ Comprehension—narrative

\_\_\_\_ Comprehension—expository

\_\_\_\_ Comprehension—listening

\_\_\_\_ Fluency—narrative

\_\_\_\_ Fluency—expository

\_\_\_\_ Vocabulary in context

\_\_\_\_ Figurative language

*Teacher notes/intervention planning:*

## Overall Summary of Yearly Progress and Recommendations

Based on this student's current skill levels, strengths and weaknesses identified by the CRI–2, classroom performance, and responses to interventions, following are the priorities for the regular classroom reading instruction:

Teacher/Examiner _____ Date _____